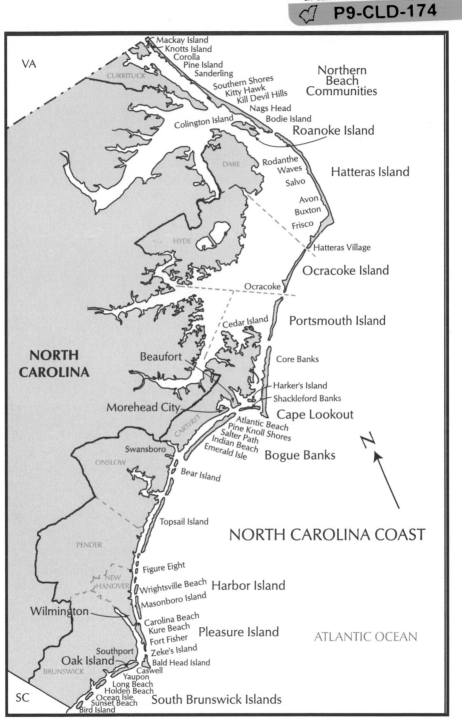

Coastal North Carolina

CONTENTS

COASTAL NORTH CAROLINA

ITS ENCHANTING ISLANDS, TOWNS, AND COMMUNITIES

TERRANCE ZEPKE

PINEAPPLE PRESS, INC.
SARASOTA, FLORIDA

To "Teach," who remains an honorary North Carolinian
(even though she reluctantly moved out of state many years ago)
because of her love for North Carolina, and most especially,
our coast. She has inspired and encouraged me throughout my life.

———————————————

Inquiries should be addressed to:

Pineapple Press, Inc.
P.O. Box 3889
Sarasota, Florida 34230

www.pineapplepress.com

Library of Congress Cataloging-in-Publication Data

Zepke, Terrance –
    Coastal North Carolina : its enchanting islands, towns, and communities / by Terrance Zepke.
        p. cm.
    Includes bibliographical references and index.
    ISBN 1-56164-298-3 (pbk. : alk. paper)
1. Atlantic Coast (N.C.)–Description and travel. 2. Atlantic Coast (N.C.)–History, Local. 3. Islands–North Carolina. 4. North Carolina–Description and travel. 5. North Carolina–History, Local. 6. Atlantic Coast (N.C.)–Guidebooks. 7. North Carolina–Guidebooks. I. Title.
F262.A84Z45 2004
975.6'1–dc22

                        2004003819

First Edition
10 9 8 7 6 5 4 3 2 1

Design by Ramonda Talkie
Printed in the United States of America

CRYSTAL COAST

3 LOWER COAST

INTRODUCTION

Coastal North Carolina: Its Enchanting Islands, Towns, and Communities is divided into three sections, like our coast: Outer Banks, Upper "Crystal" Coast, and Lower "Cape Fear" Coast. What is the book about? It explains how the North Carolina islands and coastal towns evolved from Native American hunting grounds to the summer retreats of colonial planters escaping the "deadly fever," to private playgrounds for the rich and elusive, and to vacation spots sought after by millions of tourists every year. The book details the history of each major community in coastal North Carolina, including sites and attractions. For each section, it lists unique opportunities for recreational, sports, and outdoor activities. As you read on, you will also learn about the lore and traditional events of these communities, and you will find quizzes and other fun ways to learn and test your knowledge.

Who might be interested in this book? Anyone who wants to learn more about these coastal communities and their unique histories and attractions. It is a useful resource for nature lovers, extreme sports zealots (think hang-gliding and kite surfing), lighthouse enthusiasts, anglers, ghost hunters, pirates at heart, bird-watchers, sun worshippers, history buffs, and those who like quirky festivals (think underwater bicycle races on top of a sunken ship and impressive holiday flotillas).

You should know that this is not a guidebook. *Coastal North Carolina* doesn't offer exhaustive lists of restaurants and accommodations, since you can get the most current information easily from tourism bureaus or visitors centers—and you can always ask the locals if you want to know who serves the best seafood. This is meant to be an educational tool, souvenir or gift book, as well as a handy reference for students, vacationers, and those looking to relocate or retire to some of these remarkable islands and towns.

I wrote this book for two simple reasons. The main reason was to share North Carolina's coastal history and reveal the true character of each of these coastal hamlets. Can you believe that big incentives and dirt-cheap prices were once offered to encourage people to move to many of our islands and beaches? Did you know that we have the only seaside ghost town in the United States, or that America's tallest lighthouse is at the Outer Banks, or that the first airplane flight occurred here?

The second reason I wrote this book was that, as part of my research, I had to spend a lot of time at the coast taking scenic ferry rides over to lovely islands, hiking through picturesque maritime forests, exploring incredible historical sites, visiting nifty museums and other tourist attractions, strolling along pretty boardwalks and wooden piers, and checking out numerous beaches. There are more unique activities, interesting festivals, and good old-fashioned seafood celebrations here than you can possibly imagine. So all my research for this book was "hard work," but I did it for you—and I would gladly do it all over again! I hope you enjoy Coastal North Carolina as much as I did.

ACKNOWLEDGMENTS

Quinn Capps, Outer Banks Visitors Center
Janis Williams, Carteret County Tourism Development Authority
Karen Sphar, Southport-Oak Island Area Chamber of Commerce
Jeanette Masters, Greater Topsail Chamber of Commerce
Mitzi York, South Brunswick Islands Chamber of Commerce
Connie Nelson, Cape Fear Coast Convention & Visitors Bureau
Margie Brooks, Hyde County Chamber of Commerce
Patricia Howarth, Bald Head Island
Figure Eight Realty (especially Brooke and Kira), Figure Eight Island
Mariann Dellerba, North Carolina Division of Travel and Tourism
Steve Massengill, North Carolina State Archives
My family, who accompanied me on various research trips
The locals, who gave me advice, leads, and directions
And, as always, the "gang" at Pineapple Press

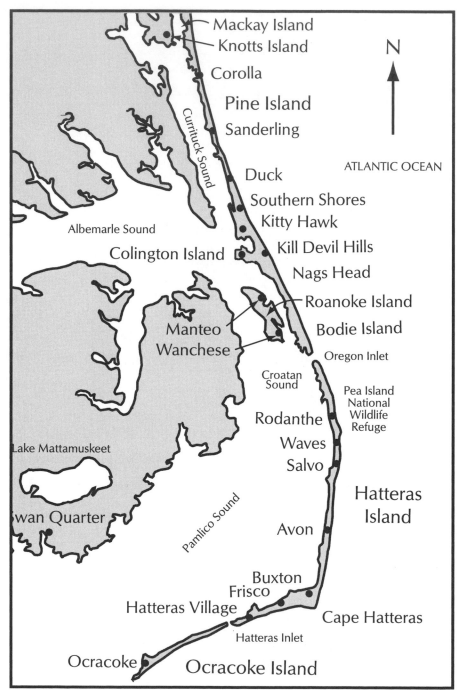

The Outer Banks

1

Outer Banks

More than seven million visitors frequent the Outer Banks every year. That's a lot of people descending on a relatively small area. The Outer Banks is made up of three counties: Currituck (northern Outer Banks), Dare (central Outer Banks), and Hyde (lower Outer Banks). Dare is the largest of the three counties with 391 square miles of land and over 31,000 residents. Currituck County encompasses 255 square miles of land, most of it on the mainland, and has a population of 19,500. Hyde County extends 634 square miles, but its population, comprised mostly of Ocracoke Island's 700–800 inhabitants, is relatively small.

The Outer Banks is a cluster of islands comprised of narrow ribbons of sand connected to the mainland by private boats, state-operated ferries, and man-made bridges. The only exception is Bodie Island, which is a peninsula adjoined to Virginia. Bodie, Hatteras, and Ocracoke Islands are barrier islands, separated from the mainland by a system of sounds. Roanoke Island and Colington Island are floating in the sound west of the barrier islands.

There has long been great debate as to which islands make up the Outer Banks. Everyone knows the Outer Banks ends at the Virginia border, but the confusing issue is where it begins. Some suggest the Outer Banks begins at Ocracoke Island. Others claim the "Southern" Outer Banks starts at Beaufort and Bogue Banks. Still others believe the area becomes the Outer Banks somewhere between Beaufort and Ocracoke Island.

The Albemarle-Pamlico Sounds system that separates the Outer Banks from the mainland is the second largest estuary in the United States, second only to the Chesapeake Bay. The sounds are made up of three thousand square miles of surface water and thirty thousand square miles of watershed. The Albemarle-Pamlico Sounds system is comprised of Albemarle, Pamlico, Currituck, Croatan, Roanoke, Bogue, and Core Sounds, which get their origins from inlets and rivers. This system is very important because of the fish, plant life, shellfish, and wildlife that reside in it. It is one of the most fertile estuaries in the U.S.

North Carolina has used ferries to link island communities to the mainland since the 1920s. The ferries were privately owned until 1934 when the state began funding them. In 1947, the Department of Transportation established the North Carolina Ferry Division. Our ferry system has grown to become one of the largest in the U.S. More than 2.5 million people use it every year.

The 1930s brought three big changes to the Outer Banks. First, bridges were built to link the isolated barrier islands to the mainland. Second, the federal government created the Civilian Conservation Corps (CCC). Many CCC workers were sent to the Outer Banks to perform tasks such as planting vegetation and rebuilding dunes to thwart coastal erosion. Third, the plan to develop national seashores was hatched, which brought about Cape Hatteras National Seashore and Cape Lookout National Seashore.

The Outer Banks provide many things to see and do for all ages and interests, and tourists are fully appreciative. In fact, tourism nudges out commercial fishing as the single most important industry.

FAST FACTS

OUTER BANKS This string of barrier islands is comprised of **Currituck, Dare,** and **Hyde Counties**. The residents of these communities are known as "bankers." The Outer Banks are 827 miles from Toronto, Ontario; 607 miles from

Atlanta, Georgia; 359 miles from Charlotte, North Carolina; and 169 miles from Richmond, Virginia. The place to learn all about the history and heritage of the Outer Banks is the **Graveyard of the Atlantic Museum** on Hatteras Island. 252-986-2995. www.grave yardoftheatlantic.com

Officially runs from **Easter to Thanksgiving**. However, many attractions, accommodations, restaurants, and souvenir shops are closed or have limited hours except during the summer.

TOURIST SEASON

From the top of America's tallest beacon, **Cape Hatteras Lighthouse** (Cape Hatteras National Seashore, 252-252-473-2111, www.nps.gov/caha), or atop the tallest dune system along the eastern seaboard, **Jockey's Ridge** (Nags Head, 252-441-7132, www.jock eysridgestatepark.com).

BEST VIEW

Cape Hatteras National Seashore is a 30,000-acre preserve full of beaches and marshes, which can simply be enjoyed or explored at length. Coquina Beach offers swimming, bathing, and picnic facilities, as well as the *Laura A. Barnes* shipwreck display. Lifeguards are on duty at Coquina Beach during the summer. Birdwatchers will delight in the abundance of birds and waterfowl. Most of Hatteras, Ocracoke, and Bodie Islands, including their lighthouses, are part of the seashore, which became America's first designated National Seashore in 1953. The National Park Service offers many interesting programs during the summer such as guided nature walks and fishing trips. Camping is permitted in the seashore but not on the beach. However, Jet Skis and Wave Runners are not allowed. NC 12, Hatteras Island. 252-995-4474. www.nps.gov/caha

MOST POPULAR ATTRACTION

There are many exceptional events held in and around the Outer Banks every year, but the most unique has to be **Swan Days**. This is a two-day celebration held at Lake Mattamuskeet National Wildlife Refuge every December in honor of the annual homecoming of thousands of Lake Mattamuskeet swans. There is a 10K walk, arts and crafts booths, concessions, in-depth presentations, and guided tours of the refuge where participants may see bears,

MOST UNIQUE ANNUAL EVENT

geese, deer, and other wildlife. The refuge is about one hour from the Outer Banks. 38 Mattamuskeet Road, Swan Quarter (Hyde County mainland). 252-926-4021. www.mat tamuskeet.fws.gov

MOST IMPORTANT INDUSTRIES

Tourism and commercial fishing.

MOST IMPORTANT HISTORICAL EVENT

The Wright Brothers made the first successful flight on December 17, 1903, in Kitty Hawk. The **Wright Brothers National Memorial** is located in Kill Devil Hills. 252-441-7430. www.nps.gov/wrbr

ISLANDS & TOWNS

1. KNOTTS AND MACKAY ISLANDS

History

KNOTTS ISLAND

The first Outer Banks post office was established on **Knotts Island** in 1833. Most inhabitants were seamen operating out of Currituck Inlet. There was a tavern on the south side of Knotts Island that reportedly was a hangout for rogues and pirates.

In the early 1900s, many residents of Knotts Island made their money guiding and chaperoning wealthy men on hunting and fishing trips. Fishing, raising livestock, and growing gardens was a way of life for all island inhabitants.

Knotts Island as seen across Currituck Sound 1956

The livestock were allowed to roam the island freely, foraging for food. Wealthy part-time residents such as Joseph Knapp did not like the animals grazing on their land. They claimed the animals caused significant destruction to their property. The islanders, already resentful of their affluent neighbors, relied heavily on these animals for food and disregarded their claims. Fences were erected, but holes were cut in them and the hogs and cows went where they pleased. There was a great deal of hostility on both sides, but in the end it was resolved by allowing the livestock to continue to roam while their owners paid a nominal fee for grazing privileges. In 1938, a main road to the island was built. A few years later electricity was extended to the island.

There is a road onto Hatteras on the Virginia side but North Carolina visitors arrive by scenic ferry ride.

There are no historic sites on Knotts Island, but there are a few vineyards and roadside fruit stands. These are all easy to find and there is no danger of getting lost because the main road loops around the heart of the island and signs are posted to direct you where to turn off to area attractions. Fishing is good on the island, especially for big-striped bass. A permit is needed, which can be obtained at Knotts Island Market (near the ferry).

Mackay Island National Wildlife Refuge, just south of the Virginia state line, was established in 1960 as a protected place for migratory birds. Nature lovers and bird watchers may use the canal system, which extends

MACKAY ISLAND

nearly twenty miles. In addition to boating, canoeing and kayaking, fishing is permitted. There is a public boat ramp. Walking, hiking, and bicycling can be done along the Kuralt Trail and the Marsh Loop Trail, which run through a small part of the 8,646-acre refuge. Located on the north side of Currituck Sound along the Atlantic Flyway, the refuge accommodates ducks, geese, tundra swans, raptors, shorebirds, and wading birds, as well as many species of reptiles and amphibians.

This uninhabited island got its name from former owner, John Mackie, who bought it in 1761. Before Mackie purchased the land, it was known as "Orphan's Island." Upon Mackie's death in 1823, the property changed ownership many times. Thomas Dixon, author of *The Birth of*

a Nation, owned the island from 1916–1918. He sold it to wealthy publisher and wildlife conservationist, Joseph P. Knapp, who built a mansion, swimming pool, large boat house, and golf course. They have all been destroyed over the years. Knapp founded Ducks Unlimited, Inc., which is a nationally recognized waterfowl conservation organization. The land was later sold to the state with the understanding that it would remain a wildlife refuge.

Mackay Island was once part of Knotts Island, formerly known as Knots and

A heron on Mackay Island Mackeys Islands. Today, they are separate entities. The separation occurred in 1728 when the boundary line dividing Virginia and North Carolina was determined. The lower part of Knotts Island was put in North Carolina, while the northeast tip of the island and most of Mackay Island became part of Virginia.

Knotts Island is five miles from Currituck and can be reached by car using Hwy. 158/168 or by ferry. To reach the ferry terminal, take Hwy. 158/168 and watch for ferry signs around the town of Currituck. Once on the island, look for well-posted signs to the wildlife refuge or vineyards.

As you disembark the ferry, you'll see long-time island icon Knotts Island Market. It has a little bit of everything, including gasoline pumps, an ATM, fish bait, hardware, movie rentals, groceries, a pizzeria, and a deli. The folks who work here know everything that's going on, so ask them if you need directions or advice. Breakfast, lunch, and dinner are served here. You can also pick up some deli sandwiches and picnic fixings.

Sites and Attractions–Knotts & Mackay Islands

Mackay Island National Wildlife Refuge and **Kuralt Trail and Marsh Loop Trail** (suitable for walking, hiking, picnicking, and canoeing). Mackay Island. 252-429-3100. http://mackayisland.fws.gov

Martin Vineyards. Established 1977, this is a small operation that offers free, informal wine tastings and tours, fruit picking, and a picnic area. 213 Martin Farm Lane, Knotts Island. 252- 429-3542. www.martinvineyards.com

Moon Rise Bay Vineyard offers free, informal tours and tastings. 134 Moonrise Bay Landing, Knotts Island. 252-429-WINE (9056). No website available.

The Peach Basket is a seasonal roadside fruit stand. Knotts Island. No telephone or website available.

Atlantic sunrise in North Carolina

2. NORTHERN BEACH COMMUNITIES (CURRITUCK BANKS)

History

Long before the colonists arrived, the Poteskeet were using Currituck Banks for hunting and fishing. However, the early settlers wanted to raise cattle and did not want the Native Americans coming to hunt. Citing ownership of the land, some of the residents refused to let the Native Americans on it. The Poteskeet appealed to the North Carolina Council, who ruled in their favor on March 10, 1715.

During the 1700s, captains were supposed to sign in with the Port Currituck collector, but most ignored this law since there was no collector's office! Currituck Banks residents had great difficulty with the British during the Revolutionary War. British privateers repeatedly attacked them and a local militia had to be formed. Proud Bankers called this the "Currituck Liberty Plains" during the war.

The area from old Currituck Inlet and the Virginia line to Bodie Island was once collectively called Currituck Banks. Some still refer to it this way. Over the years, some of the Currituck Banks communities have disappeared and new ones have evolved. The Banks extend across two counties, Currituck and Dare, because of the way the county lines have been drawn.

A note about access. Although Currituck County's Outer Banks are open to the public, it is a bit tricky for those coming from the north to access them because there is no way to get there from Virginia, except by boat. Many years ago, Virginia and North Carolina considered building a road to extend from Sandbridge, Virginia to Corolla, North Carolina. However, it was decided not to pursue this transportation method. So, only longtime property owners with special permits can drive through the gated, protected lands that lie between Carova Beach and Sandbridge. Everyone else must take NC 12, which joins with US 158 at Kitty Hawk, 1.5 miles east of the Wright Memorial Bridge. It is a 10-minute drive from Kitty Hawk through Southern Shores to Duck, except during the summer when you should anticipate it taking up to 30 minutes. It is 10 miles from Kitty Hawk to the Currituck County border, and then 11 miles to where the road ends at Corolla.

Kitty Hawk is just across the Wright Memorial Bridge. To its south is Kill Devil Hills and to the north lies Southern Shores. The four-mile town made famous by Wilbur and Orville Wright is packed full of tourist amenities such as golf courses, a fishing pier, maritime forest, restaurants, and lodging. These places are denoted by mile markers (not street addresses) because most can be found along US 158 and NC 12. However, locals have dubbed US 158 "The Bypass" and NC 12 "Beach Road," so beware of this when asking for directions or distances. The first mile marker (MM) or milepost (MP) is close to the Kitty Hawk Aycock Brown Welcome Center.

CAROVA SWAN BEACH

Carova and Swan Beach have been described as "the last frontier" of Currituck County. The two small communities are situated between Currituck Sound and the Atlantic Ocean, extending due north of Corolla to Virginia. They are in the northernmost part of Currituck County. The area was once untamed territory, inhabited only by some wild horses and fishing encampments from the late 1600s to the mid 1900s. After much debate, the land was surveyed in 1728 to determine what land belonged to North Carolina and what land was part of Virginia.

Development began in Carova in 1967 and extended to Swan Beach and North Swan Beach. Carova remains the largest development. While many vacation homes and rental properties have been built here, development is limited because there are no paved roads, only a system of dirt roads that run well behind the dunes. Since NC 12 ends just north of Corolla, the only way to get to Carova or Swan Beach is with a four-wheel drive vehicle. Only a few dozen families reside here year-round, although an exact number of permanent residents is difficult to determine. Records indicate there are seventy-five registered voters in Swan Beach and Carova.

Another factor that prevents excessive development is that the Nature Conservancy owns almost seven thousand acres in Currituck County, including a substantial tract of land in this area. Because the Currituck Wildlife Refuge and Currituck Banks Estuarine Reserve are located here, it is doubtful that a paved road will ever connect these communities to the rest of the northern beaches. What's more, the Virginia border is due north of Carova and a state line fence extends from the sound to the ocean. Just on the other side of the border lies Back Bay Wildlife Refuge and False Cape State Park.

Part of the beach area is called Wash Woods because of all the ancient tree stumps that protrude haphazardly from the sand. They are all that remains of Soundside, a barrier island that was once filled with a maritime forest. As the islands shifted to the west, the forest was alternately under water and above sea level. The result is a "wash woods." A lifesaving station was put into operation at Wash Woods during the nineteenth century. The former station is now a Swan Beach vacation property. Wash Woods is due south of Swan Beach.

COROLLA

Corolla was once the largest community on the Outer Banks. Still, it was nothing more than a sleepy fishing village. The only so-called development was when Currituck Lifesaving Station, formerly known as Jones Hill and Whalehead, was built in 1874. The following year, Currituck Lighthouse was erected and the village was offi-

Currituck Beach

cially named Corolla. Several names were bantered around before choosing "corolla," which describes the inner petals of a flower. It seemed fitting to name the idyllic hamlet after the best, and least known, part of a flower. A post office was built near the lighthouse to serve Corolla area residents. Hunters came from near and far to pursue the waterfowl attracted to Currituck Sound.

By the turn of the century, Corolla's population had reached about two hundred. Grid electricity was the only option for area residents until the 1950s. One telephone was used by everyone—and only outgoing calls could be made! Currituck County residents placed grocery orders every week with the postmaster, who operated a general store out of his house. As recently as 1973, Currituck's twenty-three miles of beautiful beaches was still considered a "no man's land," the longest stretch of prime, undeveloped coastal land on the eastern seaboard.

The Currituck Lighthouse was built in 1875 and stands 162 feet tall.

This all came to an end when Winston-Salem developer, Earl Slick, bought 636 acres for $2 million. He purchased the land from Texas oil tycoon, Walter B. Davis. Within two years, Slick had a guardhouse constructed on the only road, which kept everyone except Currituck County residents from entering the area. Lawsuits were filed against this action and were ultimately heard by the North Carolina Supreme Court. Slick eventually loss the court case and the state took possession of the road on November 1, 1984. The first order of business was to destroy the guardhouse, once again opening Currituck beaches to the public. This led to extensive development. When the road and beaches opened up to public access, there were only 171 permanent residents and 4,271 tourists per year. Just ten years later, the permanent population had catapulted to 620 and tourism had increased to 19,370 area visitors and daytrippers per year. However, the permanent population of Corolla has leveled off to about five hundred. There are more than one hundred businesses and several residential communities in Currituck County, which remain unincorporated. In these Currituck County communities, the average house can accommodate a dozen people and has more than three thousand square feet of living space. Many of these homes are rented out during the summer months.

SANDERLING **Sanderling,** Dare County's northernmost community, is located five miles north of Duck. This three hundred acre private community was established in 1978, although Caffey's Inlet Lifesaving Station was erected in Sanderling as early as 1874. Since 1985, the historic lifesaving station houses the Sanderling Inn's restaurant. The inn is considered one of the premier lodging options along the Outer Banks with afternoon tea, conference facilities, and soundside racquet and swim club.

Immediately past Sanderling is another exclusive and private development, Palmer's Island Club. This thirty-five-acre subdivision has nearly two dozen estate homes situated on huge lots. Since the Outer Banks is particularly vulnerable to nor'easters and hurricanes, the five-thousand- to ten-thousand-square-foot homes are designed to easily endure winds of 120 miles per hour. One can only imagine the insurance premiums on the mandatory homeowner, hurricane, and flood policies!

Duck, as you may gather, is named after the many **DUCK** ducks that come here. It is also a migratory stop for many kinds of waterfowl, ranging from loons to swans. Duck was primarily a hunter's paradise and fishing village until the early 1990s. While it wasn't officially incorporated until 2002, it has long been a vibrant, coastal community. As in many towns along the upper Outer Banks, there is in Duck a mix of cozy, wooden beach cottages and brand new brick mansions.

The landscape of this former fishing village used to present a very different view. It was heavily sprinkled with

Fishing the Outer Banks 1909

small gardens and livestock, grown and raised to supplement the sporadic fishing incomes of its inhabitants. During the Depression, Outer Banks families began harvesting blue crabs and eels. Fishermen would go out early in the morning to trap them using crab pots and eel crates. These sea creatures, especially blue crabs, remain the source of a profitable livelihood.

The first post office opened in 1909 but closed down in 1950. Development began in the 1970s, tourism began to flourish in the late 1980s, and by the 1990s, many shops and restaurants had opened. The biggest development is Barrier Island Station, a timeshare resort. If you look just beyond these commercial and residential dwellings, you'll note the Atlantic Ocean to one side of the road and Currituck Sound on the other side. In between, is a constricted strip of sand that accommodates the two-lane highway and all development.

Mosquitoes are a common problem in the islands, especially during the summer. The best remedies for mosquito bites are toothpaste, Vicks VapoRub©, witch hazel, and baking soda mixed with water to create a paste. Apply a small amount directly to the wound(s) and the itching will soon subside.

SOUTHERN SHORES

Southern Shores is ideally located north of Kitty Hawk and south of Duck. It is one of the premier Outer Banks addresses. Southern Shores was the first planned community on the upper Outer Banks. Frank Stick and his son, David, who were developers, avid outdoorsmen, artists, and historians, bought these four square miles of land in 1947 for $30,000. It was named by Frank Stick, who thought "southern shores" would hold great appeal to northerners. It is now valued at more than $430 million, so it seems he was right.

Stick spent eight years developing Southern Shores, which includes single-family homes, two marinas, and a golf course. His goal was to provide a satisfactory respite for both people and nature. Most feel he more than achieved his objective. Perhaps, if you have the opportunity to witness the dogwoods in full bloom during spring or catch a glimpse of singing mockingbirds and red-breasted cardinals, you'll agree. Southern Shores was officially incorporated in 1979.

The most popular (if dubious) theory about **Kitty Hawk** is that it was originally called "Killy Honk" or "Killy Honker" by area Native Americans who came here hunting goose. Documents dating back to the eighteenth century state that this area was called Chickahauk, a name that was later adopted by the town located between Southern Shores and Kitty Hawk. Others believe the town got its name from the area raptors that preyed on kitty wren.

Whatever its name origin, Kitty Hawk was clearly a fishing village. As in most of Currituck's Outer Banks, fishing families here earned their living by farming and raising livestock. This bustling tourist town was more agricultural during the 1800s and up to the mid-1900s than one might imagine. Kitty Hawk Lifesaving Station was erected in 1874 and the U.S. Weather Bureau opened a satellite station here in 1875. That's what drew the Wright Brothers to this part of North Carolina. The nearby weather station provided them with essential information about weather conditions, including local wind patterns. This weather facility operated until 1904. Good thing this was one year *after* the Wright Brothers' first successful flight!

Being so isolated, Outer Banks families at the beginning of the twentieth century had to be able to successfully complete many tasks, ranging from farming to boat building. If you want to imagine just how cut off this area was at that time, think about what Wilbur Wright went through to reach Kitty Hawk in 1900. He came by train from Dayton, Ohio, to Elizabeth City, North Carolina. In Elizabeth City, he used a boat service to reach the Outer Banks. The boat trip alone took two days! Orville Wright joined his brother several weeks later and they set up camp in Kitty Hawk Village to begin their aviation experiments in neighboring Kill Devil Hills.

The post office opening a station is always a good indicator of progress. The first Kitty Hawk post office opened in November 1878. A second station was established in 1905 to serve the fast-growing community. In 1993, the biggest Outer Banks postal facility was built in Kitty Hawk.

In 1924, the first Kitty Hawk school was constructed thanks to the passing of a bond referendum. This one school accommodated elementary and high school students until a central high school was built in Manteo. Middle school students were bussed to Kill Devil Hills. Elementary students in the Outer Banks continue to go to school in Kitty Hawk. It is a long commute to Manteo for high school students, but such is the trade-off for life here at the Outer Banks.

During the early 1920s, the first bridge linking Kitty Hawk to the mainland was constructed. Several Elizabeth City businessmen formed the Wright Memorial Bridge Company and bought seven miles of beach just north of the village of Kitty Hawk. Several years later, a three-mile wooden bridge jutted out from the mainland over Currituck Sound to Kitty Hawk. This changed everything. Tourists could now easily reach the beach community by paying a per-car fee. A fee is no longer charged to cross this bridge.

It's hard to get lost in Kitty Hawk for two reasons. First, it's only four miles from sound to sea. Second, mile-post markers (MP) indicate where things can be found; for example, the Aycock Brown Welcome Center is located at MP 1 1/2. When asking for directions, it is worth knowing that most locals refer to NC 12 as Beach Road and to U.S. 158 as the Bypass. Also, roads here are named after the first families of Kitty Hawk, for example, the Herbert Perry Road and Elijah Baum Road.

Storm and erosion damage has been extensive in the Outer Banks. Kitty Hawk beaches are the narrowest in the area thanks to these factors. The lifesaving station, now a private home, had to be moved to the other side of the road to safeguard it. Many homes have succumbed to the damaging effects of Mother Nature. Sadly, Kitty Hawk loses an average of one home per year to severe storms and erosion loss. This is because federal law does not allow owners to rebuild closer than 60 feet from a beach's first line of vegetation.

KILL DEVIL HILLS

There are many legends about how **Kill Devil Hills** got its name. One legend has it that it was named after Devil Ike, a local man who claimed to chase the devil into these hills to retrieve his stolen shipwrecked cargo, the lethal rum. He also claimed he had to kill the devil to regain possession of his goods. Some say that mariners thought that navigating the area's shallow waters were "to kill the devil to navigate." Another legend has it that the three hills were named after a nearly lethal kill-devil rum that washed ashore from a shipwreck. Some say that a visiting Virginian, William Byrd, claimed he drank rum that was strong enough to kill the devil himself. Yet another legend is about a banker who traded his soul to the devil for a bag of gold; regretful of his decision, he climbed to the top of one of the hills and tried unsuccessfully to kill the devil.

The Wright Brothers National Memorial was built in 1932 as a tribute to the Wright Brothers' contribution to aeronautics.

Whatever its name's origin, Kill Devil Hills was the most desirable spot on the Outer Banks for the Wright Brothers' aviation experiments. They resided in Kitty Hawk but came here to conduct their flight trials. This five-mile municipality is where the magnificent "First in Flight" Wright Brothers Memorial Monument is located. Kill Devil Hills, just south of Kitty Hawk and due north of

Nags Head, was also the first incorporated community of the Outer Banks, becoming so on March 6, 1953. However, considerable tax increases over the following two years caused citizens to repeal the decision through the state judicial system. The North Carolina Supreme Court ruled against the citizen petition in 1956, so Kill Devil Hills remained incorporated. Kill Devil Hills still has one of the highest property tax rates in Dare County.

The Kill Devil Hills Lifesaving Station was established in 1879. Until the 1930s, most of the population were the men serving at the lifesaving station and local fishermen. The town's growth accelerated when bridges were completed in the 1930s, thereby adjoining the mainland to the coastal communities. Prior to this, there was no way for cars to reach the area, nor was there passenger ferry service to Kill Devil Hills. Thus, the Wright Brothers's historic flight on December 17, 1903, was witnessed by only a few schoolchildren and local fishermen and their families.

Slowly, things changed. A post office was built in 1938, and from the late 1950s to the 1970s there was a big real estate boom. It started with developers setting up

Aerial View of Wright Brothers National Memorial, Kill Devil Hills 1963

"offices" under colorful beach umbrellas perched atop folding tables. They would sell each lot for roughly $250. How times have changed! There's been so much development here that a stretch along U.S. 158 has been dubbed "French Fry Alley" because of all the fast food franchises. The first franchise was McDonald's, which opened in 1978.

Kill Devil Hills has been home to the Dare County Reverse Osmosis Water Treatment Plant since 1986. This vital facility provides water for the county's northern communities.

COLINGTON ISLAND

The eastern tip of the small **Colington Island** is one mile west of the Wright Brothers Memorial. It is connected to Kill Devil Hills by a bridge that extends over

Colington Creek. To its west lie four sounds: Currituck, Albemarle, Croatan, and Roanoke. To the north is Kitty Hawk Bay and to the south is Buzzard Bay.

Sir John Colleton obtained a land grant from the British government for this two-mile-long and 2.5-mile-wide island in 1633. Colleton had ambitious plans for his land. He partnered with three other men to establish a colony and grow tobacco and corn, raise livestock, and plant grapes for a winery. But a wicked nor'easter storm or hurricane on August 27, 1667, destroyed the crops and buildings on Colleton Island. The next few years saw similar disasters; there was either insufficient rainfall or it was too rainy, and more nor'easters and hurricanes plagued the area.

Thomas Pendleton bought the land in 1750. Before he could do anything with it, he died, leaving it to his heirs. By the 1800s, people realized that this area was best suited for fishing. The fishing communities of Great Colenton and Little Colenton emerged on both ends of the island, which became separated by Dividing Creek in 1769. A post office, tiny school, and general store opened in 1889. Later, a second store opened on the other side of the island. A steamer would come through once a week, delivering supplies to the eighty island residents. Inhabitants could feed themselves and make a living hunting deer, rabbit, and waterfowl, as well as by fishing, trapping eels and crabs, and raking oysters. Most had vegetable gardens, and the two island stores sold baking supplies, clothing, and other essentials that couldn't be farmed or trapped. Locals guided Northerners on fishing trips and sold muskrat pelts to buyers who came down from New York stores.

Big Colington and Little Colington, as the island communities are now called, are linked to the mainland by bridges. The island's curvy main road is paved and extends the length of the four-mile island. Bridges link Little Colington and Big Colington. A Washington, D.C., developer bought 550 acres on the north side of Colington Island in the early 1960s. His intent was to build a residential community, but due to financial difficulty, the land was auctioned off to American Central Corporation of New York in 1965.

The first subdivision, Colington Harbour, was established that same year. This development houses more than two thousand people in a gated community. Many other developments have occurred since that time, but most didn't happen until the late 1980s and early 1990s, and none are as large as this one. The shame of it is that along the way developers destroyed most of the island's maritime forest, filled in wetlands, and made canals and boat basins as they pleased. Long-time residents are struggling to accept all the changes that have occurred, such as increased traffic and yuppie eateries.

Nags Head bicycle path

NAGS HEAD

Local legend has it that **Nags Head** got its name because inhabitants used to tie a lantern to a Banker pony's neck (also known as a nag's head) and then ride the animal back and forth along the beach. Ships would think this light belonged to another vessel, so they would head in that direction. Of course, they would be wrecked on the shoals and then the local inhabitants would pillage the ship's cargo.

In the 1830s, a Perquimans County planter bought two hundred acres for one hundred dollars and built the first Nags Head summer home to escape the deadly fever. In 1838, the first hotel, which could comfortably accommodate two hundred guests, was erected. The Nags Head Hotel built a boardwalk extending to the steamship dock, where guests arrived. Later, they laid a rail system so that mule-pulled carts could spare patrons the mile-long walk from the pier to the hotel. The two-story edifice housed a bowling alley, ballroom, big porches, and pier. The Nags Head Hotel eventually was "consumed" by a natural phenomenon, Jockey's Ridge. Near the end, the hotel gave patrons a discounted rate if they were willing to shovel some sand to reach their rooms!

By the mid-1850s, nearly six hundred people resided year-round at Nags Head. A post office was established in 1884. By the 1900s, hundreds of homes had been built in Nags Head, including many right on the beach. These were built on log foundations so the dwellings could be rolled back, if need be. Because the Outer Banks is a narrow ribbon of shifting sand, erosion and tide patterns could merit a home being moved further back two or three times during a homeowner's life. Today, houses are no longer built on logs but are relocated by raising the home off the ground, loading it onto a flatbed truck, and transporting it to the new destination—usually just a few feet or yards away.

Sand Skiing at Jockey's Ridge, Nags Head
by the Elizabeth City Majorettes 1960

Nags Head became an incorporated town in 1961. It boasts a few impressive developments, such as South Ridge and The Village at Nags Head. It remains a very popular spot for summer vacationers for a couple of reasons. One is that Nags Head is the southernmost of the northern beach communities, making it centrally located to both the northern and southern Outer Banks. Daytrippers appreciate this convenience. Additionally, there is good fishing and excellent hang-gliding here, as well as a lovely beach and old-style beach cottages.

Nags Head Beach Cottage Row Historic District consists of wooden cottages with wraparound porches, gabled roofs, and painted shutters. These privately owned residences are all that is left of a bygone era.

According to a recent article in the *News & Record* (Greensboro, North Carolina), our barrier islands are in greater jeopardy than most of us imagine. Stan Riggs, an East Carolina University geologist, informed the North Carolina Coastal Resources Commission that beach renourishment efforts will be to no avail in the long run. Riggs predicts that in the next 50–150 years there will be no more barrier islands because of hurricanes and higher sea levels. The geologist even goes so far as to say that one category five storm or ten years of steady storms would wipe out low-lying islands.

Sites and Attractions–Northern Beach Communities

Currituck Lighthouse was the last beacon built on the Outer Banks. It was lit on December 1, 1875. Requiring one and a half years to build and several appropriations totaling $178,000, the beacon stands 162 feet tall, has 214 steps, and a 50,000-candlepower lamp that can be seen for up to 18 nautical miles. It is one of four beacons placed at intervals from Cape Henry, Virginia, to Cape Hatteras. Currituck Lighthouse is located thirty-four miles south of Cape Henry, and thirty-two and a half miles north-northwest of Bodie Island Lighthouse.

Because Currituck Sound was (and is) very shallow, the big vessels that brought in the bricks and other building supplies had to anchor as far as eight miles out. Shallow-bottomed boats carried the materials the rest of the way to the dock. From the dock, the one million bricks and other supplies were carried by a cart on the tramway, which extended from the wharf to the lighthouse site.

The stone and timber piling foundation goes as far as seven feet below the ground and the base walls are five feet, eight inches thick, decreasing to three feet at the parapet. Since the four Outer Banks lighthouses so closely resembled one another, the Lighthouse Board ordered them painted with different patterns to make them easily distinguishable to mariners. Since the other lighthouses were already painted with black-and-white vertical, horizontal, and checkered patterns, the Board decided to leave this lighthouse natural, probably to avoid the expense of repainting it from time to time. And so it remains today.

Originally, the beacon was fueled by a mineral oil lamp with five concentric wicks. Automated in 1939, the electric light now has a flash pattern of three seconds on, seventeen seconds off. A generator provided electricity until grid electricity reached Corolla in the 1950s.

The Outer Banks Conservationists are responsible for the massive renovation efforts on the lighthouse, keepers' houses, and outbuildings. The tower is open for climbing, seasonally, and there is a museum and gift shop in one of the former keeper's residences. Corolla. 252-453-4939. www.currituckbeachlight.com.

Duck Pier Field Research Facility is an 1,840-foot-long pier and research facility used by the U.S. Army Corps of Engineers. The former U.S. Navy bombing site is a perfect place for studying the effects of man-made jetties, erosion, beach nourishment projects, and so forth. It is situated on 173 federally-owned acres, due north of Duck. Approximately a dozen employees and scientists are stationed here and have several spectacular tools at their service, including a 35-foot-tall Coastal Research Amphibious Buggy (CRAB) and a 150-foot research vessel. In 1994, over 100 scientists from around the world gathered here to conduct experiments and review the results of fifteen years of studies. Northernmost tip of Duck. 252-261-6840, ext. 401. http://www.frf.usace.army.mil/

Historic Corolla Village features a few of the original historic buildings completely renovated so they reflect what the tiny community once looked like, such as Corolla Chapel, where religious services are still held, and Corolla Schoolhouse. Corolla (behind Currituck Lighthouse). No phone or website available.

Kill Devil Hills Lifesaving Station was built in 1878, after the U.S. Lifesaving Service mandated that lifesaving stations should be constructed every 7 miles along the perilous Outer Banks shoreline. It was moved 30 miles north of its original location in Kill Devil Hills to Corolla in 1986. The structure has particular historical significance because the Wright Brothers frequented it during their time at the Outer Banks. The lifesaving crew, who lived in the station, befriended the Wright Brothers and assisted in some of their aviation experiments. The old lifesaving station, located near the Currituck Lighthouse and Corolla Village, is now used as a retail shop. No phone or website available.

The Outer Banks Center for Wildlife Education is an educational center and museum highlighting area waterfowl, ecology, and wildlife. Its mission statement is "to educate North Carolina's citizens in the area of wildlife resources through increased awareness, knowledge and skills that result in understanding, commitment, informed decisions, and constructive actions to ensure the stewardship of the state's wildlife resources." Corolla (across the boat dock from Whalehead Club). 252-453-0221. www.ncwildlife.org

The Whalehead Club affords visitors a rare glimpse into the "lifestyles of the rich and famous" and takes them back in time to when this area was little more than a remote fishing and hunting mecca. The 20,000-square-foot mansion was built in 1925 by wealthy railroad industrialist Edward Collins Knight Jr. for his wife, Marie Louise LeBel, who was refused admission to the all-male Lighthouse Hunt Club. The exorbitantly expensive, retaliatory hunt club cost almost $385,000 to build in 1925. Among its many features is an elevator, five chimneys, fifteen bedrooms, copper roof shingles, corduroy walls, Tiffany lighting fixtures, fresh and salt water for therapeutic baths, and a swimming pool.

Despite the numerous amenities and square footage, the Knights never entertained large numbers of people. Instead, they spent quiet winters at the property they called Corolla Island Club from 1925 to 1934. Although the Knights resided in New York much of the year, Mrs. Marie Louise Knight did not fit in with New York society and preferred spending time here. She was likened to Mae West because she used to holster pistols and walk around the wild vegetation that surrounded the house shooting at snakes and rodents. She also liked to drink and it is rumored that servants sometimes had to use the elevator to get her up to her bedroom. As was typical, Edward and Marie had separate bedrooms, but what is interesting is that he had no lock on his door but she had a lock on hers!

The beautiful home sat empty for many years following their deaths because relatives did not know what to do with it. They eventually sold the house in 1940 to Ray Adams of Washington, D.C., for a reported $25,000. Adams renamed it the Whalehead Club. He rented the property to the Coast Guard during World War II for use as a training base, and it was later used briefly as a private school for boys. For nearly a decade, it served as a research facility for a rocket fuel testing company. After that, it once again sat dormant until Currituck County took ownership and began restoring it. The county's efforts earned the grand old structure a spot on the National Register of Historic Places. Corolla (adjacent to the Currituck Lighthouse, facing the sound). 252-453-9040. www.whaleheadclub.com

Wright Brothers National Memorial was built in 1932 as a tribute to the Wright Brothers' contribution to aeronautics. The memorial has a visitors center with a gift shop and numerous exhibits, including a replica of the Wright flyer devoted to the Wright Brothers's efforts, as well as a lecture presented by a knowledgeable park service employee. Also on the site are replicas of the Wright Brothers' camp and work area.

The Wright Brothers owned a bicycle shop in Dayton, Ohio. They graduated from building bicycles to building gliders and airplanes. They needed a place to test their equipment, a location that provided optimal flying conditions. They wrote to Captain Bill Tate at the Kitty

Hawk Weather Station to inquire. He responded with such enthusiasm and encouragement that Wilbur Wright made the long, arduous journey arriving on September 13, 1900. He set up camp in Kitty Hawk Village, near Captain Tate's home. Orville arrived a couple of weeks later.

During the next three years the men conducted several experiments, modifying their glider accordingly. They returned to Dayton in the winters to work at their bicycle shop and build equipment such as an engine or propellers. The Wright Brothers perfected their aircraft and made their fourth trip to Kill Devil Hills in September 1903. They were ready to make their first test flight on December 14, 1903. It wasn't successful because Wilbur stalled the plane when he brought the nose up too fast. Three days later, Orville piloted the plane and it stayed airborne for twelve seconds. The brothers took turns and by the fourth flight at noon, Wilbur stayed in the air for 59 seconds and went 829 feet.

From the weather station, Orville sent this message out on the telegraph: "Success Four Flights Thursday Morning. All Against Twenty-One Mile Wind. Started from Level With Engine Power Alone. Average Speed Through Air Thirty-One Miles. Longest 59 Seconds. Inform Press. Home Christmas. Orville Wright." US 158, MP 8, Kill Devil Hills. 252-441-7430. www.nps.gov/wrbr

---

3. ROANOKE ISLAND

History

This twelve-mile-long and three-mile-wide island holds the most historical significance of the Outer Banks, and arguably, the entire United States of America. History books credit Jamestown, Virginia, as the first colony in the New World. However, Roanoke Island is where the first colony was attempted. In 1585, Sir Walter Raleigh's cousin, Richard Grenville, brought six hundred men to the

New World. He left them under the command of Ralph Lane and returned to England. Sir Francis Drake visited this new colony on his way back to England from Florida. Things were going so badly, especially as far as battling the area Native Americans, that the men abandoned their colony and returned with Drake to England.

Two years later, Raleigh sent Grenville back to the New World with another group of settlers. The new colonists immediately began work on Fort Raleigh and settled down in their new homeland. Grenville soon returned to England. John White, who had been chosen as governor of this new colony, was forced to return to England for supplies. Surviving in the New World was harder than the colonists had expected. Due to the war between England and Spain, White was called to duty and was unable to return to the new settlement until 1590. Meanwhile, his daughter, Eleanor Dare, gave birth to the first English child in the New World, Virginia Dare, on August 18, 1587.

White was in for the surprise of his life when he returned to find that all of the settlers had mysteriously disappeared. Fort Raleigh stood empty and there was no sign of life. The only clue was the word "Croatoan" carved on a board. This was especially strange because the pre-arranged signal was to carve a cross. The cross represented danger and so it would be known that the colonists had to flee from danger. So what did this clue mean? Were the settlers all right? Had they relocated voluntarily or had danger come so suddenly that there was no time to carve a cross?

We'll probably never know. John White had to return to England before he had time to conduct a thorough search of surrounding islands. His initial search turned up nothing and a later investigation also revealed nothing. It was like the men, women, and children just vanished into thin air! Many theories have been brought forth over the years, but no definitive answers have been found as to what happened to the Lost Colony.

For many years, the island consisted of three communities: Upper End, Lower End, and California. The parcel of land known as California extended from Burnside Road to Bowserstown Road. No one knows how or why this part of the island got its name. Relocated African Americans ended up here and a group of African-American businessmen bought California to ensure its residents retain their homes. Eventually, the island encompassed two communities: Manteo and Wanchese. Both were named after Native Americans who helped the early settlers. **Manteo** was incorporated in 1899. Soon thereafter, a post office and courthouse were established. The courthouse you see today was built in 1904 to replace the original structure.

Manteo Main Street 1947

Fort Huger was established at Weir Point during the Civil War. It was one of the biggest fortifications built by the Confederates during this war. The Union troops won control of this fort in 1862 and a settlement for runaway slaves was set up on the northern end of the island from 1862–1867.

During the 1800s, Roanoke Island was a busy port. Steamer ships carrying freight, passengers, and mail arrived daily from Norfolk, Virginia. The Washington Baum Bridge was constructed in 1928. It joined Roanoke Island to the Outer Banks beaches. Also, paved roads stretching from Elizabeth City to Manteo were completed. Big economic growth and development would soon have occurred had it not been for the Depression and WW II. Bootleggers operated a thriving business out of the area during Prohibition, but they were the only ones who benefited financially since they didn't pay taxes on their ill-gotten gains!

Five major fires have wrecked havoc on the Roanoke Island waterfront at Manteo. Oil tanks stored at the docks accidentally ignited, causing severe fires. Fire-fighting personnel and equipment did not exist until the mid-1930s. Prior to this, townsfolk passed buckets of water down a line. As you can imagine, this would be a pretty ineffective approach against a fuel-based fire.

The picturesque island has come a long way since those dark days. Fifteen hundred crepe myrtles and live oaks can be appreciated by those passing along U.S. 64 onto Roanoke Island. England's Princess Anne visited in 1984, as did former North Carolina Governor Jim Hunt and renowned anchorman Walter Cronkite, during a special celebration.

WANCHESE

Wanchese, located on the southern end of the island, remains a quiet fishing community. Visitors will instantly sense the difference between it and other Dare County "touristy" communities. The simple, wooden fishing cottages have been home to many generations of Wanchese families and serve as a stark contrast to the expansive rental properties being built elsewhere along the Outer Banks.

Wanchese

In addition to commercial fishing, boat building is an important industry. On the harbor's east side is Wanchese Seafood Industrial Park, a state-owned boat-maintenance complex, seafood plants, boat builders, and state fisheries operations. This is the only facility of its kind in America. On the mainland, near the Croatan Sound Bridge, are two more fishing communities: Mann's Harbor and Stumpy Point.

Roanoke Island can be reached by private boat, car, or airplane. Dare County Regional Airport is on the north side of the island (Airport Road, 252-473-2600). Motorists have several options. The most popular route is U.S. 64/264. Terrible traffic problems have recently been addressed with the construction of a $90 million, 5.2-mile bridge, Virginia Dare Memorial Bridge, extending from Manns Harbor to Manteo. This means vacationers have a shortcut to area beaches and are no longer forced to follow 64 through Roanoke Island. Also, a state-of-the-art Tourism Information and Welcome Center was recently built to greet visitors as soon as they enter Roanoke Island.

On February 7, 1862 approximately 11,000 Union militia arrived at Roanoke Island to attack a Confederate stronghold. The Confederates were vastly outnumbered but put up a good fight at what is now the Nags Head Manteo Causeway. The Union army already controlled much of the Outer Banks so the Confederates desperately needed to maintain their position. However, after a few hours they were forced to surrender and Roanoke Island came under the control of Union forces.

After Union troops seized Roanoke Island, they proclaimed that slavery was contraband, which meant that any slaves that ran away would be protected by Union forces. The Federals also promised to aid all runaway and freed slaves by paying the men $8 a month, plus rations and clothing, to build Fort Burnside on the north end of Roanoke Island. Women and children were entitled to $4 a month plus rations and clothing. Soon, more than one thousand runaway and freed slaves had come to Roanoke Island.

(continued on next page)

About three thousand African Americans lived in the village, which contained a little church, school, hospital, store, and five to six hundred homes. The Union gave the villagers possession of all unclaimed lands. Some even enrolled in the Union's first African-American unit. The budding community came to an end three years later when the government returned the lands to their prior owners. Worse still, the government removed many of the freed slaves from the island because they had no land and no means to earn a living. Some stayed and tried their hand at fishing, hunting, and farming.

Sites and Attractions–Roanoke Island

The Elizabethan Gardens is ten acres of botanical gardens filled with one thousand types of exotic plants and flowers. The formal gardens were designed by Richard Webel and Umberto Innocenti to show off indigenous Outer Banks shrubs, trees, and flowers. It was cleverly designed so as to bloom year-round. Thus the gardens could be open all year. Some outstanding features include

The Elizabethan Gardens

a splendid fifteenth-century fountain, gazebo, and pool. There are restrooms and a gift shop on site. Off US 64, Roanoke Island. 252-473-3244. www.outerbanks.com/eliza bethangardens

Fort Raleigh National Historic Site includes five hundred acres of Lost Colony fort remains and a visitor's center with a museum. There is also a trail (Thomas Hariot Nature Trail) with historical placards along the route. Off US 64, Roanoke Island. 252-473 5772. www.nps.gov/fora/

Freedmen's Colony Site and **Fort Huger**. Freedmen's Colony was a settlement for runaway slaves from 1862–1867. Signs posted along a two-mile trail tell its story. Entrance is well posted near the entrance to Elizabethan Gardens. Nearby Fort Huger was one of the biggest Confederate fortifications in the area. Most of it now lies underwater at Weirs Point, a beach. Northern end of Roanoke Island at Weirs Point. No phone available. www.roanokeisland.com

Illuminations Summer Arts Festival provides various shows, including jazz concerts, dance shows, and dramas in an outdoor pavilion. The audience is encouraged to bring a blanket or folding chairs and a picnic. Off US 64, Roanoke Island. 252-475-1500/1506. www.roanokeisland.com

The Lost Colony is America's oldest outdoor drama. It theorizes what happened to those early colonists. The long-running drama opened in 1937 and was penned by Pulitzer Prize playwright Paul Green. It has been attended by celebrities and dignitaries. North Carolinian Andy Griffith began his acting career in this prestigious production. Over the years, more than three million folks have attended this show, which includes spectacular costumes, dancing, singing, and fireworks. Off US 64, Roanoke Island. 800-488-5012 or 252-473-3414. www.thelostcolony.org

North Carolina Aquarium on Roanoke Island is one of three impressive state aquariums, complete with numerous exhibits and gift shops. This 68,000-square-foot aquarium houses all kinds of marine life and shipwreck replicas. Kids and adults will delight in watching many interesting-looking fish, endangered sea turtles, sharks, barracudas, otters, and alligators. Presentations which can be appreciated by all ages are often given. It underwent a huge renovation in 2000 and opened with the theme "Waters of the Outer Banks." The crowning gem of this aquarium is a 180,000-gallon ocean tank center with a replica of the *USS Monitor* shipwreck and many varieties of reef fish. There is also a large atrium that highlights the aquatic life of the state's rivers, sounds, and marshes. 374 Airport Road, Roanoke Island. 252-473-3494. www.ncaquariums.com

North Carolina Aquarium on Roanoke Island

North Carolina Maritime Museum on Roanoke Island has exhibits pertaining to boatbuilding and area's rich maritime history. There are a number of small watercraft on exhibit such as the 1883 *Creef Shad* boat, spritsail skiffs, and a 1948 Davis Runabout. The facility opened in 1996 and is located in the George Washington Creef Boathouse. The boatbuilding operation and museum are staffed by volunteers. The building suffered significant damage as a result of Hurricane Isabel in 2003 but has been repaired. 106 Fernando Street, Roanoke Island. 252-475-1500. http://www.ah.dcr.state.nc.us/sections/maritime/branches/roanoke_default.htm

Roanoke Island Festival Park and the *Elizabeth II* includes Roanoke Adventure Museum, an 8,500-square foot museum with gift shop; an art gallery, boardwalks for area exploration, a settlement site, a film, and a replica of the ship that carried the lost colonists to the New World in 1585. The film depicts the history and culture of the island's inhabitants and the art gallery offers an ever-changing array of displays. The *Elizabeth II* is a sixty-nine-foot sailing vessel that is owned by the state but was built using private donations. The wooden ship cost $750,000 to build—considerably more than the original ship cost! During the summer, Elizabethan-costumed guides offer tours of its two decks and share interesting stories. Additionally, the North Carolina School of Arts holds its annual arts festival at the park. There are many children's performances as well. 1 Festival Park, Roanoke Island. 252-475-1500 or 475-1506. www.roanokeisland.com

Roanoke Island Festival Park Adventure Museum

Nearby Towns

BATH

Bath, founded in 1705, is one of the state's oldest towns. As Charleston is known as the "City of Firsts," so is Bath. It had the state's first public library, port, shipyard, church—and resident pirate! It is believed that Blackbeard lived here briefly and was quite a celebrity. One of his fourteen wives is said to have been from Bath. Bath soon became a major port because of its strategic location on the Pamlico Sound. Four buildings dating back to the original township are on the National Register of Historic Places. Stop in at the Historic Bath State Historic Site on Carteret Street to see a film explaining the town's history and also to pick up self-guided walking maps or take a guided tour. Take NC 92 or the Pamlico ferry to get here. Bath Visitor Center. 252-923-3971.

Residents of historic Edenton enjoy the scenic beauty afforded by Albemarle Sound.

Edenton, established in 1690, is also one of the oldest towns in the state and among the oldest in the United States. It was incorporated in 1715 as "the Towne on Queen Anne's Creek." The name was later changed to Edenton in honor of former North Carolina Governor Charles Eden. Its residents have had a hand in shaping our history, from Joseph Hewes, who signed the Declaration of Independence, to Hugh Williamson, who signed the U.S. Constitution in 1787. Edenton, which calls itself "the South's prettiest small town," has a rich history and is well worth a visit. It is about a forty-five minutes' drive from Roanoke Island, on Albemarle Sound at the mouth of the

EDENTON

Chowan River. Motorists can reach it by taking NC 32 from the north or south, or Hwy. 17 from the east or west. Be sure to visit Historic Edenton State Historic Site (252-482-2637), which has tourism information and walking or trolley tours, and the Edenton Museum, which is down the street from the historic site (252-482-2637, www.edenton.com).

ELIZABETH CITY

Elizabeth City is perched on the banks of the Pasquotank River, whose name means "where the currents divide." The waterfront town is the headquarters of the biggest Coast Guard facilities in the U.S., has five historic districts, and was featured in Norm Crampton's *The 100 Best Small Towns in America*. Elizabeth City can be reached from the west on US 158 or Hwy. 17 from the north or south. Elizabeth City Chamber of Commerce. 252-335-4365. www.elizcity.com.

WASHINGTON

Washington is fifteen minutes northwest of Bath and is another historic town, founded in 1775. This scenic city was named after former President George Washington. The Beaufort county seat was moved from Bath to Washington in 1785, which catapulted its commerce and growth. Much of the town was demolished during the Civil War, rebuilt after the war, and then destroyed again by fire in 1900. Several blocks of buildings are included on the National Register of Historic Places. Washington City Chamber of Commerce. 252-946-9168. www.pamlico.com/washington

4. BODIE ISLAND

History

In the 1720s, North Carolinian Mathew Midgett was issued a land grant for Bodie Island. Midgett owned the island until his death in 1734, at which time it was inherited by his sons. Over the years the island has called Bodys Island, Body Island, Bodies Island, Micher Island, and Cow Island. Legend has it that the island got its name because of all the bodies that washed ashore from area shipwrecks.

Some believe it was named after someone who had something to do with the lighthouse, perhaps someone who was part of its construction or who served as a keeper? Over the years there have been three lighthouses here and several inlets have opened and closed. In fact, the island has changed shapes a few times over the years due to the ever changing inlets.

The 9.5-mile-long island has served many purposes: lifesaving (both a lighthouse and lifesaving station were erected on the island); military combat during the Civil War; hunting (several gun clubs utilized it over the years); and finally, being part of the Cape Hatteras National Seashore. It was truly an island until 1819, when Roanoke Inlet closed, thereby connecting it with the northern peninsula beaches. It has been part of the seashore since it was established in 1953. It is uninhabited, except by waterfowl, wildlife, and a few Coast Guard personnel.

Sites and Attractions–Bodie Island

Bodie Island Lighthouse is a 150-foot structure that is positioned one half-mile from the ocean and just north of Oregon Inlet. The brick sentinel with alternating black-and-white painted bands that we see today is actually the third Bodie Island Lighthouse. Because Oregon Inlet continually shifts southward, the remains of the two original lighthouses have long since been washed away. The first beacon was so poorly constructed it was inadequate from the time it was lit in 1848. The second beacon was built in 1859, less than eleven years after the original tower. Unfortunately, the Confederates destroyed the lighthouse when they were forced to retreat. They did not want the Union to be able to use it, so they blew it up.

The third and final beacon was constructed in 1872 at a cost of $140,000. It included a large duplex and several outbuildings. This dwelling accommodated three keepers and their families. According to the Outer Banks Lighthouse Society, most of the keepers' families only lived in the house during holidays and school vacations, not just because of the cramped quarters, but also because there was no school or church nearby and Bodie Island was so remote.

Bodie Island Lighthouse is located just north of Oregon Inlet in the Cape Hatteras National Seashore.

The wall that separated the two keepers' quarters has been removed, and the former living room now serves as a visitor center. The center has lighthouse exhibits and maritime displays, restrooms, and a gift shop. On occasion, the lower portion of the beacon is open to the public.

The lighthouse was originally a fixed light illuminated by a vapor lamp. A large container of kerosene oil was lugged every day from the oil shed to the tower and then up its 214 steps to the lantern room. The lamp was filled and the wick was cleaned, trimmed, and then lit. Until the 1920s, a keeper stood watch from the watch tower each night. He kept warm in this room, located just below the lantern room, by using a coal stove. This meant he also had to haul coal upstairs each night, in addition to the lamp oil. The keeper went on duty each night as soon as the lamp was lit, just before sunset, and remained on duty until shortly after sunrise.

When electricity replaced oil in the early 1930s, the steady beam was replaced by a flashing light and the oil shed became home to a generator. In 1932, a one-thousand-watt bulb was installed, along with an automatic changer for when the bulb burned out. In the 1950s, the lighting system changed once again, becoming an automated 160,000-candlepower beam.

The Coast Guard has turned over most of the grounds and all buildings, including the lighthouse, to the National Park Service. A nearby U.S. Lifesaving Station, erected in 1874, is now used by Park Service personnel serving this area of the Cape Hatteras National Seashore (see Hatteras Island for more information). There is a clearly marked trail that originates at the Bodie Island Lighthouse and extends through the marsh to the sound, providing a scenic stroll. Eight miles south of the US 158/US 64 intersection, west of NC 12, Bodie Island. 252-441-5711. http://www.nps.gov/caha/bodielh.htm

Laura A. Barnes, built in 1918, was a 120-foot schooner that was wrecked during a voyage from New York to South Carolina. A nor'easter forced the ship aground due north of Coquina Beach, but the crew survived the shipwreck. It was one of the last schooners built in the U.S. The National Park Service moved the remains of the ship to Coquina Beach in 1973 and put up informational signs at the site. NC 12 at Coquina Beach, Bodie Island. 252-473-2111. www.nps.gov/caha/capehatteras.html

The Outer Banks has more than two million acres of bays and sounds, which puts it just behind Alaska and Louisiana in estuarine acreage. The Albemarle Sound is the largest freshwater sound on the East Coast. The Outer Banks also has three other significant sounds: Currituck, Roanoke, and Croatan.

Commercial fishing has always been an important part of coastal life.

Oregon Inlet Coast Guard Station. At one time, there were two lifesaving stations at Oregon Inlet. The Oregon Inlet Station was on the south side of the inlet and the Bodie Island Station was to the north of the inlet. The Oregon Inlet Station still exists, but is in the great jeopardy due to its proximity to the inlet. The Bodie Island Station was razed to make way for the new Coast Guard Station. The 10,000-square-foot structure was constructed in the 1990s. In the Cape Hatteras National Seashore, behind the Oregon Inlet Fishing Center, on Bodie Island (8 miles south of Whalebone Junction, NC 12). 800-272-5199 or 252-441-6301. www.oregon-inlet.com

5. HATTERAS ISLAND

History

The lower Outer Banks is a far bigger stretch of sand than the upper portion. Hatteras Island covers thirty-three miles, from Oregon Inlet to Hatteras Inlet, and is made up of seven townships: Rodanthe, Waves, Salvo, Avon, Buxton, Frisco, and Hatteras Village. As in most of the Outer Banks, fishing and tourism are the primary industries here. There is only one, two-lane road, NC 12, so traffic on this thoroughfare is heavy during tourism season.

However, the only real hardships to life here are the nor'easters and hurricanes. When they hit (or seriously threaten to), tourists flee or forgo planned vacations. Considering that hurricane season runs from June to November, and that the main tourist season is June to September, one can see how damaging this can be to the local economy. In the past several years, Hurricanes Andrew, Hugo, Dennis, and Isabel have done significant damage to the area in terms of tourism. Erosion also threatens the island. America's tallest beacon, Cape Hatteras Lighthouse, had to be moved in 1999 from the beach to the other side of the highway to protect it from the encroaching sea.

What makes living or visiting this area worth the risk and aggravation? The first thing is its beach. Hatteras has been named one of the top ten beaches in America by Stephen "Dr. Beach" Leatherman, who rates beaches based on fifty criteria including sand quality, water temperature, cleanliness, and proximity of amenities. "Dr.

Beach" has a Ph.D. in coastal science and is director of Florida International University's Laboratory for Coastal Research.

Another good reason to come to Hatteras is that some of the best fishing can be found here. The Outer Banks has the honor of being "Billfish Capital of the World." World-record fish have been caught at Cape Point. This also means you'll enjoy some of the best fresh seafood you've ever eaten! Also, Cape Hatteras National Seashore and Pea Island National Wildlife Refuge are paradises for nature lovers. The beaches here are more pristine and less crowded than more centrally-located state beaches. What's more, you won't find high-rise timeshare condominium complexes and towering neon signs indicating "bargain beachwear."

Cape Hatteras National Seashore

One of the biggest reasons development hasn't been more extensive here is that the Bonner Bridge, which juts over the Oregon Inlet, wasn't built until 1963. That means that until the 1960s, the only way to get from Hatteras Island to the mainland was by private boat. While this thwarted tourism, it wasn't a problem for most residents who owned boats because they made their living through commercial fishing. These ingenious inhabitants reaped anything and everything they could to make money, including whale oil, crabs, oysters, turtles, and seaweed. They also had their own vegetable gardens and livestock which freely roamed the island to graze.

At one time, there was only one community, Chicamacomico (also called Chicamacomico Banks), that extended from Oregon Inlet to Avon (formerly

Kinnakeet). By the early 1900s, this had separated into three communities: **Rodanthe, Waves, and Salvo.** The largest is Rodanthe, which is home to the Chicamacomico Lifesaving Station and a fishing pier. The Confederates came to Rodanthe—then known as Chicamacomico—in 1861 in hopes of recapturing Fort Hatteras and Fort Clark. They had lost these important fortifications to the Federals during an earlier naval assault. During this attack, the Confederates had pushed the Union troops all the way up to the part of the island that is now Buxton. More Union troops arrived at the southern end of the island, forcing the Southern Rebels to retreat north. These battles were named "The Chicamacomico Races."

**RODANTHE
WAVES
SALVO**

The Chicamacomico Lifesaving Station was established in 1874 as one of seven stations that were built along the Outer Banks. The crew saved many lives over the years, but one of its most daring and heroic deeds happened in 1918 when an English tanker, *Mirlo*, caught fire after being torpedoed by the Germans. Forty-two sailors were saved by the crew of Chicamacomico.

Chicamacomico Lifesaving Station

The first of several name changes occurred in 1874 when the post office changed the town's name from Chicamacomico to Rodanthe, although the lifesaving station maintained its name. Something to do with easier spelling! By the turn of the nineteenth century, Rodanthe had become three separate communities: North Rodanthe, South Rodanthe, and Clark. Much later, North Rodanthe became Rodanthe and the other two villages were renamed as Waves and Salvo. The subsequent name changes came about in 1939 when the post office opened a branch in South Rodanthe. To avoid any confusion with North Rodanthe, the name was changed to Waves. When a post office opened in Clark in 1901, its name was changed to Salvo.

AVON

The next village, **Avon,** is separated by ten miles of undeveloped National Park Service land. This can be confusing to tourists because some locals still call it by its former name, Kinnakeet. As in its neighboring communities, the post office changed Kinnakeet's name when it opened a branch here in 1883. The government decided the Native American names were too hard to spell and pronounce. One of the seven lifesaving stations deemed necessary along the Outer Banks, Little Kinnakeet Lifesaving Station, was placed here in 1874. To its south, Big Kinnakeet Lifesaving Station was erected five years later. Avon is home to the ever popular windsurfing spot, the Canadian Hole. Millions of folks from all over the world have come here over the years to experience its superior conditions (see Recreational Activities for more information).

Buxton 1952

BUXTON

Buxton is the hub of Hatteras Island because it offers the only school, medical facilities, and Dare County government satellite offices, as well as the U.S. Weather Bureau Station. America's tallest beacon, Cape Hatteras Lighthouse, is located here. The point of land that juts out to the Atlantic Ocean at Cape Hatteras is Cape Point, which is one of the best fishing spots on Hatteras Island and a place where surfing competitions are held annually. This village is also home to Buxton Woods, a spectacular maritime forest with extensive nature trails that runs through Frisco (see Nature Preserves, Sanctuaries, and Parks for more information).

Frisco is the next village to the south. Its appeal is the solitude. One of its few commercial enterprises is the Frisco Native American Museum and Natural History Center (252-995-4440, www.nativeamericanmuseum.org). An ancient Native American village has been discovered near the museum, and excavations are ongoing. Formerly known as Trent, the postal service changed the town's name to Frisco when it opened an office here. It is unclear why the government changed the name since Trent was not difficult to spell or pronounce. Some surmise there must have been another Trent in the state, or something similar to it, that might have caused confusion. Army Air Service General Billy Mitchell used the Frisco airstrip to bomb battleships found off the coast on September 5, 1923. This successful event helped in the founding of the modern-day U.S. Air Force.

FRISCO

Hatteras Village is the southernmost village on the island and the location of the ferry terminal to Ocracoke Island. At the terminal, there is a marina filled with all kinds of tourist shops, restaurants, and a hotel. Additionally, the impressive Graveyard of the Atlantic Museum is located here. Hatteras Landing and Hatteras Village are the biggest shopping centers on Hatteras Island. You won't find any superstores, monster home supply centers, or three-story shopping malls. That's what makes the Outer Banks so great. With just a few exceptions, there are only mom-and-pop establishments: independent restaurants and gas stations, local honky-tonks, family-operated motels and guesthouses, quaint arts and crafts stores, and old-fashioned grocery stores.

HATTERAS VILLAGE

Hatteras Inlet was created by the same 1846 storm that brought about Oregon Inlet. As a link between Pamlico Sound and the ocean, it made the area less dangerous because it wasn't as difficult to cross the Gulf Stream. Previously, ships had had to go way out past Cape Point to avoid the strong Gulf Stream and its accompanying winds, or go very close to shore. Sailing too close to shore was just as hazardous as going farther out to sea—perhaps more so because of the treacherous Diamond Shoals. Records show that ships sometimes had to wait for days or weeks to get around Cape Point if conditions weren't favorable. And, at one time, one hundred vessels couldn't get around Diamond Shoals for twenty-six days. The sea traffic was detained north of Cape Hatteras for nearly a month!

Hatteras Village was originally known as Hatteras. Hatteras was one of the rare island communities that kept its original name after the postal service set an office there. Later, it came to be called Hatteras Village to avoid confusion with Cape Hatteras, which is located thirteen miles north of the village, or with Hatteras Inlet, which is located four miles south of the village, at the end of the island. Some of the best fishing along the Outer Banks is at Hatteras, which is why it hosts numerous fishing tournaments each year (see Traditions for a list of tournaments and fishing information).

The island still celebrates its unique history, including two annual Christmas celebrations. Residents celebrate the holiday on December 25 and again on Old Christmas, which occurs during the first week of January. Many unusual events take place during Old Christmas, a tradition dating back to medieval England.

There was no highway joining any of Hatteras Island's communities until 1953, when the Cape Hatteras National Seashore was established. Prior to this time, these townships had nothing to do with each other. In fact, they competed on every level, from lifesaving stations to fishing. The only common denominator was Mirlo Beach.When the seashore was established, the state government proposed that a highway be built which would run the length of the island. However, the government wanted a consolidated school system in exchange for building NC 12 through Hatteras Island. The islanders declined the government's offer, enjoying their independence. It was many years before the schools were combined and the communities no longer competed with one another.

In 2003, Hurricane Isabel tore through the Outer Banks and hit this island especially hard. An inlet was created between Hatteras Village and the rest of Hatteras Island. Homes, businesses, and NC 12 were destroyed or heavily damaged at Hatteras Village. Although some experts said it shouldn't be done, the inlet was filled in and most of the homes, businesses, and highway were eventually repaired and rebuilt.

Hatteras Island is accessible by car from the north on NC 12. Simply cross the Herbert C. Bonner Bridge. From the south, it can be reached only by private boat or state ferry via Ocracoke Island. There is a small airstrip in Frisco for private aircraft, Billy Mitchell Airport.

Seven lifesaving stations were established on the Outer Banks in 1874. They were located at Jones Hill (Currituck Beach Lighthouse), Caffey's Inlet (Duck), Kitty Hawk Beach, Nags Head, Bodie Island, Chicamacomico, and Little Kinnakeet (Avon). The men patrolled the beach twenty-four hours a day and kept vigil from their station's towers. This was an important and dangerous job and the men knew it. Most of them were longtime Outer Banks residents and/or seamen. In 1876, all seven men of the Jones Hill Lifesaving Station were lost during a rescue mission.

Eleven more stations opened by 1879: Deal's Island, Old Currituck Inlet, Poyners Hill, Paul Gamiels Hill, Kill Devil Hills, Tommy's Hummock, Pea Island, Cedar Hummock, Big Kinnakeet, Creeds Hill, and Hatteras. Pea Island Station was the only all-African-American station, not just on the Outer Banks but in the country. Thanks to the efforts of all these heroic men, thousands of lives were saved. Some of these stations still exist as private residences or businesses and Coast Guard property.

Sites and Attractions–Hatteras Island

Altoona **Wreck** is the remains of an 1878 shipwreck. The crew members and most of the cargo were saved but the vessel was lost. There's not much left of the wreck but the hull can still be seen. SUVs and ATVs may come on the beach at Cape Point (ramp 44), near Cape Hatteras Lighthouse or take the easy, ten-minute walk from the road.

Cape Point, Buxton, Hatteras Island. 252-473-2111.
www.nps.gov/caha/capehatteras.html

Cape Hatteras Lighthouse is America's tallest lighthouse and a source of great pride among North Carolinians.
Amidst much controversy, in 1999-2000 it was moved
2,900-feet west-southwest, about 1,600 feet from the shoreline, because of serious erosion. This is the second Cape
Hatteras Lighthouse. The first beacon was commissioned
in 1793, but it took nearly nine years to complete due to
bad weather and illness among the crew that was building
it. The beacon was finally lit in 1803. However, it was too
short and its lighting apparatus
was insufficient to fulfill its
obligation. Despite several
modifications, the lighthouse
had too many shortcomings to
overcome. In 1824, Diamond
Shoals Lightship was stationed
nearby for the first time to
serve as additional aid for
mariners. Additionally, the
keeper who had been criti-
cized for not doing his job
properly was replaced.

After the Civil War, it was
decided that a better lighthouse had to be built. Work
began in 1868 on a new beacon modeled after the light at
Cape Lookout which would
be located six hundred feet
further inland than the original lighthouse and thus be bet-

*Cape Hatteras Lighthouse
is America's tallest beacon.*

ter protected from erosion. Bricks and other supplies were
brought in to the isolated island by barge, and a tram railway was built to haul materials to the construction site.

The new tower was designed to be a whopping 198
feet tall, comparable to a skyscraper. Despite outbreaks of
malaria among the building crew members and the loss of
some construction materials in a shipwreck, work continued at a rapid pace and the $150,000 conical tower light,
equipped with a first-order Fresnel lens, made its debut on
December 18, 1870. The original beacon was destroyed

after the new lighthouse was lit. The octagonal base of brick and granite, which measures twenty-four by forty-five feet six inches, was left natural. The black-and-white bar-ber-pole paint job, or "candy striping" as it is more com-monly described, was added in 1873 to make the light-house more distinctive by day. Today, the flashing beacon is automated, but at the time Hatteras was built, the keep-er had to wind weights suspended on heavy cables in order to rotate the thousand-prism lens.

By the 1920s, erosion had once again become a major problem. A steel frame tower was built further inland and Cape Hatteras Lighthouse was shut down on May 15, 1936. In 1948, the former beacon was reactivated when it was determined there was still a need for it. The light was taken out of the steel tower and put back into Cape Hatteras Lighthouse. The steel tower was dismantled.

It's a great view from the top of the lighthouse, but visitors should be in good health to attempt the climb up its 257 steps! A visitor's center, museum, and gift shop are located in the former keepers' quarters. Off NC 12 at Buxton. 252-995-4474. www.nps.gov/caha

Chicamacomico Lifesaving Station is one of the seven original lifesaving stations that once operated along the Outer Banks. This station and its outbuildings are con-sidered to be among the most complete U.S. Lifesaving Service/Coast Guard Station complexes on the Atlantic Coast. The original building was turned into a boathouse when the new shingle-style station was built in 1911. Both have been renovated and are listed on the National Register of Historic Places. This large complex serves as an excellent reminder of these heroic men and the tremen-dous service they once provided. One of their biggest res-cues was that of the crew of an English tanker, *Mirlo,* when it was torpedoed by the Germans in 1918. The station was closed in 1954. Nowadays, volunteers with the nonprofit Chicamacomico Historical Association operate the on-site museum and gift shop and maintain the station. Summer programs, including lifesaving reenactments, are offered. NC 12, Rodanthe, Hatteras Island. 252-987-1552. www.chi camacomico.org

Diamond Shoals Light Tower. The shoals once held a lighthouse, but pounding waves so violently struck the offshore rocks which held the lighthouse that federal officials gave up the project. Three lightships have been stationed on the shoals since 1824. The first sank in an 1827 gale. The second held its ground from 1897 until German submarines sank it in 1918. The third beamed until 1967 when it was replaced by the current light tower. Diamond Shoals, the rocks around the tower, are the southern end of the treacherous near-shore sandbars off Hatteras Island. Its bright beacon blinks every two seconds from a steel structure set twelve miles out in the sea. There has been talk for some time by the Coast Guard of tearing down the structure because it has suffered so much abuse that it is becoming structurally unsafe to maintain and may eventually become a navigational hazard, but so far no initiative has been taken. This is because of the high costs that would be involved in destroying and removing the old tower. You can't really visit this attraction because it is in the Atlantic Ocean. However, you can see this unusual light tower from the eastern shore of Cape Point and from the top of the Cape Hatteras Lighthouse. No telephone or website available.

Deep sea fishing at Diamond Shoals 1948. Diamond Lightship can be seen in the background. Several lightships were stationed here from 1827–1967 but either broke free of their moorings or were hit by passing ships, and one was sunk by a German submarine.

Frisco Native American Museum and Nature Center is a good place to learn more about Native Americans and discover what the Outer Banks was like when they were the only inhabitants. Artifacts include weapons, jewelry, pottery, and more. There are also nature trails around the property and a lovely gift store featuring Native American crafts and local interest books. NC 12, Frisco, Hatteras Island. 252-995-4440. www.nativeamericanmuseum.org

Graveyard of the Atlantic Museum was a long time in the making but it was well worth the wait. The 19,000-square-foot, hurricane-proof facility provides an excellent overview of Outer Banks history, especially from 1545 to 1945, and is a must-see for visitors. The purpose of this nonprofit museum is to preserve the maritime history and heritage of the Outer Banks. NC 12, Hatteras Village, Hatteras Island. 252-986-2995. www.graveyardoftheatlantic.com

Enjoying the Outer Banks beach

6. OCRACOKE ISLAND

History

This sixteen-mile-long island, which ranges from a half-mile to two miles wide, looks out over Silver Lake. It is bordered to the west by Pamlico Sound, to the east by the Atlantic Ocean, to the north by Hatteras Inlet, and to the south by Ocracoke Inlet. The southern beaches are the most popular with fishermen and four-wheel-drive vehicles including all-terrain vehicles (ATVs). Go farther north and you might not spot anyone else on the beach for quite some distance. This stretch of sand is best for beach-combers and sunbathers.

Ocracoke Beach

Interestingly enough, Ocracoke Island and Hatteras Island were once one and the same. The land mass was called Croatan. Some maps even indicate that Ocracoke Island, Hatteras Island, and Portsmouth Island were one giant island, Wokokon—named after a Native American tribe that came for its abundant seafood. Others theorize the island was named after the villainous buccaneer, Blackbeard. The pirate's final confrontation against the Royal Navy, led by Lt. Robert Maynard, took place here in 1718. As Maynard waited for the first light of day to proceed into battle, it is reported that he yelled out several times, "O Crow Cock! O Crow Cock!" Blackbeard was killed during this skirmish when his ship ran aground and he was outmaneuvered by the British Royal Navy.

This bit of coastline is one of the trickiest along the eastern seaboard. It has been dubbed "Graveyard of the Atlantic" because hundreds of ships have been wrecked along the Outer Banks. The many area lighthouses and lifesaving stations in the area were built to help alleviate the danger. Still, "lightering" pilots were needed to assist mariners across the shallow shoals.

In 1715, an act was passed to establish Ocracoke Island as a port. Local fishermen, who knew the waters well, became "lightering" pilots, directing guides safely past the Ocracoke Inlet. On November 11, 1719, John Lovick, Secretary of the Colony of North Carolina and a Deputy of the Lord's Proprietors, was given a land grant for the 2,110-acre Ocracoke Island. By 1730, more people began arriving on the island. Inhabitants earned a living fishing, piloting, and farming cattle and sheep.

North Carolinian William Howard bought the island on July 30, 1759, for £105 and moved to Ocracoke. Soon thereafter, island squatters were issued land grants for 20 acres apiece. Wallace Howard, who had inherited the land from his father, sold several parcels to island families.

In 1770, Ocracoke became part of Carteret County, until it was transferred to Hyde County in 1845. Ocracoke Inlet played a significant role in several wars, including the Revolutionary War, the Civil War, and World War II. Fort Ocracoke, on Beacon Island, endured a naval attack in 1861. Ocracoke residents were divided over the issue of slavery, so men fought in both the Union and Confederate troops. By November 1779, the Ocracoke Militia Company was established to protect the Ocracoke Inlet. During World War II, a naval base and radar tower were built on Ocracoke. It wasn't uncommon for islanders to see ships on fire as a result of U-boat assaults. One of the most significant attacks occurred on May 11, 1942, when 37 British sailors were killed by a German submarine torpedo.

In the late 1700s, the North Carolina General Assembly passed an act to build the Ocracoke Lighthouse. However, construction was delayed because the federal government took control of all navigational aids away from the state government in 1790. It wasn't until 1823 that the much-needed beacon was lit. Several lifesaving stations were also constructed on the island in the late 1800s and early 1900s. In 1808, the first school was built, and in 1840, the first post office was established.

By the 1820s, Ocracoke Island had become a major shipping port. However, less than thirty years later, the island population dwindled to 536 and only a small percentage still made a living as pilots. It's interesting to note that the population has barely changed in more than 150 years. In the late 1800s, a clam factory was opened on the island and records indicated it employed up to four dozen islanders. It operated until the early 1900s.

In 1940, a Coast Guard station was built and served the area for many years. During World War II, the navy operated a training and combat base on Ocracoke. The dredging of Cockle Creek and the creation of Silver Lake Harbor in 1931 significantly altered the fate of Ocracoke. It changed the economic emphasis from fishing to tourism. The island's highway was built in 1957, which furthered development and tourism.

Most amenities and necessities can now be found on the island, including a school for K-12 grades and a grocery store. Until recently, islanders had to go to the mainland to do their grocery shopping. Until the grocery store opened, only convenience items could be purchased on Ocracoke.

Only about 10 percent of the island is privately owned, including Ocracoke Village. The remaining land is owned by the National Park Service. Capitalizing on its rich history and attractions, this former fishing community has about 750 permanent residents, many of who own gift shops, bed-and-breakfast inns, lakeside cottages, seafood restaurants, and charter fishing companies. About forty thousand tourists visit the island each year. Ocracoke has been named one of the top ten beaches in America by Stephen "Dr. Beach" Leatherman, who rates beaches based on fifty criteria including sand quality, water temperature, cleanliness, and proximity of amenities.

It's interesting that the island has endured the same hurricanes and nor'easter storms as the rest of the Outer Banks, yet minimal property damage has occurred and no lives been lost in these fierce storms.

Getting to Ocracoke

Ocracoke Island is accessible only by ferry, boat, or private plane. If coming from the north, take NC 12 south until it dead ends at the end of Hatteras Island, which is where the Hatteras-Ocracoke Ferry Terminal is located. If coming from the east, take US 64 to Plymouth and then NC 32 South to NC 45 South. This takes you to US 264 South. Follow the highway to Swan Quarter and watch for Ocracoke-Swan Quarter ferry terminal signs. If coming from the west, follow the above directions along US 64 and US 264, or take US 70 East to NC 12 North and follow it to the Cedar Island-Ocracoke ferry terminal.

The ferry terminal delivers passengers to the north end of the island, which is a scenic twelve-mile drive to Ocracoke Village. The free ferry ride lasts about forty minutes. Only thirty vehicles can fit on the ferry, so reservations are strongly advised during the summer. You can obtain a ferry schedule and information at 800-368-8949 or 252-986-2353 or www.ncferry.org.

There are two toll ferries, Cedar Island and Swan Quarter. Each requires a two-and-a-half-hour ride and bring you into the Ocracoke Village terminal. For ferry service to Ocracoke from Cedar Island, call 800-856 0343. For ferry service to Ocracoke from Swan Quarter, call 800-771-1094.

The speed limit in the village is 20-25 MPH and is strictly enforced. You will not need a vehicle if you plan to stay in Ocracoke Village, where most of the shops and restaurants are located. Everything in the village is within easy walking distance. Another option is to rent a bicycle or kayak for further exploration. The best place to park is in the NPS parking lot, at the southern end of the village.

Ocracoke Harbor

Sites and Attractions–Ocracoke Island

British Cemetery is a final resting place for four men who served aboard *HMS Bedfordshire,* an anti-submarine trawler sent by Winston Churchill to help the Americans fight the Germans. In 1942, a German sub torpedoed the *HMS Bedfordshire* and it sank about forty miles from Ocracoke. Thirty-seven enlisted men and officers drowned in this conflict, but only four bodies were recovered. However, this graveyard serves as a reminder of all the men who came to America's aid during this hard-fought war. A memorial service is held on site every year. This cemetery has been deeded over to the British Government and is maintained by the British War Graves Commission. British Cemetery Road, Ocracoke Village, Ocracoke Island. 252-928-4531. No website available.

Hammock Hills Trail is a 0.75-mile trail that meanders through a maritime forest. The trailhead is three miles north of Ocracoke Village on NC 12, Ocracoke Island. No telephone or website available.

Ocracoke Interpretive Trail is a self-guided tour of Ocracoke Village's historic sites, which include Teach's Hole, where the legendary pirate Edward "Blackbeard" Teach was killed, Ocracoke Lighthouse, Silver Lake Harbor, Howard Street, and the British Cemetery. It is best done by foot or bicycle because parking is scarce and the unpaved roads are narrow. Ocracoke Village is on the National Register of Historic Places. The historic houses have several distinctive features: picket fences to keep live-stock out of vegetable gardens; wide porches, nicknamed "pizers" by Ocracokers; cisterns for collecting rainwater; and rear or detached kitchens so as to keep strong odors and heat away from the home. The wooden houses were often constructed using materials confiscated from area shipwrecks Free maps can be picked up at the Ocracoke Island Visitors Center, which is on NC 12, Ocracoke Village. 252-928-4531. No website available.

Ocracoke Lighthouse is a squat white tower that was constructed in 1822 and lit the following year. It was built by Noah Porter of Massachusetts and cost $11,359.35, including the three-room keeper's quarters. The beacon rises seventy-five feet above sea level and is made of brick covered with plaster. Before plaster was invented, keepers boiled a glue and rice mixture and used it to coat and pro-tect the brick. The light is a fixed white light that is emit-ted from a fourth-order Fresnel lens. It is the oldest con-tinuously operating light in the state (people often get con-fused because Bald Head Lighthouse is indeed older but it is no longer an active aid to navigation) and the second oldest continuously operating light on the East Coast, although the original flashing third-order Fresnel lens was briefly removed during the Civil War. Confederate troops did not want the beacon to be useful to the Union. The lighthouse was automated in 1946. The eight-thousand-can-dlepower light is visible fourteen miles out to sea The tower is not open to the public, nor is the former keeper's house because it now accommodates NPS personnel. However, the property, including a boardwalk that extends from the parking lot to the beacon, is open to the public. NC 12, Ocracoke Village, Ocracoke Island. 252-928-4531. www.outer-banks.com/lights/nocracoke.cfm

Ocracoke Preservation Society Museum and Gift Shop provides informative exhibits and a short film introducing visitors to the island's history. The Ocracoke Preservation Society is a nonprofit organization whose goal is to preserve the island's rich cultural and historical her-itage through education. It was founded in 1983 and since that time has raised money and awareness for the

Ocracoke ponies and Save An Old House Fund, which restores historic dwellings. The society also offers summer talks from its front porch.

The museum is housed in a historic structure, a circa 1900 two-story house that was once owned by David Williams. Williams was the first captain of the U.S. Coast Guard Lifesaving Station on Ocracoke. The former dwelling, which was moved to its new site in 1989, is now part of the Ocracoke Historic District. The facility opened in 1992. The museum occupies the first floor, while the second floor is a research library and administrative offices. It is located on Silver Lake, at the edge of Ocracoke Village and across from the ferry docks. Ocracoke Island. 252-928-7375. www.ocracokepreservation.org

Ocracoke Preservation Society Museum and Gift Shop

Ocracoke Ponies. These once-wild ponies were corralled in 1959 into a 180-acre field to protect them from motorists. The horses are an important part of the island's history and so their well-being is of great concern to islanders. No one knows for sure how these animals got to Ocracoke. It is widely believed that the horses swam ashore to flee sinking Spanish ships stranded on area sand bars. They may have been brought by early settlers. Island inhabitants once used them as work animals. They were also used by the Coast Guard and Lifesaving Station personnel for beach patrol. What's interesting is that

Ocracoke ponies have different physical attributes than other horses, such as seventeen ribs instead of eighteen, five lumbar vertebrae instead of six, and unusual size and markings. For many years, Ocracoke Island held an annual roundup, commonly known as pony penning. Now that the ponies have been permanently rounded up, visitors may see them from a viewing stand on NC 12, seven miles south of the Hatteras-Ocracoke Ferry Terminal. The National Park Service places four ponies in this viewing area so that visitors may see them up close. The roughly two dozen ponies are rotated regularly into this viewing area. This is also a good chance for NPS personnel to observe them and make sure they remain in good health. 252-928-4531. www.ocracoke-nc.com/ponies

About an hour from the Outer Banks is **Somerset Plantation** in Washington County. Visitors will appreciate this antebellum structure and grounds, which includes walking trails and boardwalks leading to the water. Somerset Place was once one of the biggest rice plantations in the state, requiring more than three hundred slaves to work it. The two-story house was fourteen rooms filled with period antiques and six outbuildings. What is unique about this former plantation is that both sides are equally presented, so visitors may see what it was really like for both the owners and slaves. School groups get

Somerset Place

to grind corn by hand, cook cornbread in an iron skillet, make candles, and much more. 2572 Lake Shore Road off US 64, Creswell (near Pettigrewe State Park). 252-797-4560. www.ah.dcr.state.nc.us/

RECREATIONAL ACTIVITIES AND SPORTS— THE OUTER BANKS

In this section you will find listings of boat ramps and marinas, along with some resources for practicing fishing, golf, tennis, and adventure sports in the Outer Banks. This information is not meant to be comprehensive since it is constantly changing and the venues are sometimes too numerous to list here. For the most complete and up-to-date list of venues, companies, and outfitters, contact the **Outer Banks Visitors Bureau** at One Visitors Center Circle, Manteo. 800-446-6262. www.outerbanks.org

The Outer Banks is a paradise for nature lovers, fishermen, and sports enthusiasts. From kayaking to kitesurfing and pier fishing to offshore charters, conditions are idyllic nearly year-round along this stretch of coast. Some fun and memorable ways to explore the Outer Banks are from the air with an exciting flightseeing tour, along the waterways aboard a scenic boat tour, or on horseback through a maritime forest. Flying over America's tallest beacon, Cape Hatteras Lighthouse, seeing dolphins swim alongside your boat/canoe/kayak, or taking an early morning ride through beautiful Buxton Woods are unforgettable experiences.

BOATING

For boating enthusiasts, there are several public boat launches along the Outer Banks.

- Soundside end of Wampum Drive, Duck
- Bob Perry Road, Kitty Hawk Bay
- MP 1/4 at the Kitty Hawk Sports Paddling Center, Kitty Hawk
- Avalon Beach, off Bay Drive, Kill Devil Hills

- Washington Baum Bridge on Nags Head-Manteo Causeway
- Thicket Lump Marina, near Thicket Lump Lane in Wanchese
- The foot of the bridge that leads to Roanoke Island Festival Park, Manteo
- Oregon Inlet Fishing Center, Avon Boathouse
- Hatteras Wind N Surf, Avon
- Oceanside end of Lighthouse Road, Buxton
- Frisco Cove, Frisco
- Between Cedar Island/Swan Quarter ferry docks, Ocracoke Island

There are also several piers and marinas along the Outer Banks. For a complete listing, check out www.outerbanksfishing.com/ or www.outerbanks.com. A list of marinas from north of Oregon Inlet to the south follows:

Anchorage Inn and Marina. Ocracoke Island. 252-928-6661. www.theanchorageinn.com/

Doughs Creek Marina, The Waterfront. Manteo, Roanoke Island. 252-473-3320 No website available.

Frisco Cover Marina and Campground. Frisco, Hatteras Island. 252-995-4242. No website available.

Hatteras Harbor Marina (south of Oregon Inlet). Hatteras Island. 252-986-2166. www.hatterasharbor.com

Hatteras Landing. Hatteras Island. 252-986-2205. No website available.

Manns Harbor Marina. Manns Harbor. 252-473-5150. No website available.

Oden's Dock Hatteras Island (Pamlico Sound). 252-986-2555. www.odensdock.com

Pirate's Cove Yacht Club. Manteo/Nags Head Causeway. 252-473-3906. www.fishpiratescove.com

Salty Dawg Marina. Manteo 252-473-3405. www.saltydawgmarina.com

Teach's Lair. Hatteras Island (Pamlico Sound). 252-986-2460. No website available.

Thicket Lump Marina. Wanchese, Roanoke Island. 252-473-4500. www.thicketlumpmarina.com

Village Marina and Campground. Hatteras Island (Pamlico Sound). 252-986-2522. www.villagemarina-hatteras.com

---

FISHING

Just name what you want and you can find it here. Surf fishing off a pier? Half-day or full-day charters? Largemouth bass? Billfish? Bluefin tuna? Many fishing world records have been accomplished along this part of the Outer Banks: a 405-pound lemon shark, a 94-pound red drum, a 13-pound Spanish mackerel, a 31-pound bluefish, and a 348-pound bluefin tuna, just to name a few. The Outer Banks has been referred to as "The Billfish Capital of the World." Outer Banks anglers can hope to catch mahi mahi, blue or white marlin, amberjack, striped bass, yellowfin tuna, sailfish, king or Spanish mackerel, shark, barracuda, and wahoo.

Headboats can be used for inshore or offshore fishing and are an alternative to charters. These boats hold up to fifty passengers, so you pay significantly less than a charter that takes six to eight people out.

FISHING SCHEDULE

JANUARY
FEBRUARY

January and February: trout, sea bass, some grouper, some snapper, blue fish, bluefin and yellowfin tuna, oysters, clams

MARCH

March: grouper, sea trout, sea bass, bluefish, croaker, bluefin and yellowfin tuna, oysters, some snapper, some clams

APRIL

April: bluefish, channel bass (red Drum), grouper, snapper, croaker, sea trout, sea mullet, some king mackerel, some wahoo, some oysters, some clams

MAY

May: king mackerel, bluefish, grouper, cobia, tuna, dolphin, some wahoo, crabs, soft crabs, some sea mullet, some blue marlin

June: blue marlin, white marlin, dolphin, wahoo, cobia, king mackerel, bluefish, tuna, flounder, snapper, grouper, Spanish mackerel, crabs, soft crabs, shrimp

July: dolphin, wahoo, blue marlin, sailfish, white marlin, snapper, grouper, sea mullet, flounder, bluefish, Spanish mackerel, shrimp, crabs, some soft crabs

August: blue marlin, white marlin, dolphin, wahoo, tuna, grouper, snapper, bluefish, Spanish mackerel, flounder, some croaker, speckled trout, spot, shrimp, crabs

September: white marlin, blue marlin, tuna, grouper, snapper, Spanish mackerel, king mackerel, spot, bluefish, speckled trout, sea mullet, some channel bass, shrimp

October: king mackerel, tuna, bluefish, snapper, grouper, channel bass, spot, speckled trout, some flounder, oysters, some shrimp

November: king mackerel, tuna, bluefish, speckled trout, flounder, snapper, grouper, clams, some sea mullet, oysters

December: tuna, bluefish, flounder, speckled trout, oysters, clams, sea trout, some sea bass, some snapper, some grouper

FISHING RESOURCES

North Carolina Division of Marine Fisheries offers hunting, fishing, and boating licenses and permits as well as general information. 3441 Arendell Street, Morehead City. 800-682-2632 or 252-726-7021. www.ncfisheries.net

North Carolina Wildlife Resources Commission offers educational programs, wildlife services, and information on hunting, fishing, and boating. 322 Chapanoke Road, Raleigh. 919-733-7291. www.ncwildlife.org

Oregon Inlet Fishing Center. Offers a convenience store, fuel, parking lot, and several boat launches. Many local fishermen run inshore and offshore charters and headboats from here. In Cape Hatteras National Seashore, on Bodie Island, 8 miles south of Whalebone Junction, NC 12. 800-272-5199 or 252-441-6301. www.oregon-inlet.com

Fishing Facts. Offshore fishing charters began in North Carolina during the 1930s.

The number of offshore fishing charters has gone from 230 in 1999 to more than 400 in 2003. That's an increase of 80 percent!

Hatteras Island is one of the best fishing places along the Outer Banks.

It is estimated that in 2003 roughly two million people came to the Outer Banks to fish.

GOLF

There are a few good courses in the Outer Banks area, most notably the Currituck Club.

Duck Woods Country Club has a par 72 course that is considered somewhat challenging. 50 Dogwood Trail, Kitty Hawk. 252-261-2609. No website available.

Goose Creek Golf and Country Club is a par 72 course. US 158, Grandy (20 minutes from Kitty Hawk). 800-443-4008 or 252-453-4008. No website available.

Holly Ridge Golf Course is a par 63 course with plans to make some holes more challenging. It is an especially good course for beginning golfers. US 158, Harbinger. 252-491-2893. No website available.

Mill Run Golf and Country Club is about five miles south of the NC/VA state line. While it's not a particularly challenging course, its year-round low green fees and idyllic setting make it well worth playing. US 168 near Moyock and Currituck. 800-MILLRUN or 252-435-MILL. No website available.

Nags Head Golf Links is a par 71 course overlooking Roanoke Island. Golf schools are offered three or four times a week during the summer. 5615 S. Seachase Dr., Nags Head. 800-851-9404 or 252-441-8073. www.nagsheadgolflinks.com

Ocean Edge Golf Course is a nine-hole course that can be played like an eighteen-hole course simply by playing it twice. The par 30 course is open to the public year-round with very affordable rates. NC 12, Frisco. 252-995-4100. No website available.

Sea Scape Golf Links is a beautiful par 72 championship course. 300 Eckner St., Kitty Hawk. 252-261 2158. www.seascapegolf.com

The Carolina Club is a par 72 course that offers scenic vistas. US 158, Grandy. 252-453 3588. www.thecar olinaclub.com

The Currituck Club has been named one of the top North Carolina courses by *Golf Magazine* and *Golf Digest*. It is a par 72 course that is located on six hundred acres of Currituck Sound wetlands. Lessons, clinics, and golf schools are offered throughout the year. NC 12, Corolla. 888-453-9400 or 252-453 9400. www.thecurrituck club.com

TENNIS

There are several public tennis courts along the Outer Banks. A list of the places open to the public is given below.

Cape Hatteras School allows the public to use its courts after school hours. NC 12 at Buxton, Hatteras Island. For more information, call the Outer Banks Visitors Center at 877-298-4373 or visit the school website at www.outer-banks.com/hatteras-school

Manteo High School's tennis courts are available to the public after school hours. Wingina Avenue at US 64/264, Manteo, Roanoke Island. 252-473-5841. www.dare.k12.nc.us

Pine Island Racquet Club has the only indoor tennis courts on the Outer Banks and is open to the public. NC 12, between Corolla and Duck. 252-453-8525. No website available.

Other courts can be found at the following locations:

Near the Kill Devil Hills Fire Department at MP 6 on US 158 (two hard surface courts)

Beside the Kill Devil Hills Water Plant on Mustian Street (four hard surface courts)

Off US 158 at MP 10½, Nags Head (one public court)

ADVENTURE SPORTS

For the adventurous, the Outer Banks offers a number of options, including rock-climbing walls, skydiving, hang gliding, kitesurfing, parasailing, scuba diving, surfing, and windsurfing. There are many companies and outfitters that offer lessons, equipment rentals, etc., to help you enjoy these activities. To obtain a current listing, contact the Outer Banks Visitors Bureau.

Jockey's Ridge is a favorite spot for **hang-gliding**. The launching method of choice for Outer Banks hang gliders is to run down the slope until airborne.

Kitesurfing, also known as kite-boarding, is the latest craze in watersports. The Outer Banks provides a perfect setting for this sport because of the wind conditions and shallow sounds.

You know a place dubbed "The Graveyard of the Atlantic," because its home to more than 1,500 shipwrecks, is going to have good **scuba diving**. Some shipwreck sites are federally protected and can be visited but not touched. Others offer hands-on exploration and may even yield an artifact or two! Of course, any diving enthusiast knows that where there are shipwrecks, there is lots of marine life. Sharks, whales, dolphins, and hundreds of colorful fish can be spotted along the Outer Banks. At Avon, there is even a coral reef.

The Outer Banks is known for outstanding **surfing**. The best conditions occur from mid-August through November because the severe storms and nor'easters create rough waters and big waves. Conditions are especially good around piers because of the surrounding sandbars.

The **Canadian Hole** is the most popular place along the Outer Banks for **windsurfing.** Those addicted to the sport come from near and far for the chance to surf here. Fifty to one hundred surfers are gathered here on any given day. All the brightly-colored sails bobbing along the water make a fantastic spectacle. This windsurfing paradise was formed in the 1960s when a severe storm cut an inlet across Hatteras Island. Dredging had to be done to rebuild the highway. This resulted in carved troughs near Pamlico Sound. The troughs extend as deep as five feet. It's called the Canadian Hole because thousands of Canadians come every fall to experience the optimum windsurfing and sailboarding conditions. It is 1.5 miles south of Avon on NC 12.

Windsurfing in the Outer Banks

NATURE PRESERVES, PARKS, AND SANCTUARIES–THE OUTER BANKS

Alligator River National Wildlife Refuge can be appreciated by all, especially children, photographers, and nature lovers. Two-hour after-dark tours of the refuge are offered some nights during the summer. A refuge employee meets participants on the mainland and, after a short discussion, drives visitors several miles into the refuge where the vehicle stops and its passengers can hear the night cries of the endangered red wolf among other refuge inhabitants. The refuge takes on a whole other face after dark, and this tour provides a fun and safe way to experience it. The refuge is user-friendly for daytime independent exploration because it has two good walking trails with boardwalks: Sandy Ridge Wildlife Trail, which originates at the south end of the Buffalo City Road, and Creef Cut Wildlife Trail, which begins on US 64 at the intersection of Milltail Road. Dare County mainland at US 64 & Milltail Road. 252-473-1131. http://alligatorriver.fws.gov/

Audubon Wildlife Sanctuary at Pine Island extends more than five thousand acres and is open year-round. Nature lovers may explore it by bicycle or walking and hiking. Visitors may be rewarded with sightings of deer, foxes, waterfowl, and more in this wetland habitat. There are no public facilities or a parking lot, and while the trail is said to be maintained, it is not an easy walking trail, so sturdy walking or hiking shoes are advised. However, visitors may park at the Sanderling Inn and, if they enter the sanctuary from the inn, they will find this part of the trail is the best maintained. Off NC 12, between Duck and Corolla. 919-929-3899. www.ncaudubon.org/

Bodie Island Dike Trail and Pond Trail originates at the Bodie Island Lighthouse and extends through the marsh to the sound. It is a scenic and enjoyable stroll if you are wearing insect repellent. Off NC 12, Bodie Island. 252-441-5711. www.nps.gov/caha/dike.htm

Buxton Woods Nature Trail extends three-quarters of a mile into Buxton Woods. The trail is marked with signs explaining the area's natural history and ecology. A picnic and grilling area is located near the trail. Buxton Woods is the most significant maritime forest in North Carolina because of its size—500 acres. Visitors will notice many different species of trees, birds, and mammals. Off NC 12 at Buxton, Hatteras Island. 252-995-4474. www.hatteras-nc.com/buxton

Family campground in Cape Hatteras National Seashore 1960

Cape Hatteras National Seashore is a thirty-thousand-acre preserve that was established in 1953. It is full of beaches and marshes that can be explored at length. Coquina Beach offers swimming, bathing, and picnic facilities. Lifeguards are on duty at Coquina Beach during the summer. Birdwatchers will delight in the abundance of birds and waterfowl. Most of Hatteras, Ocracoke, and Bodie Islands are part of the seashore, which was the America's first designated National Seashore. The NPS offers many interesting programs during the summer, such as guided nature walks and fishing trips. Camping is permitted in the seashore, but not on the beach. Jet Skis and WaveRunners are not allowed. The seashore is about six miles south of the US 158 and US 64 intersection, west of NC 12. 252-995-4474. www.nps.gov/caha/capehatteras.htm

Currituck Banks National Estuarine Reserve. Currituck Banks is a twenty-two-mile stretch of some of the most diverse, protected habitats for migratory waterfowl in the country. Many hunt clubs were built here in the late nineteenth century to take advantage of the abundance of geese, ducks, and swans. The banks are famous for the large concentration of winter snow geese and tundra swans. Several islands are part of the reserve, including Monkey, Mary, Swan, and Narrow Islands. The reserve is open to the public during the day, and hiking, swimming, fishing, and nature study may be enjoyed. Currituck Banks is just north of Corolla in Currituck County and is accessible by four-wheel-drive vehicles. NC Division of Coastal Management. 919-733-2293. http://www.ncnerr.org/

Currituck National Wildlife Refuge is a 3,213-acre refuge that accommodates wild boar, deer, waterfowl, wild horses, and more. There are no public facilities, but it is open to the public during daylight hours. Just north of Corolla on NC 12. NC Division of Coastal Management. 919-733-2293. http://mackayisland.fws.gov/currituck/

Great Dismal Swamp National Wildlife Refuge covers almost six hundred miles in North Carolina and Virginia. It is the only live peat bog in North America, and as such contains some of the wildest land on the eastern seaboard. Its name came from Colonel William Byrd II, who said in 1728 that the place was so dismal that no one could or would want to inhabit it. Nonetheless, a group of men bought the land in the late 1790s and began to drain the forty thousand acres to convert it to useful farmland, but this proposition became too expensive and the men decided to make use of its timber to sell for building supplies. In order to do this, canals had to be built such as the Jericho and Dismal Swamp Canals. The swamp forest was later abandoned for easier lumbering areas and it returned to its natural state. In 1973, the land was donated to the Nature Conservancy, which gave it to the federal government to be used as a wildlife refuge. The land now encompasses 109,000 acres. There is a welcome center, which offers several programs and a short film. Hiking, biking, fishing, birding, and boating can be accomplished in the refuge. You may even be lucky enough to spot a bear! 757-986-3705. http://greatdismalswamp.fws.gov/

Jockey's Ridge State Park is one of the top tourist attractions on the Outer Banks. More than a million visitors come every year to see the eastern seaboard's tallest dune, which became a park in 1975. It is always changing, but at a recent measurement it was 1.5 miles long and approximately one hundred feet high. It is believed to have gotten its name because the tall dune permitted an excellent view of a horse racetrack. Jockey's Hill is on a land grant dating back to 1753. Today, hang gliders come here from all over to enjoy the dune and wind patterns. Kite flying is also a popular past time and sandboarding is permitted seasonally. There are walking trails and a visitor's center museum with gift shop. Visitors need shoes, flimsy sandals, or flip-flops to walk through the sandy terrain. There is a 350-foot boardwalk to accommodate baby strollers and wheelchairs. Natural history programs and special kids' programs are offered in the summer. US 158, MP 12, Nags Head. 252-441-7132. www.jockeysridgestatepark.com

More than one million visitors come to Jockey's Ridge State Park every year to see the eastern seaboard's tallest dune.

Lake Mattamuskeet National Wildlife Refuge is about an hour and a half from Roanoke Island, but it is a beautiful place that rewards those who make the commute. Alligators, swans, geese, bald eagles, peregrine falcons, and many other animal species come here. Winter is the best time to see migratory birds. The swans won't let you get too close, but, if by chance you do, be careful because they may attack. Fishing and hunting are permitted seasonally and there are three boat ramps available. There is an old pumping station from when the lake was drained for farming. This endeavor was never successful, so the government bought the land and made it a refuge in 1934. 38 Mattamuskeet Road, Swan Quarter, Hyde County mainland. 252-926-4021. http://mattamuskeet.fws.gov/

Lake Mattamuskeet

Mackay Island National Wildlife Refuge was established in 1960 as a protected place for migratory birds. Nature lovers and bird watchers may utilize the canal system, which extends nearly twenty miles. In addition to boating, fishing is permitted. There is a public boat ramp. Hiking and bicycling trails are also provided but only extend through a small part of the 8,646-acre refuge. Kuralt and Marsh Loop Trails are perfect for walking, hiking, picnicking, and canoeing in the river. Take the NC ferry over from Currituck and follow signs. 252-429-3100. http://mackayisland.fws.gov/

Merchants Millpond State Park is 3,233 acres with much to offer visitors: bass fishing, hiking, canoeing, camping, a picnic area with grills, two hundred species of birds and other wildlife, remains of an old gristmill, a public boat launch, restrooms, and ample parking. Access from US 158, NC 32 and NC 37, Gatesville. One hour and forty-five minutes from Outer Banks. 252-357-1191. www.ils.unc.edu/parkproject/visit/memi/home.html

Nags Head Woods Ecological Preserve is a 1,400-acre maritime forest filled with many reptiles, bird species, mammals, and unusual flora and fauna. There are five miles of walking trails that meander through heavily wooded forest and wetlands, as well as a visitors center, operated by the Nature Conservancy, gift shop, and parking lot on site. Special summer programs are offered, such as kayaking and day camp for kids. No camping or picnicking is permitted and dog walking or bicycling is restricted to Old Nags Head Woods Road. Ocean Acres Drive (west of US 158), Kill Devil Hills. 252-441 2525. www.nature.org

Pea Island National Wildlife Refuge

Pea Island National Wildlife Refuge is a haven for bird-watchers and nature lovers. The 5,915-acre refuge draws more than 400 species of birds, sea turtles, geese, ducks, pelicans, and all kinds of flora and fauna, including the wild pea vine. The North Pond Trail is a mile-long trail that affords a good glimpse into the refuge. There is ample parking at the visitor center, as well as rest-rooms and a gift shop, and this is where a complimentary map and Birding Checklist can be obtained. Special programs such as guided walks and canoe rides are offered during the summer. No guns, camping, driving, or hunting is permitted at any time of year. Fishing, crabbing, and boating are allowed in the sound but not the ponds. Dogs are permitted in designated areas on leashes, but owners should be careful because there are insects and snakes throughout the refuge. Off NC 12, four miles south of Bonner Bridge on northern side of Hatteras Island. 252-987-2394. http://peaisland.fws.gov/

A word of warning. Please do not try to drive or camp in restricted areas. The National Park Service (NPS) is very protective of preserves, refuges, etc. For example, you are not allowed to walk or drive over sand dunes for any reason. During certain times of the year the Outer Banks is home to migrating birds and nesting turtles. Many of these animals are endangered or threatened. You can be prosecuted for disturbing them. All beaches are public as long as public access is provided. A private boat may get you onto a private island's public beach, but remember that if you pass the high tide mark you are trespassing. Camping is allowed only in designated areas and often requires a permit or sign-in with the local NPS office. The best thing to do is to keep an eye out for signs instructing you. Forbidden areas are clearly marked. Also, it is a good idea to stop in at the nearest visitors center or NPS office to verify policy.

STRANGE TALES AND GHOSTS

Many good books have been written on Outer Banks legends and lore. A list of these publications can be found under Additional Resources at the end of this book. Some tales are simply meant to be enjoyed, while others, like "The Ghost Ship of Diamond Shoals" (from my book *The Best Ghost Tales of North Carolina)* are the reason the saying "truth is stranger than fiction" was coined.

In years past, mariners dreaded navigating the waters surrounding North Carolina's Outer Banks, a succession of skinny islands stretching roughly 175 miles from Virginia southward to Cape Lookout. They dubbed the area "Graveyard of the Atlantic" because over six hundred ships had sunk there. Mariners relied heavily on lighthouse keepers, lifesaving stations, and the Coast Guard crew to keep them afloat or rescue them when the sea tried to take them. These men knew that how well they performed their duties meant the difference between life and death.

When the crew at the Hatteras Inlet Coast Guard Station was awakened by an alarm on January 31, 1921, they moved quickly and efficiently. The surfman on lookout duty was letting them know that he had spotted a ship in distress. The lookouts at Big Kinnakeet, Creeds Hill, and Cape Hatteras Coast Guard Stations also noted the ship off in the distance. Men representing all four stations were sent in two rescue boats. The huge, five-masted schooner appeared to be stuck on the outer tip of Diamond Shoals and was slowly sinking.

The rescuers noted that no distress signal had been given and that there weren't any signs of life aboard the vessel. They could get only within a quarter mile of the ship due to the high surf and rough swells. The men circled it several times, calling out for a response from someone aboard, but the rescuers received no answer. Finally the men returned to the station and sent in the report.

A quick investigation revealed that the craft was the *Carroll A. Deering*, a three-year-old ship launched in Maine. The owner, G.G. Deering Company, was notified, and it authorized the Coast Guard to go aboard and find out what was wrong. Coast Guard cutters *Seminole* (stationed in Wilmington, North Carolina) and *Manning* (stationed in Norfolk, Virginia) as well as the wrecking tug *Rescue* (stationed in Norfolk, Virginia) were dispatched to the shipwreck, but it was four days before the men were able to board because of the bad weather. The ship had suffered quite a bit of damage during that time. Once the officials were able to search the ship, they made some eerie discoveries.

Everything seemed to be in place except some key items. The ship's log and navigational instruments were missing. Nothing seemed to indicate that there had been a problem or reason for a quick departure, except that dinner had been served in the dining hall and it didn't look like anything had been eaten. Cooking pots remained on the stove of the galley, but the fire that kept the food warm had long expired. Everything was cold to the touch. The only living thing the search party found was a cat.

Someone called out that the yawl boat (lifeboat) was missing, and all the men scrambled up to the top deck. They discovered that the anchors were also missing. The cables that connected the steering wheel to the rudder had been cut. It would have taken an ax to cut through the thick rope cables. Why would anyone do that? There was also a gash on the outside of the ship near where the ladder had been positioned. The continuous beating the vessel was taking from the combination of the wind and the pounding waves was driving the ship aground at a rapid rate.

The rescuers scooped up the gray cat and made a hasty retreat. When the ship's condition and the strange circumstances were reported to Coast Guard headquarters, a major search was initiated all along the coast. Every inch of water, including tiny bays and inlets, was searched. No further wreckage of any kind was discovered. Despite an investigation that lasted many days, nothing else from the ship was ever found. No one known to be aboard the *Carroll A. Deering*, which has been nicknamed the "ghost ship," was ever heard from again.

It was discovered that the skipper of the ship, Captain F. Merritt, had gotten very sick en route from Newport

News to Rio de Janeiro. He had put in at Lewes, Delaware, and was taken to a hospital. Captain W.M. Wormell was brought aboard to assume Captain Merritt's duties. The vessel delivered the cargo (coal) to Rio de Janeiro and then sailed on to Barbados. Upon arrival, the captain learned there was no cargo to pick up at Barbados. The ship was to return to Newport News.

Carroll A. Deering

The investigation proved that the *Carroll A. Deering* left Bridgetown, a port in Barbados, on January 9, 1921. Aboard were the captain, the first mate, and eight members of the crew. A friend or acquaintance of Captain Wormell gave testimony during the investigation that the skipper had told him he anticipated trouble. Wormell also told him that his first mate, Officer McClellan, was no good. While in port, the crew got rip-roaring drunk and McClellan was arrested, but the captain arranged his release and they set out.

Carroll A. Deering was logged as passing the Cape Fear Lightship, which was positioned at Wilmington, on January 23, 1921. No problems or oddities were noted. Six nights later the Cape Lookout Lightship sighted the ship. It is strange that it would have taken the vessel six days to go just seventy miles north.

Even more strange is the brief conversation that occurred between the watch officer of the Cape Lookout Lightship and the *Carroll A. Deering*. Someone on the Deering shouted through a megaphone that the captain had requested other ships steer clear of the vessel because she had lost her anchors during a storm. The lightship tender thought this was odd because no storms had been reported. Members of the crew were spotted on deck, although they didn't appear to be busy. The ship seemed to be making good time, yet nothing more was seen or heard of the *Carroll A. Deering* until the Hatteras Coast Guard spotted the foundering ship on January 31, 1921.

As if all of this were not enough of a mystery, it was discovered that a passenger boarded in South America. However, the investigation didn't uncover the name of the secret passenger. The ship was only permitted to carry ten men, as per its registration under U.S. maritime regulations, so that would probably explain why the eleventh passenger wasn't documented.

The shipwreck was added to navigational charts as a possible hazard to mariners. Despite the best efforts of the U.S. Navy, the Justice Department, and the Commerce Department, what happened could not be discovered. Many speculated it must have had something to do with piracy, but there were no signs of an altercation and the ship's captain appeared to be above reproach. His daughter, Miss Wormell, took part in the investigation. Above all, she didn't want her father's name forever linked to piracy or negligence.

A break in the mystery came one day when a bottle with a message washed ashore at Cape Hatteras and was found by a local resident. The note said that pirates had attacked the *Carroll A. Deering*, and those who survived the attack were put into lifeboats without oars or provisions. The government investigated the note, despite the fact that they considered it ludicrous that pirates would seize a ship at Hatteras in 1921.

The inquiry resulted in a confession by the man who wrote the note and put it in a bottle, and then claimed to have found it on the shore. In the end, the government concluded that the crew left the sinking ship on a lifeboat and must have been lost at sea while trying to escape. That sounds plausible except that no trace of the yawl or the men was ever found; not even a lifejacket or an article of clothing or a piece of the boat—nothing.

Miss Wormell still contends that the crew encountered foul play, although there is no outstanding evidence to support that claim. Ultimately, the government has stopped looking for answers and says that the mystery is only another that the sea provides so frequently.

The owners of the sunken ship hired Merritt Chapman Wrecking Corporation to salvage some of the items, which were sold at an auction. Later, a nor'easter scattered the remaining hulk all over the shoreline. Locals grabbed up usable wreckage. Remnants from the shipwreck helped build many houses along the Outer Banks. The stern sank and is part of the Graveyard of the Atlantic. The Coast Guard used explosives to blow up the remaining wreckage to keep it from being a navigational hazard.

Although the physical evidence of the mysterious ship is long gone, legend has it that strange sounds are sometimes heard when storms blow through Hatteras in February. Some say it's just the wind, but others believe it may be the spirits of the crew of the *Carroll A. Deering* still trying to tell us what happened to them.

North Carolina Coast

TRADITIONS–THE OUTER BANKS

Outer Bankers are justifiably proud of their heritage, which is celebrated with long-standing traditions. Every year dozens of events are held, including historical reenactments, folk festivals, art shows, fishing tournaments, special holiday celebrations, surfing, kite-flying, sand castle competitions, and more. Further information can be obtained about these events by contacting the appropriate tourism resources found in Additional Resources at the end of the book.

JANUARY **Dare County Schools Annual Art Show.** Gallery Row, Nags Head.

FEBRUARY **Civil War on the Outer Banks**. Spectacular reenactment complete with many vendors and activities for all ages. Roanoke Island Festival Park, Manteo.

Frank Stick Memorial Art Show. Gallery Row, Nags Head.

A Literary Evening. Literary events vary each year. Gallery Row, Nags Head.

On February 7, 1862 approximately eleven thousand Union militia arrived at Roanoke Island to attack a Confederate stronghold. The Confederates were vastly outnumbered, but put up a good fight at what is now the Nags Head Manteo Causeway. The Union army already controlled much of the Outer Banks, so the Confederates desperately needed to maintain their position. However, after a few hours they were forced to surrender and Roanoke Island came under the control of Union forces.

MARCH **Dare County Photography Show** highlights the work of local amateur and professional photographers. Nags Head.

Easter Egg Hunt. Classic children's Easter egg hunt. Nags Head.

Kelly's Midnight Easter Egg Hunt. Kelly's Outer Banks Restaurant's egg hunt and party for adults only (21 and older). Nags Head.

Pirate's Cove Fishing School joins students and experts for programs on inshore and offshore fishing. Nags Head.

Quilt Extravaganza: Priceless Pieces of Past and Present features the work of recent local quilters and quilts dating back to the Roosevelt administration's WPA. Roanoke Island.

St. Patrick's Day Parade. Irish music, food, and parade. Nags Head.

APRIL

Inner-Tribal Powwow Journey Home is a gathering of fifty to a hundred tribes from North Carolina and across the U.S., organized by the Frisco Native American Museum. Dances, music, food, crafts, exhibits, and more are held during the weekend event. Buxton, Hatteras Island. www.nativeamericanmuseum.org

Outer Banks Folk Festival is a good way to keep the folklore and traditions of this area alive. Roanoke Island Festival Park, Manteo.

Outer Banks Senior Games. Thomas A. Baum Senior Center, Kill Devil Hills.

MAY

Hang Gliding Spectacular and Air Games is the oldest continuous hang gliding competition in the United States. It takes place over four days at Currituck County Airport and Jockey's Ridge State Park in Nags Head. www.kittyhawk.com

International Miniature Art Show. Gallery Row, Nags Head.

Jaycees Beach Music Festival kicks off the season with beach music, beach events, food, and more. Roanoke Island.

Nags Head Woods 5K Run and Post-run Beach Party. Nags Head.

Ocracoke Invitational Surf Fishing Tournament. Ocracoke Island.

Surf Fishing

Pirate's Cove Memorial Weekend Tournament. Roanoke Island. www.fishpiratescove.com

JUNE

Dare Day Festival is held in honor of Virginia Dare and others who were part of the mysterious Lost Colony. Local musicians perform, food vendors are on hand, and all kinds of games are offered. Downtown Manteo, Roanoke Island.

Elizabeth R is a one-woman show depicting the life of England's Queen Elizabeth I. It runs from June to August. Elizabeth Gardens, Roanoke Island.

Hatteras Marlin Club Billfish Tournament fishing tournament. Hatteras Village on Hatteras Island.

OcraFolk Festival

OcraFolk Festival includes storytellers, artists, musicians, demonstrations, and more. Ocracoke Island.

Rogallo Kite Festival honors the inventor of the Flexible Wing Flyer, Francis Rogallo. The event includes children's competitions, stunt kites, lessons, workshops, and more. The event lasts two days. Jockey's Ridge State Park, Nags Head.

Wanchese Seafood Festival is a joyous event complete with music, children's game, arts and crafts, lots of fresh seafood, booths, and the annual Blessing of the Fleet. Wanchese, Roanoke Island.

Youth Fishing Tournament for ages four to twelve. Piers from Kitty Hawk to Nags Head.

Best Body on the Beach Contest. Kitty Hawk.   **JULY**

Fireworks Festival and Fair. July 4th festivities. Corolla.

Fireworks in Hatteras Village. July 4th festivities. Hatteras Island.

Ocracoke Parade

Independence Day Parade and Fireworks Display. July 4th festivities. Ocracoke Island.

Manteo Waterfront Independence Day Celebration provides music, food, street dance, children's games, contests, evening fireworks, and more for July 4th. Roanoke Island.

Sand Sculpture Contest. All ages welcome to compete in building extraordinary sand sculptures. Ocracoke Island.

Wright Kite Festival offers free kite-making workshops, kite flying lessons, children's games, and more. Wright Brothers National Memorial, Kill Devil Hills.

AUGUST

Alice Kelly Memorial Ladies Only Billfish Tournament. Roanoke Island.

Herbert Hoover Birthday Celebration. Fun events honoring former President Herbert Hoover. Roanoke Island.

Kitty Hawk Heritage Day Celebration is an arts and crafts festival with music, food, games, and more. The Promenade, Kitty Hawk.

National Aviation Day A celebration of the Wright Brothers' achievements. Wright Brothers National Memorial, Kill Devil Hills.

New World Festival of the Arts. brings together nearly one hundred artists to show and sell their work to the public. Roanoke Island.

Quagmire's Annual Sandcastle Contest is a fun event that can be appreciated by all ages. Quagmire's Restaurant, Kill Devil Hills.

Senior Adults Craft Fair. Kill Devil Hills.

Virginia Dare Birthday Celebration is a day filled with special events honoring Virginia Dare and her place in history. Additionally, the cast and crew of the outdoor drama, *The Lost Colony,* are on hand to add to the festivities. Roanoke Island.

Virginia Dare Night Performance of *The Lost Colony*. A local infant is chosen to portray Virginia Dare (the first white child born in the New World) during this special once-a-year celebration. Roanoke Island.

Watermelon Regatta and Race. Nags Head.

SEPTEMBER

"Allison" White Marlin Release Tournament. Roanoke Island.

The Lost Colony

East Coast Kitesurfing Championships. SEPTEMBER
Hatteras Island.

ESA Eastern Surfing Championships.
Location varies.

Hatteras Village Civic Association Surf Fishing Tournament. Hatteras Island.

Kitty Hawk Kites Annual Boomerang Competition. Kill Devil Hills.

Ocean Fest (also known as Outer Banks Surf Kayak Rodeo) takes place for five days in August or September and celebrates the ocean through surf kayaking and rodeo competitions, a boat show, local art show, seafood, and more. Hatteras Island.

Oktoberfest at the Weeping Radish Restaurant and Brewery is a fun event filled with Oktoberfest beer, food, activities, German Oompah band, and traditional dancing. Roanoke Island. www.weepingradish.com

Outer Banks Surf Kayak Festival. Kill Devil Hills.

Outer Banks Triathlon is the ultimate test for athletes: bike 15 miles, run 3.1 miles, and swim 0.6 miles. Roanoke Island.

OCTOBER

Artrageous Art Extravaganza Weekend. All kinds of art are showcased and sold over this weekend, which also includes food, music, children's auction, and vendor booths. Dare County Recreation Park, Kill Devil Hills.

King Mackerel Festival and Fishing Tournament takes place in October or November. Hatteras Island.

Nags Head Surf Fishing Club Invitational Tournament lasts two days. Nags Head.

Outer Banks Stunt Kite Competition This is something to see! Jockey's Ridge State Park, Nags Head.

Red Drum Tournament. Hatteras Island.

Wings Over Water Festival is a three-day event highlighting area wildlife and ecology. Includes field trips, workshops, and more. Roanoke Island.

NOVEMBER

Cape Hatteras Anglers Club Individual Surf Fishing Tournament. Hatteras Island.

Chicamacomico Lifesaving Station Christmas Lighting. Hatteras Island.

Chowder Cook-off and Oyster Roast. Kill Devil Hills.

Christmas Arts and Crafts Show lasts two days. Kitty Hawk.

Elizabethan Tymes: A Country Faire is an Elizabethan-style street fair. Roanoke Island.

Kites with Lights includes Christmas carols, hot cider, cookies, and more. Jockey's Ridge State Park, Nags Head.

Kitty Hawk Fire Department Turkey Shoot and Pig Pickin'. The Promenade, Kitty Hawk.

Manteo Rotary Rockfish Rodeo. Roanoke Island.

Surf and Sand Triathlon is a land and water competition. Nags Head.

Town of Nags Head Festival of

Thanksgiving consists of a 5K run, parade, children's contest, street party complete with food and music, and more. Nags Head.

Wildfest is a celebration of the area's wildlife. Roanoke Island.

Wings Over Water Festival offers bird-watching outings, nature excursions, workshops, and other related activities to commemorate the area's abundant waterfowl. Lasts three days. Several Outer Banks locations.

Rodanthe residents celebrate Christmas twice: once on December 25th and again on Old Christmas, which is the first week of January. Old Christmas has been observed for more than one hundred years in this community. It is thought to have begun back in 1752, when the English Crown adopted the Georgian calendar, shortening the year by eleven days. Local lore has it that the isolated Hatteras towns were not informed of the change until years afterwards, and, in true Outer Banks spirit, refused to adopt the change. Celebrations include the appearance of "Old Buck," a stuffed bull that is part of a custom dating back to Medieval England.

International Icarus is an international art show. Gallery Row, Nags Head.   **DECEMBER**

Lighting of the Town Tree and Christmas Parade is a fun event filled with all the things of the season: hot cocoa, carols, candy and cookies, music, boat parade, and Santa Claus. Roanoke Island.

Ocracoke Historic District Christmas Tour. Ocracoke Island.

Pirate's Cove Yacht Club New Year's Eve Bash offers live entertainment, heavy hors d'oeuvres, party favors, and more. Manteo, Roanoke Island.

DECEMBER

Roanoke Island's Performances of the Season is a week-long event filled with concerts and performances given by the North Carolina School of the Arts and Roanoke Island Festival Park. Roanoke Island Festival Park.

Sanderling Inn New Year's Eve Celebration offers live entertainment, heavy hors d'oeuvres, party favors, and more. Sanderling.

Swan Days is a two-day celebration of the annual homecoming for thousands of Lake Mattamuskeet swans, complete with arts and crafts booths, concessions, 10K walk, presentations, and guided tours. Lake Mattamuskeet Lodge at Lake Mattamuskeet National Wildlife Refuge (one hour from Outer Banks). Hyde County.

Wright Brothers Anniversary of First Flight offers different celebratory events each year. Wright Brothers National Memorial, Kill Devil Hills.

TEST YOUR KNOWLEDGE

Quiz

Just for fun, test your knowledge by taking this quiz.

1. Name the six biggest hurricanes to hit North Carolina since the 19th century.
2. What was the most devastating nor'easter to hit the Outer Banks?
3. Where is the Canadian Hole? (Hint: It is the best windsurfing spot.)
4. Where was Blackbeard killed?
5. What is the name of America's tallest lighthouse?
6. Where is the only seaside ghost town in North Carolina?
7. Where is the Wright Brothers National Memorial located?
8. Where do more than one million visitors come every year to see the eastern seaboard's tallest dune?

9. What is the name of the twenty-thousand-square foot mansion built by Edward Knight when his wife was rejected from the local all-male hunt club? Where is it located?

10. What is the date the Wright Brothers made their first successful flight?

11. How many lighthouses still exist along the Outer Banks? Name them if you can.

12. What are the two biggest industries of the Outer Banks?

13. How many lost colonists were there?

14. Which Outer Banks community has so many fast food franchises that it has been nicknamed "French Fry Alley" (Hint: It is along US 158.)

15. Which Outer Banks community has the most vineyards?

16. What Outer Banks lighthouse holds the honor of being the oldest continuously operating light in the state?

17. Where is the best fishing in the Outer Banks?

18. How many Outer Banks inlets are there?

19. What is the significance of the British Cemetery and where is it located?

20. True or False: The Outer Banks has one million acres of bays and sounds.

[Answers are found at the end of the chapter.]

FUN WAYS TO LEARN

Teachers and parents may wish to tackle the activities below to teach their kids or students about North Carolina's coastal history and nature.

• Build a miniature recreation of **Fort Raleigh**. A good illustration of the fort and its surrounding moat are detailed at the National Park Service website, www.nps.gov/fora. This site also provides instructions on how kids can receive free Junior Park Ranger badges at Fort Raleigh National Historic Site.

• Write or tell a story theorizing what happened to the crew aboard **The Ghost Ship of Diamond Shoals** (read this story in Strange Tales above). Have fun with this—take a wild guess! A follow-up discussion as to whether or not pirates still exist could follow.

• Photocopy pictures of famous **Outer Banks folks and attractions** found in magazines, travel planners, brochures, and books, such as Blackbeard, Orville and Wilbur Wright, the Currituck Lighthouse, Chicamacomico Lifesaving Station, Native-American Chief Manteo, Elizabeth Dare, Fort Raleigh, Queen Elizabeth, and Sir Walter Raleigh. Paste these cutouts onto pieces of paper with the person's name or historic site labeled on the back side. Can you guess them all?

• Discuss the timeline of the **Wright Brothers**' aviation experiment, from when they thought up the idea while working at their Ohio bicycle shop to their first successful flight. This should include a discussion of how monumental a task this was. After all, there was little interest in flying at that time because it seemed so inconceivable that people would chose to fly the sky rather than sail the ocean. In order to achieve their goal, these two young men had to fully understand weather, wind conditions, gravity, engineering, piloting, and more.

The National Park Service Wright Brothers Memorial website, www.nps.gov/wrbr, is very helpful. It offers an electronic field trip to the memorial and a teacher's lesson plan that includes many activities such as how to design a small glider using popsicle sticks, fabric, and paper, and more.

• Use a kite-flying book to make a class kite or individual kites and then spend an hour or two outside learning to fly them. If possible, take a field trip or vacation to test the kites at **Jockey's Ridge.**

• Make this year's **Christmas tree theme** the Outer Banks and make or buy ornaments such as pine cones, birds (seagulls, snowy egrets, herons), seashells, ships, pirates, treasure chests, fish, fishermen, wild ponies of Ocracoke or Currituck, airplanes, lighthouse keepers, and lighthouses. Simple paper or cardboard cutouts shaped and colored like famous Outer Banks folks could be made. Some colorful examples include a Native-American chief (Manteo or Wanchese) and a pirate captain, such as Blackbeard or Stede Bonnet.

PIRATES

Some great places to visit to learn about Outer Banks history are the Frisco Native American Museum in Frisco, the Graveyard of the Atlantic Museum in Hatteras Island, and Somerset Plantation in Creswell (Washington County). The **Outer Banks History Center** is a great place to check out if you are seriously interested in history. They have an extensive collection of rare books, photographs, maps, and much more. Roanoke Island Festival Park, Manteo. 252-473-2655. www.ah.dcr.state.nc.us/sections/archives/arch/obhc/default.htm

Pirate activities are fun ways to learn about history. Here are some ideas:

• Have kids dress in pirate clothing and assign them different roles as pirate crew to illustrate how piracy worked. Elect a pirate captain and let him or her be Blackbeard or Anne Bonny (in this day and age we can have female pirate captains). Have him or her select the crew: quartermaster, boatswain, gunner, sailing master, first mate, surgeon, carpenter, musicians, and sailmakers. The remaining kids will be supporting crew.

• Explain what each crew member does. The *boatswain* was in charge of rigging, sails, and ship maintenance. The *gunner* was in charge of the ship's armament. The *sailing master* was in charge of navigation. The *first mate* is second in charge to the captain. The *surgeon, carpenter, musician,* and *sailmaker* are self-explanatory. Explain the pirates rules of conduct. Yes, even pirates had some rules! See complete list of rules below.

• Explain mutiny and let kids vote on whether they're happy with their leader or not. If the crew doesn't like the way the captain is performing, they can vote him out. It happened all the time, except to Blackbeard. No one dared cross the man nicknamed "Black-faced Devil"!

• Use index cards to ask pirate-related questions, such as

❖ Did pirates actually make victims and mutinous pirate crew members walk the plank? (Not typically. Instead, they usually marooned them on a desert island without food or water.)

❖ What is the word for mariners who were granted permission to attack other ships, if they shared the loot with their government? (Privateers. Many seamen and pirates were commissioned as privateers and given Letters of Marque by the Crown to help raise wartime funding! These letters were official documents that proved England had authorized the privateer to capture and/or sink enemy ships. Without such authorization, the conduct was considered piracy and was punishable by law.)

❖ New Providence was a very popular pirate hangout spot in the 1600s. It has since changed names to what? (Nassau, Bahamas.)

❖ Was the most popular pirate ship name *Adventure?* (No. *Revenge* was the most commonly used name.)

❖ What is a Jolly Roger? (A ship's flag that reflected the origin of a ship. Pirates used scary symbols, such as skull and crossbones, to induce merchant ships to surrender.)

❖ Did pirates normally bury their treasure? (No. They spent it on food, drink, lodging, and fun whenever they put in at port. Also, pirates sometimes went weeks between "gigs" due to slim pickings or ship repairs.)

❖ What was it about Blackbeard's appearance that made him so feared by other pirates and seamen? (When going into battle, he tied lit fuses to his head that caused smoke to billow out under his hat and around his head. Additionally, he had a thick black beard, was tall and muscular, and often sported several pistols and cutlasses holstered to his body.)

❖ What is a doubloon? (A valuable gold coin, a form of Spanish currency dating back to the sixteenth and seventeenth centuries.)

❖ What does "pieces of eight" mean? (A piece of eight was a silver coin. Sixteen of them equaled one doubloon.)

❖ True or False: Keel hauling is when a ship had to be turned on its keel to be cleaned. (False. Keel Hauling was a strict pirate punishment used only for very serious infractions. The victim's hands and feet were bound by rope and the victim was dragged under the bottom of the ship. The result was that the victim either drowned or was badly cut on the sharp barnacles attached to the bottom of the ship.)

Pirates Rules of Conduct

Each pirate captain had the right to post his own set of rules. Some captains had only a few guidelines while other captains expected their crews to adhere to many rules and regulations.

The following is a typical eighteenth-century Pirate Code of Conduct.

1. Every man shall obey civil command; the captain shall have one full share and a half in all prizes; the master, carpenter, boatswain and gunner shall have one share and quarter.

2. If any man shall offer to run away, or keep any secret from the company, he shall be marooned with one bottle of powder, one bottle of water, one small arm and shot.

3. If any shall steal anything in the company, or game, to the value of a piece of eight, he shall be marooned or shot.

4. If at any time we should meet another marooner (that is a pirate), that man that shall sign his articles without the consent of our company, shall suffer such punishment as the captain and company shall think fit.

5. That man that shall strike another whilst these articles are in force, shall receive Mose's Law (that is, forty stripes lacking one) on the bare back.

6. That man that shall snap his arms, or smoke tobacco in the hold, without a cap to his pipe, or carry a candle lighted without a lantern, shall suffer the same punishment as in the former article.

7. That man that shall not keep his arms clean, fit for an engagement, or neglect his business, shall be cut off from his share, and suffer such other punishment as the captain and the company shall think fit.

8. If any man shall lose a joint in time of an engagement, he shall have four hundred pieces of eight; if a limb, eight hundred.

9. If at any time you meet with a prudent woman, that man that offers to meddle with her, without her consent, shall suffer present death.

There were 335 pirate attacks internationally in 2001. Countries with the highest number of attacks: Indonesia, India, Bangladesh, Malaysia, and Nigeria. In South America, pirates are commonly called "river rats." Two years ago, three masked pirates boarded two-time America's Cup sailing champion Peter Blake's yacht on the Amazon River. Blake was killed when he challenged the pirates, who made off with money, a spare engine, and wristwatches.

QUIZ ANSWERS

1. Hurricane of August, 1879
    San Ciriaco Hurricane, 1899
    Hurricane Hazel, 1954
    Hurricane Fran, 1996
    Hurricane Floyd, 1999
    Hurricane Isabel, 2003

2. Ash Wednesday Storm, March 7–9, 1962

3. Hatteras Island

4. Ocracoke

5. Cape Hatteras Lighthouse

6. Portsmouth Island

7. Kill Devil Hills

8. Jockey's Ridge, Jockey's Ridge State Park

9. The Whalehead Club, Corolla, adjacent to Currituck Lighthouse

10. December 17, 1903

11. Currituck, Bodie Island, Cape Lookout, Cape Hatteras, and Ocracoke. Give yourself a bonus point if you remembered Diamond Shoals Light Tower!

12. Fishing and tourism

13. 111 (including the first white baby born in the New World, Virginia Dare)

14. Kill Devil Hills

15. Knotts Island

16. Ocracoke Lighthouse

17. Off Hatteras Island (while many Outer Banks locales offer excellent fishing opportunities, Hatteras Island is rated highest among serious anglers)

18. Six: Oregon Inlet, Hatteras Inlet, Ocracoke Inlet, Swash Inlet, Drum Inlet, and Beaufort Inlet.

19. British Cemetery is the final resting place for four men who served aboard *HMS Bedfordshire,* an anti-submarine sent by Winston Churchill in 1942 to help the Americans fight the Germans. A German sub torpedoed the *HMS Bedfordshire,* and it sank about forty miles from Ocracoke. Thirty-seven enlisted men and officers drowned in this conflict, but only four bodies were recovered. However, this graveyard serves as a reminder of all the men who came to America's aid.

20. False. The Outer Banks boasts more than two million bays and sounds!

Sunrise at the Outer Banks

Inlets determine the fate of the Outer Banks. Since these barrier islands were first formed, countless inlets from sea to sound have opened and closed. This is due to hurricanes, nor'easters, and shifting patterns of sand and water. Once upon a time, there were more than two dozen inlets between Morehead City and Virginia. Today, there are only six Outer Banks inlets: Oregon Inlet, Hatteras Inlet, Ocracoke Inlet, Swash Inlet, Drum Inlet, and Beaufort Inlet. There is no way that man can control them. Federal, state, and local governments, as well as private citizens, have spent millions and millions of dollars trying to redirect or stabilize these inlets by dredging and building jetties. The long-term success of these efforts seems bleak.

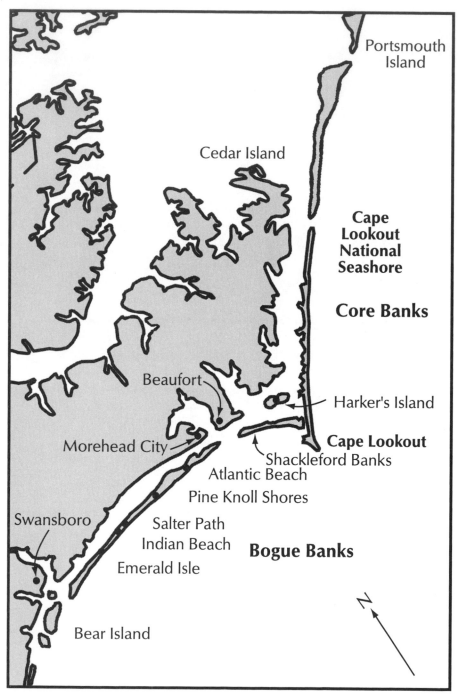

The Crystal Coast

Crystal Coast

2

The towns and beaches in the part of the North Carolina coast commonly referred to as the Crystal Coast, Upper Coast, or Southern Outer Banks are mostly located in North Carolina's biggest and fastest growing county, Carteret, while a few are in Onslow and Pamlico Counties. These beach communities are appealing, in large part, because of their geographical location. Due south lies the scenic Cape Fear River, historic Wilmington, and its unique area islands. To the north, the Outer Banks and Pamlico Sound area are the ultimate destination for both nature lovers and adventure-seekers. Centrally located to all of these beaches and towns are Beaufort and Morehead City.

There are eighty-one miles of beaches extending from Cape Lookout National Seashore to Emerald Isle where visitors may enjoy swimming, boating, diving, golfing, kayaking, bird watching, fishing, exploring historic sites, and shopping. *Rodale's* has named this area the "Number One Wreck Diving Site in North America" and the Clean Beaches Council has rated it "clean and safe." Furthermore, *National Geographic Traveler* deemed it "One of Fifty Best Places in a Lifetime."

What this coastline lacks in historic sites it more than compensates for with parks, seashores, and recreational areas. For example, Cape Lookout National Seashore extends fifty-eight miles and includes wild ponies, a seaside ghost town, all kinds of wildlife and waterfowl, a historic lighthouse, and pristine beaches. Fort Macon State

Park is one of the most visited places in the state and boasts both the remains of a Civil War fortification and a lovely beach with lots of good fishing and peaceful sunbathing. Hammocks Beach State Park is one of North Carolina's best kept secrets and is well worth a visit to picnic, hike, swim, and explore. Cedar Island National Wildlife Refuge is home to many wonderful species of mammals and birds, including peregrine falcons, raptors, river otters, and bears. Nature and wildlife photographers may never want to leave!

Other places of interest include the North Carolina Maritime Museum at Beaufort, North Carolina Aquarium at Pine Knoll Shores, and Beaufort Historic Site. These are all impressive places that will provide visitors with an excellent overview of the cultural and maritime history of the Crystal Coast. Additionally, there are hundreds of restaurants, accommodations, souvenir and gift shops, and recreational companies or outfitters catering to tourists.

FAST FACTS

TOURIST SEASON

Tourist Season officially runs from **Memorial Day to Labor Day**. Most rental agencies on the east end of Bogue Banks and in other areas of Carteret County base rental rates on two seasons: off season and in season. However, some rental agencies on the western tip of Bogue Banks use a four-season schedule: mid season (May to mid-June, mid-August to September), in season (mid-June to mid-August), low season (September to November, March to April), and off season (December to February).

MOST POPULAR ATTRACTION

More than one million visitors come to **Fort Macon State Park** every year, making it the most visited park in North Carolina. It is located at the eastern tip of Bogue Banks because the fort was erected to safeguard the Beaufort Inlet and harbor. The octagonal-shaped, brick-and-stone edifice cost a whopping $463,790 when it was built in 1834. Its outer walls are nearly five feet thick and enclose twenty-six, five-sided rooms, also called casemates. A 1924 Act of Congress gave the fort and land to North

Carolina to be used as a public park. The four-hundred-acre park opened in 1936 and was the state's first public park. There are nice beaches, birding, swimming, superb fishing, a bathhouse with restrooms, a nature trail, a museum and gift shop, a concession stand, and a picnic area complete with grills. The museum may be explored independently or by taking a tour. MM 0, NC 58, Atlantic Beach, Bogue Banks. 252-726-3775. www.ils.unc.edu/parkproject/visit/foma/home.html

BEST VIEW

The best view of the area is from the **Cedar Island–Ocracoke Ferry**. The vessel carries passengers and vehicles on the enjoyable two hour and fifteen minute ride between the Crystal Coast and Ocracoke Island. During this time, there is ample opportunity to see small islands, birds, pleasure crafts, and more. Cedar Island Ferry Terminal, 252-225-3551; Ocracoke Island Ferry Terminal, 252-928-3841 or 1-800-BYFERRY. www.ncferry.org

MOST UNIQUE ANNUAL EVENT

We have a tie! **St. Patrick's Day Pet Parade** in downtown Morehead City takes place in the morning but includes events throughout the day, among them contests for the "Best Dressed Pet" and "Best Look-A-Like Pet/Pal." Morehead City. 252-808-2398. www.downtownmoreheadcity.com

The **Fourth of July Underwater Bike Race** on the wreck of the *Indra* is a unique event sponsored by Discovery Diving Company, one of the largest diving companies on the eastern coast. Beaufort. 252-728-2265. www.discoverydiving.com

MOST IMPORTANT INDUSTRIES

Tourism and commercial fishing. Boat building is a close third.

MOST IMPORTANT HISTORICAL EVENT

Confederate defeat at Fort Macon. On April 25, 1862, the Union launched its land and sea attack on Fort Macon. The Confederates were no match against the big arsenal and manpower of the Federals. Beaufort was occupied by Union forces for the remainder of the war. Losing control of Fort Macon was devastating to the Confederates, and no doubt played a substantial role in the outcome of the war.

Down East is the nickname given to the area of land that extends from Beaufort (North River) to Cedar Island. None of the communities that comprise Down East are incorporated, so the area is governed by Carteret County, as well as Pamlico and Onslow Counties.

ISLANDS & TOWNS

7. BEAUFORT

History

Beaufort is the third oldest town in North Carolina and was named for Englishman Henry Somerset, the Duke of Beaufort. Visitors will note that the streets are also named after English royalty. The town was founded in 1709, but wasn't officially incorporated until 1722. By that time, Beaufort had become an important port and so a customs office was opened. Because it is nearly three hundred years old, Beaufort has an engaging history.

During 1747, the town successfully fended off two separate pirate attacks thanks to its excellent militia. Beaufort citizens largely supported the Patriots during the Revolutionary War, so many privateers used Beaufort's port. A saltworks facility was built near the town so that the people would no longer be dependent on England, which had previously supplied them with salt. Beaufort was captured by the British for ten days in 1782, but the courageous townsfolk succeeded in driving them onward to Charleston.

During the War of 1812, many Beaufort area residents were granted authority to be pirates! Actually, the U.S. government provided them letters of marque. This practice was common worldwide during times of war. Governments would license citizens to raid enemy ships in exchange for sharing the cargo with the government (or, in other countries, with the crown). These citizens were known as privateers. One could say they were authorized to be pirates on behalf of our government. This was done under the logic of having to finance a lengthy war. You can imagine what liberties were taken by all those involved!

The most famous Beaufort citizen turned privateer was Captain Otway Burns, who commandeered cargo worth millions from 1812 until 1814. On June 29, 1814, the British captured Captain Burns' ship, the *Snap Dragon*, but not Burns. Burns wasn't aboard on this occasion, so he escaped punishment. He gave up privateering and opted to stay in Beaufort, where he became a wealthy ship-builder and merchant.

Beaufort, NC

During the 1800s, Beaufort became a prominent port for commerce as well as a desirable location for vacationers. Many wealthy planter families spent summers here. In 1851, the swanky, three-story Atlantic Hotel was constructed on the harbor. A railroad was built in 1858, thereby bringing in more summer visitors. Many Beaufort homes became boarding houses during the summer to accommodate them.

When the Civil War erupted, Beaufort was important to blockade runners because it was the only waterway to the Outer Banks held by the Confederates and it was isolated from New Bern, which was held by the Union. Union General Ambrose Burnside desperately wanted to win Beaufort and Beaufort Inlet, and the Confederates were equally desperate to hold on to it. In early 1862, Burnside sent federal troops led by General John Parke to take control of several cities, including neighboring Morehead City. Next, Union forces crossed Newport River and claimed Beaufort early in the morning.

The only thing that stood in the Union's way to Beaufort Inlet was Fort Macon. General Parke sent word to his adversary, Confederate Colonel Moses White, that he should surrender immediately. Knowing the importance of Fort Macon, Colonel Moses prepared for battle. On April 25, 1862, the Union launched its land and sea attack on Fort Macon. The Confederates were no match against the big arsenal and manpower of the Federals. With a heavy heart, Colonel Moses admitted defeat late that afternoon. Beaufort was occupied by Union forces for the remainder of the war.

After the war, the port city reestablished itself as a perfect summer resort and fishing mecca. A processing plant for menhaden was established because many important oils came from this fish found in Core Sound. Rum, molasses, and lumber were also key exports. The Atlantic Hotel accommodated many patrons until a hurricane annihilated it in 1879. It was later rebuilt in Morehead City. Two other impressive hotels were also built, the Seaside Hotel and Ocean View.

A railroad bridge was constructed in 1908 and a highway bridge was finished in 1926, bringing marine research labs to the Beaufort area. Even though Beaufort was better connected to the rest of the state than ever before, many residents left in the 1950s and 1960s. By the 1970s, town leaders realized serious revitalization must take place or Beaufort would fade into oblivion. The Beaufort Historic Association played a prominent role in balancing new and old. The Historic District was beautifully renovated. The association recognized Beaufort's historic structures with plaques that are engraved with the name of the original owner and the date the structure was built. A home must be at least eighty years old and have maintained its historic integrity and appearance in order to deserve such a plaque. Since the formation of the Beaufort Historic Association, the port city has experienced growth in both permanent population and tourism.

To get to Beaufort, take US 70 and cross the Grayden M. Paul Drawbridge. Signs are well posted. The closest commercial airport is Craven County Regional Airport in New Bern (US Hwy. 70, 252-638-8591), but private aircraft may land at Michael J. Smith Airport (NC Hwy. 101, Beaufort. 252-728-1928/2323)

Sites and Attractions–Beaufort

Beaufort Historic District can be experienced either by tour or through independent exploration. There are several historic edifices that were moved to Turner Street by the Beaufort Historical Association in order to save them from demolition. One of the most interesting structures is Hammock House, circa 1698. It is the oldest house in the city and reportedly accommodated Blackbeard during the period of time it served as an inn. Local legend has it that the "Fury from Hell" hung one of his wives from a tree in front of the inn and that her screams are still heard on breezeless, moonlit nights. I never came across this tale when I was researching *Pirates of the Carolinas,* but Blackbeard did hang out in Beaufort often, so who knows? At the time, the house sat right on Taylor's Creek (before dredging changed the water flow) and a dinghy could be tied up to the porch so a fast escape could be made simply by stepping out onto the porch and into the boat. Hammock House was also occupied by Union troops during the War Between the States. Free maps or tour information is available at the Robert W. and Elva Faison Safrit Historical Center, 100 Block of Turner Street, Beaufort. 800-575-SITE or 252-728-5225. www.historicbeaufort.com

Beaufort Historic Site is a two-acre tract with ten beautifully restored buildings in the center of town, including the Josiah Bell House, Samuel Leffers Cottage, Carteret County Courthouse, Old County Jail, and R. Rustell House, which houses the Mattie King Davis Art Gallery. The works of more than one hundred artists are displayed in the gallery. The buildings are furnished in accordance with their architectural style. Next to the old jail, an Apothecary Shop has been replicated. The medical tools and treatments you'll see will make you glad there have been so many advancements since then! Under the guardianship of the Beaufort Historical Association, the site welcomes roughly fifty thousand visitors every year. In addition to tours, workshops and reenactments are offered. The Beaufort Historic Association offers double-decker bus tours of Beaufort, seasonally. 100 Block of Turner Street, Beaufort. 800-575-SITE or 252-728-5225. www.historicbeaufort.com

Harvey W. Smith Watercraft Center is where visitors may watch boat restorations and construction or see how scale models of different types of vessels are skillfully made by experts. If you want to learn how they do it, sign up for one of the many weekend classes offered, which range from model boat building for children to boat-building carpentry. The center is an extension of the North Carolina Maritime Museum and is located across from it. 252-728-7317. www.ah.dcr.state.nc.us/sections/maritime/ or www.ncmm-friends.org

North Carolina Maritime Museum is an eighteen-thousand-square-foot museum offering educational displays, special programs in its auditorium, reference library,

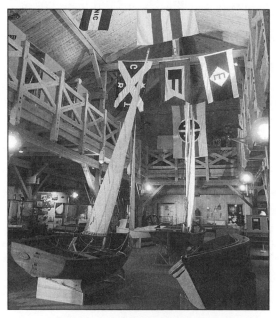

NC Maritime Museum, Beaufort

and gift shop, as well as ongoing programs and field trips. Visitors are sure to learn a great deal by examining its informative exhibits. No matter what your interests are, you won't want to miss the Blackbeard exhibit, which features artifacts from his flagship, *Queen Anne's Revenge.* 315 Front Street, Beaufort. 252-728-7317. www.ah.dcr.state.nc.us/sections/maritime/ or www.ncmm-friends.org

The Old Burying Ground, which dates back to 1731, is one of Beaufort's most fascinating sites. The cemetery was declared full in 1825, and the state government decreed that no more burials could occur here. It ordered Beaufort to construct a new cemetery, but the residents kept right on burying their loved ones there until the early 1900s. Among the distinguished personalities buried in the cemetery are privateer Captains Joshiah Pender and Otway Burns as well as the crew of *Crissie Wright,* who froze to death when the ship sunk at Shackleford Banks. 400 Block, Ann Street, Beaufort. 252-728-5225. www.historicbeaufort.com

Grave of Otway Burns Beaufort

Robert W. and Elva Faison Safrit Historical Center provides video presentations, exhibits, tourism information, the Old Beaufort Museum Gift Shop, and more. This is an excellent point of origin for visitors. 100 Block of Turner Street, Beaufort. 800-575-SITE or 252-728-5225. www.historicbeaufort.com

Nearby Towns

There are some small residential developments and fishing communities around Beaufort that may be of interest to tourists or those thinking of relocating to the Beaufort area.

LENNOXVILLE   **Lennoxville** is a small, waterfront residential community that originates at the east end of Front Street in Beaufort. The town of **North River** lies north of

NORTH RIVER
SOUTH RIVER   Beaufort on Merrimon Road. **South River**, north of North River is a hunting and fishing mecca that is for the most part privately owned. To the west of South River is

MERRIMON   **Merrimon,** which borders the scenic Neuse River.

ORIENTAL   **Oriental** is in Pamlico County, just across the Neuse River. The town is situated among six creeks: Smith, Camp, Raccoon, Green, Whittaker and Pierce Creeks—so it's the place to live or visit if you're a boater. In fact, nearly six thousand Intracoastal Waterway vessels stop here every year. It's no surprise that it is known as the "Sailing Capital of North Carolina." The permanent population has declined to less than one thousand residents, but they like the quiet community, which is named after the *USS Oriental,* a Yankee cargo ship that sank in stormy seas off the Outer Banks in 1862. Some years later, Rebecca Midyette, wife of town founder Louis Midyette, came across the ship's name board hanging on the wall of a private residence in Manteo, North Carolina. Mrs. Midyette liked the name, and after talking it over, the residents of Smith's Creek decided to name it Oriental.

Besides boating, there are some nifty specialty shops and restaurants. There are a few recent developments: Sportsman's Village, Sandy Point, Jonaquin's Landing, and Indian Summer. Things to see and do in Oriental include Oriental's School of Sailing, Carolina Sailing Unlimited, Pelican Players Community Theater, Pamlico Musical Society concerts, Circle 10 Art Gallery, and some exceptional annual events: Croaker Festival (July Fourth); Oriental Cup Regatta (September); Spirit of Christmas with candles, costumes, carolers, and a Tree of Lights (December); and Running of the Dragon (New Year's Eve). Oriental can be reached by a free ferry. The Cherry Branch–Minnesott Beach Ferry puts passengers just ten miles from Oriental. Oriental Town Hall is at 507 Church Street, 252-249-0555.

New Bern is a lovely city that is situated on the scenic Neuse River. It is the second oldest town in the state with more than one hundred historic sites. Originally incorporated in 1723, it has flourished into one of the biggest retirement communities and tourist spots thanks to its historical significance and location on the Intracoastal Waterway. Self-guided walking tour maps can be picked up at the Craven County Convention and Visitors Bureau, 314 Tryon Palace Drive. 800-437-5767 or 252-637-9400. www.visitnewbern.com

Tryon Palace, New Bern

New Bern Highlights

• Bellair Plantation Farm (circa 1734). 1100 Washington Post Road on NC 43 North, New Bern. 252-637-3913.

• Cedar Grove Cemetery. Queen and George Streets, New Bern.

• Christ Episcopal Church (first built in 1750 and rebuilt in 1875). You can't miss the four-sided clock, but there are interior treasures, such as a silver communion service given to the church by King George II and a 1752 *Book of Common Prayer*. 320 Pollock Street, New Bern. 252-633-2109.

• Tryon Palace Historic Sites and Gardens (1770). Pollock and George Streets, New Bern. 800-767-1560 or 252-514-4900.

• Union Point Park. South Front and East Front Streets, New Bern. 252-636-4660.

8. MOREHEAD CITY

History

Morehead City's first landowner was John Shackleford, a Virginian prospector. In 1714, he bought fourteen hundred acres in Carteret County and Morehead City. Shackleford Banks is named after this first settler. Streets and buildings have been named after other prominent settlers such as Bridges Arendell and David Shepard.

When the North Carolina government decided in 1852 that the state's railroad system should extend to this coastal area, most residents were overjoyed. Prior to this, these communities were pretty isolated from the rest of the state. In 1857, William H. Arendell, John Motley Morehead (North Carolina governor, 1841–45), and several other notable citizens formed Shepard's Point Land Company to combine their resources. Their first purchase was one thousand acres at Shepard's Point, which was subdivided into sixty home lots. The lots were soon sold during a public auction in 1857.

John Motley Morehead made a speech in 1858 before the North Carolina Legislature in an effort to get the railroad line extended to this fledging town: "The City of Morehead is situated on a beautiful neck of land or dry plain, almost entirely surrounded by salt water; its climate salubrious; its sea breezes and sea bathing delightful; its

Boat races, Morehead City 1949

drinking water good and its fine chalybeate spring, strongly impregnated with sulfur, will make it a pleasant watering place . . ." Initially, it was discussed that the railroad line would only go as far as Beaufort. Shortly after Morehead's speech, it was decided that the railroad would definitely extend to Morehead City.

Morehead City was officially incorporated in 1861 and officially occupied by Union troops as of April 26, 1862, which was the day Fort Macon fell to the Federals. It wasn't until the 1880s that Morehead City fully recovered from the effects of the Civil War. Places like Morehead City that were newly developed when the war broke out took longer to recover and prosper because they had to start all over again. In the early 1880s, commercial shipping came to the city. Also, a new Atlantic Hotel was constructed to take the place of its predecessor, which was destroyed by a hurricane. It was a beauty until it burned down during an accidental fire in 1933. The deluxe hotel had a grand foyer, the largest ballroom in the southeast, and more than two hundred guestrooms. It drew crowds from across the state and several other states, as well.

Fish Market, Morehead City

For many, many years, the residents have made their income on commercial fishing and tourism. Morehead City's Crab Point got its name because the tide brought crabs right up to the shore! The part of the city dubbed "Promised Land" is along Bridges Street. The nickname came about because of all the refugees that relocated to this part of Morehead City from Shackleford Banks when the Hurricane of 1899 destroyed their communities. A substantial charter fishing business has flourished over the last several years. Towards its tourism efforts, the port city has renovated its waterfront and increased its annual events. The city's efforts have made Morehead City the largest city in Carteret County.

To get there, take US 70, following well-posted signs into Morehead City. The closest commercial airport is Craven Regional Airport in New Bern (US Hwy. 70, 252-638-8591), but private aircraft may land at Michael J. Smith Airport (NC Hwy. 101, Beaufort. 252-728-1928/2323).

Passenger ferry departing Morehead City 1945

Sites and Attractions–Morehead City

The History Place is a big facility that is filled with many displays detailing the area's history. Guided tours last about one hour. Additionally, there is a research library which contains more than four thousand publications, boxes of archival material, and an extensive photo collection. There is an on-site gift shop and The Tea Clipper Room and Cafe, which was designed to resemble an old Victorian tea room. The museum is run by Carteret County Historical Society. 1008 Arendell Street, Morehead City. 252-247-7533. www.thehistoryplace.org

9. HARKERS ISLAND

History

Harkers Island, a five-mile-long and one-mile-wide island, was founded in 1714 when a land grant was issued to Thomas Sparrow. At that time, it was called Craney Island. Before that time, the island was home to the Corees. Its name was changed when Ebenezer Harker purchased the land in 1730 for four hundred pounds and a twenty-foot boat. To divide the land among his three sons, Harker divided it into three sections, "eastard," "westard," and "center." The island remains, at least unofficially, divided into these three parts. Few people inhabited the island until the early 1900s when Shackleford Banks residents relocated to Morehead City, Harkers Island, and a few other area communities because their homes had been destroyed by a big hurricane.

The ferry began making trips to the island in 1926, electricity reached the area in 1939, and a bridge linking it to the mainland was constructed two years later. Most locals make their living in commercial fishing and boat building. Harkers Island Fishing Center and Calico Jack's Marina are where most of the many fishing charters originate.

To get there, take US 70 to its end at Harkers Island, about fifteen miles east of Morehead City or twenty miles east of Beaufort.

Harkers Island 1950

Fishermen pulling in fish nets, Harkers Island 1910

Sites and Attractions–Harkers Island

Core Sound Waterfowl Museum opened in 1988 thanks to the efforts of the Decoy Carvers Guild. In addition to the many interesting decoy and hunting artifact exhibits and carvings, there is a gift shop, gallery, and research library on site. It is located next to the Cape Lookout National Seashore Visitor's Center on Harkers Island Rd. 1785 Island Road, Harkers Island. 252-728-1500. www.coresound.com

Legend of Decatur Gillikin. Decatur Gillikin lived on Harkers Island around the turn of the century. He was a man blessed with great physical strength. One day he was out hauling logs when he came upon a fence that blocked his path. He would have to make a one-mile detour to circumvent the fence. Instead, Gillikin picked up each of his oxen and then his cart and lifted them over the fence!

The brawny youth also had a temper and ended up in many brawls, but he never lost one. According to legend, he became a sailor on a British ship. He ended up in a fight with another sailor, who had never lost a fight until then. The patriots were so distressed by the defeat that the entire crew fought him! It is said that Gillikin beat all fifteen sailors.

10. CAPE LOOKOUT NATIONAL SEASHORE

History

Cape Lookout National Seashore consists of three uninhabited barrier islands—North Core Banks, South Core Banks, and Shackleford Banks—which extend 28,500 acres or nearly 58 miles. The seashore runs from Ocracoke Inlet on the northeast to Beaufort Inlet on the southeast. It is under the jurisdiction of the National Park Service and has been since it was designated in 1966. The islands offer many natural and historical features that can make a visit very rewarding.

In the 1740s, Spanish privateers used Cape Lookout to hide from merchant ships. The only inhabitants were a handful of whalers who had set up camps along the banks. Whale oil and blubber fetched a good amount of money and whaling was good in these waters.

Cape Lookout

During the Revolutionary War, a fort was constructed on Cape Lookout. The fortress was needed because the Cape Lookout area was the only safe harbor along the Outer Banks and Upper Coast. The stronghold was authorized by the colony of North Carolina and built by General Washington's men and two Frenchmen who volunteered to help. Named in honor of Enoch Hancock, who owned the land, the fort was used for two years. It no longer exists.

During the 1800s, Cape Lookout Lighthouse and Cape Lookout Lifesaving Station were established. A U.S. Weather Station operated here from 1876 to 1904. In 1912, a plan was devised to turn Cape Lookout into a major exporter of coal. It was decided that the railroad would be extended from Beaufort out to the cape, but first some work had to be done to increase its rock jetty. Work began on the jetty in 1914 but was halted when World War I began. It was never resumed and the coal plan was later abandoned.

CORE BANKS

Both the **North and South Core Banks** are narrow ribbons of sand that have beaches on the ocean side and marshes on the sound side. The land is accessible only by boat, and a dinghy is probably the best way to transverse the shallow waters. Like most of the Down East communities, Core Banks started out as a fishing village. Several camps were set up along Core Banks for whalers, who used to make their living harvesting whale oil from migrating whales. Portsmouth was one of the few Core Banks villages that maintained its population for any period of time. Whale Creek, Brier Hill, Jack's Place, and Three Hats Creek were basically transient fishing camps. Atlantic Lifesaving Station (formerly Core Banks Lifesaving Station) operated near Drum Inlet until it was decommissioned in 1957.

Cape Lookout

SHACKLEFORD BANKS

Located across from Beaufort Inlet, **Shackleford Banks** extends nine miles to South Core Banks. The island got its name from former owner, John Shackleford, who purchased it in 1723. By the late 1800s, two communities existed: Diamond City on the Barden Inlet side and Wades Hammock near Beaufort Inlet. The inhabitants were primarily fishing families. Their primary source of income was whale oil, which was used for lighting lamps, making lubricating oil, and making soap. Whale bone was used to make items such as umbrellas and corsets. By 1887, five hundred people lived in Diamond City. There were a school, post office, church, and stores on the island. The Great Hurricane of 1899 ended life on Shackleford Banks. It became part of the Cape Lookout National Seashore in 1986. Prior to this, shacks and blinds had been built on the island for use by hunters, fishermen, and locals looking for a secluded hideaway. The island was used as grazing grounds for livestock and a junkyard for unwanted vehicles.

The first thing the NPS did when it took control of Shackleford was to remove the old shacks and sheds, relocate the livestock, and haul off the abandoned vehicles. They towed away more than 2,500 old, broken-down trucks, cars, boats, and farm equipment! It seems this barrier island was a perfect junkyard for area residents. Also, longtime residents say that when visitors used to come to the island, they would sometimes get stuck in the heavy sand, and if they were unable to extract their vehicles, they would simply leave them! Some of these abandoned vehicles still remain on the island and the NPS has no plans to remove them.

Wild pony, Shackleford Banks

The NPS also left the wild ponies alone to roam the banks. I should hope so! After all, these descendants of Spanish mustangs, believed to have survived the shipwreck of a seventeenth-century Spanish exploration expedition, have called these banks home for centuries. The NPS did round up the horses in 1997 to test for disease, pursue a birth control program, and euthanize the unhealthy horses. Their handling of the horses has caused quite a rift with many local residents who believe the wild ponies of Shackleford Banks are an asset that should be nurtured and protected. So the NPS and the nonprofit Foundation for Shackleford Horses, Inc., now have joint custodianship of these unique animals.

Rare close-up view of a Shackleford Banks pony 1997

During the early 1900s, pony roundups or horse-pennings took place twice a year throughout Core Banks. All the horses on the island were corralled and all colts were branded. According to David Stick's *The Outer Banks of North Carolina* (University of North Carolina Press, 1958), horse-pennings or roundups were attended by nearly everyone in the area. The events were both for business and entertainment. The horses were gathered and coerced into a pen by drivers and numerous volunteers. The young colts were branded and afterwards the horse buying and trading began. After price negotiations were completed, each animal was harnessed and ridden, by professional or experienced riders, for the first time. Here's where it gets really interesting! The horse repeatedly tried to throw its rider, while the rider would strive to get the horse into a nearby creek. The creek bottom was covered with mud, which made it impossible for the animal to buck and throw the rider. The horse quickly tired of trying and not getting anywhere and was soon "broken." From then on the animal could be ridden by nearly anyone and used for various tasks. The author notes that seasonal pennings continued to be events of primary importance in all part of the Banks until state laws were passed forcing removal of the stock, beginning with the North Banks in the 1930s.

Pony roundup on beach near Beaufort 1907

Diamond City used to be on the eastern end of Shackleford Banks. It took its name from the diamond-shaped pattern found on Cape Lookout Lighthouse. Diamond City once had the biggest population of any Outer Banks community. In the center of the city stood a sand dune that was twelve hundred feet long, four hundred feet wide, and forty feet high. This massive dune sheltered the city from bad storms. The founding residents were mostly whalers and some fishermen. Their homes were made from Shackleford Banks forest timber and shipwreck timbers. Two horrific hurricanes in the late 1800s did tremendous damage to all Shackleford Banks communities, including Diamond City. The giant sand dune was destroyed and homes washed away. The residents decided to move inland to Harkers Island, Morehead City, and other area communities.

Did you know there is a six-year waiting list for Cape Lookout Lighthouse volunteer caretakers? Take heart, the waiting period for a volunteer position on Portsmouth Island is less—only two years or so!

There used to be some private residences on Cape Lookout, but the leases held by their owners have recently expired. The properties now belong to the NPS, which has granted historical leases to some groups. For example, the former Coast Guard Station is used as a field research station by the North Carolina Maritime Museum. At the time of publication, no final decision had been made as to what will happen to the rest of the buildings. Most likely, they will be used for special events and programs, museums, and to accommodate park personnel and volunteer caretakers.

Fishing party posing at Shackleford Banks (circa early 1900s)

There will be no further construction or development along the seashore. As part of the effort to keep these barrier islands pristine, there are no amenities, so visitors must bring their own provisions, i.e., food, insect repellent, and sunscreen. What you will find here is a great place for swimming, sunbathing, shelling, picnicking, bird-watching, hunting (as per regulations), and primitive camping. No pets are allowed. Private ferry service is available from different embarkation points on Harkers Island and Beaufort. Contact the Cape Lookout National Seashore for a current list of authorized companies. 252-728-2250. www.nps.gov/calo

Party at Core Banks circa early 1900s

Sites and Attractions—Cape Lookout National Seashore

Cape Lookout Lighthouse is well worth a visit. While visitors cannot climb the tower, they are able to stroll through the keeper's quarters, which contains pertinent exhibits. The first beacon was built in 1812 but was inadequate; the one you see today was constructed in 1859. It became the model for all lighthouses constructed on the Outer Banks from that point on. When all the lighthouses were finished (Cape Lookout, Cape Hatteras, Bodie, and Currituck), the Lighthouse Board painted each using a different design so each was easily distinguished from the others and recognizable by daylight. Cape Lookout's tower is painted with a black-and-white diamond-shaped pattern. The NPS uses two volunteers to assist personnel with the lighthouse each season. Responsibilities include greeting visitors, picking up debris on the beach, and watching over the beacon and former keeper's house. Volunteers live on site at the former keeper's house. Cape Lookout National Seashore. 252-728-2250. www.nps.gov/calo

There's a terrible, yet intriguing, tale about an event that took place at Cape Lookout in 1886. A three-masted schooner, *Crissie Wright,* was sailing northward when a bad storm erupted. The captain decided not to try to cross the treacherous Diamond Shoals in the terrible conditions, so he changed course for Cape Lookout Bight. Near the harbor, the main mast brace split and the ship drifted onto the shoals. The surf was too high to launch the lifeboats, so the men took to the rigging. The Diamond City residents watched helplessly as the crew struggled. Some of the whalers even tried to reach the men to help them, but their small boats were no match for the pounding surf. To make matters worse, it was a bitterly cold night, the wind was whipping fiercely, and the water was icy cold. When some of the Diamond City men got to the ship the next morning they found four men wrapped up in a jib sail. It did not save them. Three had frozen to death and the fourth man survived only to die less than a year later. So if you ever hear the Beaufort saying, "Cold as the night the *Crissie Wright* came ashore," you'll know what it means.

11. PORTSMOUTH ISLAND

History

Just south of Ocracoke Island lies Portsmouth Island. In the heart of the island lies Portsmouth Village, a seaside ghost town which, in its heyday, was the largest town along the Outer Banks and had a population of seven hundred as well as roughly one hundred buildings.

The town was established in 1753 by river pilots who were paid to help ships through the tricky inlet. Back then, a ship's cargo would make the ship too heavy to cross the inlet without going aground. So cargo would be off-loaded into local boats which would transport it across the inlet. The cargo would be reloaded after the ship had safely crossed the inlet. The first tavern on the Outer Banks opened on Ocracoke Island in 1757, most likely to accommodate these river pilots and fishermen.

In its early days, life was simple, but enjoyable, on this remote barrier island. The hub of the island was its general store. A post office was established in a corner of the store in 1840. The mail boat brought civilization to the island, from letters to household items, to even visitors. A small mariner's hospital was established on Portsmouth during the 1800s to care for sick or injured seamen. Folks played croquet on the lawn in front of the general store and post office. Beach picnics and parties were held.

In 1846, Hatteras Inlet opened up and provided a better transport alternative. Ships no longer had to unload their cargo, so lightering pilots were no longer needed. Many families were forced to leave Portsmouth to find work elsewhere. Railroads also brought about the downfall of this island community, as ships were no longer the only way to transport goods. The 23-mile-long and 1.5-mile wide island was abandoned during the Civil War. Many residents never returned when the war ended. By 1880, only 220 residents inhabited the island.

A U.S. Lifesaving Station was established on Portsmouth in 1894, which helped revive the ailing economy. Also, many families turned their homes into hunting

Portsmouth Village Lifesaving Station

lodges during the early 1900s. Hurricanes and nor'easters were problematic. A 1913 hurricane destroyed the two churches on the island. Only one, the Methodist Church, was rebuilt. A 1944 storm caused the church to lean left and flooded many residences. The NPS eventually straightened and stabilized the church's foundation. In 1937, the lifesaving station was decommissioned. It was reestablished during World War II but was once again shut down when the war ended. By 1956, there were only seventeen island inhabitants. Three years later the post office shut down.

Portsmouth Village is listed on the National Register of Historic Places. Visitors are not permitted in the remaining twenty structures (circa early 1900s), except for the Methodist Church (circa 1914). However, they will enjoy

Portsmouth

seeing the old post office, schoolhouse, Coast Guard Lifesaving Station (with its boathouse and watchtower), cemeteries, and residences. Some homes are private and some have turned in ownership rights in exchange for help with restoration and maintenance. They hold long-term leases on the properties and use them for vacationing. The oldest structure is believed to be the Washington Roberts

House (circa late 1700s), which was partially built using shipwreck timbers. Most of the homes are painted a soothing shade of yellow and evoke simpler, though not always easier, times (as separate screened dairy houses and summer kitchens certainly do remind us). The island did eventually get electricity through generators, but only some of the islanders had it. Portsmouth inhabitants worked hard, tending their gardens and livestock, fishing, and clamming.

Portsmouth Island is 250 acres at North Core Banks. The beach is roughly one mile from the village. A trail leads visitors from the beach into the heart of the village and island. Insect repellent and sunscreen are strongly advised, as well as anything else you may need, as there are no amenities on the island. There are restrooms in the Dixon-Salter House (visitors center) and environmentally-friendly flush toilets on the beach. Primitive camping, fishing, exploring, and self-guided walking tours can be accomplished here. About one thousand visitors come to see this seaside ghost town every month during season. Private ferry service is available from nearby Ocracoke Island. Volunteer caretakers watch over the village and island, as well as make minor repairs and perform maintenance work. The nonprofit Friends of Portsmouth Island works with the NPS to preserve and protect the village. They host a homecoming every other year. I had the privilege of attending one of them several years ago and met many descendants or relatives of former island residents.

Sites and Attractions–Portsmouth Island

Portsmouth Village serves as an excellent example of what homes and life were once like along this stretch of coast. The oldest structure is believed to be the Washington Roberts House (circa late 1700s), which was partially built using shipwreck timbers. Portsmouth Island is 250 acres at North Core Banks. Primitive camping, fishing, exploring, and self-guided walking tours can be accomplished. Private ferry service is available from nearby Ocracoke Island. 252-728-2250 or www.nps.gov/calo

According to *Portsmouth Island: Short Stories and History*, written by Ben B. Salter and Dot. S. Willis in 1972, in the late 1700s and early 1800s there was one road that was wide enough to accommodate a horse and cart, a few businesses, dozens of homes, and a hospital. There was a forest in the middle of the island and that is where residents went to get wood to build their homes, which were scattered all along the banks and around the island. Grapes grew big and plentiful. Fishing and oystering was good. Wild waterfowl was abundant. Horses, cattle, and sheep once roamed freely, except in fenced-in yards. And the yards were full of grass, flowering plants, and fruit trees. There was a nice beach were folks could sunbathe and picnic. Inhabitants thought Portsmouth Island was a wonderful, magical place.

12. BOGUE BANKS

History

ATLANTIC
BEACH

Bogue Banks is a thirty-mile island comprised of five towns. **Atlantic Beach** started out in 1887 as a small beach pavilion which consisted of a one-story refreshment stand that had stalls in the rear for changing clothes. Guests of Morehead City's ritzy Atlantic Hotel would come over by boat to the oceanfront pavilion. Ox-pulled carts would deliver supplies and refreshments.

Nineteen years later, wealthy businessman Von Bedsworth bought the pavilion and one hundred acres, and built the one-hundred-room Atlantic View Beach Hotel, destroyed by fire a few years later. A group of local citizens rallied together and had a toll bridge built to connect Atlantic Beach to Morehead City in 1928. This led to the construction of another beach resort which had cabanas, dining facilities, and a pavilion. Unfortunately, this was all destroyed in another fire. Shortly thereafter, a New York bank bought the property and built a new hotel.

In 1936, the toll bridge was sold to the state, which promptly suspended toll charges. A drawbridge was constructed in 1953 to replace the run-down old bridge, and in the late 1980s, the drawbridge was replaced by the Morehead City–Atlantic Beach Bridge, a high-rise bridge that allows Intracoastal Waterway traffic easy passage.

Bridge at Bogue Sound (circa 1950)

The center of town is actually the southernmost end of the Atlantic Beach Causeway and is commonly referred to as "The Circle." The Circle offers an amusement park, tourist-oriented businesses, and parking. Atlantic Beach is the biggest and oldest of the five towns on Bogue Banks.

Pine Knoll Shores starts at Mile Marker 4 (MM 4). It dates back to 1918 when Alice Hoffman bought land on Bogue Banks, which was formerly called "Isle of the Pines." She lived here, for the most part, until her death in 1953. The property was left to her niece, the wife of President Theodore Roosevelt Jr. The Roosevelts thought that any development of Pine Knoll Shores should be mindful of the surrounding nature that makes it such a special place. That philosophy has remained prevalent, even after Pine Knoll Shores was incorporated in 1973. Zoning regulations are stringent, so it has remained primarily residential. It seems

PINE KNOLL SHORES

appropriate that one of the state's three aquariums should be here. Surrounding the maritime complex is the Theodore Roosevelt Natural Area, a 265-acre maritime forest owned by the state.

NC Aquarium at Pine Knoll Shores

INDIAN BEACH   The next town you come to after leaving Pine Knoll Shores is **Indian Beach,** also incorporated in 1973. However, this coastal community has permitted both residential and commercial development, including single-family dwellings, condominiums, restaurants, and camping areas. It offers residents and visitors beautiful beaches for sunbathing, surf fishing, and water sports. Indian Beach surrounds Salter Path, thereby creating a West Indian Beach and an East Indian Beach. This can be confusing when you think you have driven through Indian Beach and Salter Beach, only to find you are back in Indian Beach!

SALTER PATH   **Salter Path**'s first inhabitants came over from Diamond City in the late 1890s. Diamond City was once a big whaling community on Shackleford Banks, where more than five hundred people lived by the 1880s. There was a school, post office, church, and a few stores. In the late 1890s, two terrible storms nearly destroyed the city. Diamond City residents decided it was time to leave the island, so they carefully tore down their homes, cutting them into manageable sections. Then, they tied them to skiffs and floated the homes over to Morehead City, Harkers Island, Salter Path, and a few other area communities, where they reassembled their houses. What they left behind was destroyed by subsequent storms.

Legend has it that the name Salter Path originated with Joshua Salter, a Broad Creek resident who often traveled by boat from the mainland to fish and hunt on Bogue Banks. Stories say he made a path from the sound side of the island, where he anchored his boat, to the oceanfront. This became known as Salter's Path. Fishing has always been a main source of livelihood for many Carteret County residents. Early Salter Path fishermen made shrimping a profitable enterprise. Surprisingly, this town remains unincorporated, despite its growth and popularity.

Bogue Sound and Inland Waterway 1957

EMERALD ISLE

It's believed that whalers and Native Americans were the first to inhabit **Emerald Isle**. In 1893, fifteen families arrived, probably from the Diamond City evacuation. These families made their homes in Middletown, which is now a small part of Emerald Isle. Emerald Isle remained sparsely populated and mostly undeveloped until the 1950s. Seeing the success of Atlantic Beach as a resort, Philadelphian Henry K. Fort bought Emerald Isle, as well as five hundred acres on the mainland, Cape Carteret. Fort planned to build a spiffy island resort and a bridge to join it to the mainland. However, Fort was unable to get support for his bridge project, so the resort plan was abandoned.

Several years later, a ferry service was launched to Bogue Banks beaches. Today, Emerald Isle is still a popular vacation spot. New housing developments are still being constructed on this part of the island.

To reach Bogue Banks, take US 70 if entering from the eastern end of the island (Atlantic Beach), or NC 24 if coming from the western end (Emerald Isle). Bogue Banks is thirty-mile-long barrier island, situated just south of Morehead City. It is separated from the mainland by Bogue Sound but linked to it by high-rise bridges located at each end of the island. NC 58 runs across Bogue Banks; mile markers(MM) along the roadside indicate where you may find a particular site. Note that NC 58 changes names at certain places along its Bogue Banks route. In Atlantic Beach, it is called Fort Macon Road. From the end of Atlantic Beach to the other side of Pine Knoll Shores, NC 58 is also called Salter Path Road. And, in Emerald Isle, it becomes Emerald Drive.

Sites and Attractions–Bogue Banks

Since most attractions in this area are nature-related, please refer to the Nature Preserves, Sanctuaries, and Parks section further down for more.

North Carolina Aquarium at Pine Knoll Shores has something for all ages, including their fun and educational half-day summer kids' program Coastal Explorer Day Camp, for ages 4–11. Live animal programs include sea turtles, snakes, and alligators. Beginning snorkeling for all ages is offered throughout the summer. Many other programs are offered during the year for both adults and children, such as interpretive beach walks, crabbing classes, canoe trips, surf fishing, nautical craft classes, birding outings, seafood cooking demonstrations, "Breakfast with the Animals" (in which kids watch animals being fed and listen to a talk about the animals), barrier island excursions(including Cape Lookout/Shackleford Banks and Hammocks Beach State Park), Aquarium Jeopardy, and much more.

You may also just spend a day visiting this state-of-the-art facility. You'll find many exciting indoor and outdoor exhibits, including a twelve-thousand-gallon "Living Shipwreck" and a "Salt Marsh Safari." Visitors will see sharks, seahorses, moray eels, river otters, sea turtles, jellyfish, octopus, and more, up close. Note: The aquarium will be closed from January 2004 until spring 2006 to undergo an extensive expansion. When it reopens, it will be three times larger and hold many more exhibits, including a 300,000-gallon ocean tank with a sunken German sub U-352 on the "ocean floor." With a viewing window of more than sixty feet in length, there will be plenty of room for everyone to get a good look! 1 Roosevelt Dr., off NC 58 at MM7, Pine Knoll Shores, Bogue Banks. 252-247-4003. www.ncaquariums.com

13. BEAR ISLAND AND SWANSBORO

History

Bear Island is situated between Bogue and Bear Inlets, at the mouth of White Oak River. The 892-acre island makes up most of Hammocks Beach State Park. It has hosted lots of folks over the years: Native Americans, whalers, fishermen, pirates, privateers, planters, soldiers, and vacationers. The Tuscarora attacked area colonists from strategic hideouts in and around Bear Island during the Tuscarora Wars in 1711 and 1713. Eventually, they were driven out and the hostilities ended. However, pirates and Spanish privateers became a problem, launching attacks from these barrier islands as merchant ships passed by en route to various ports.

BEAR ISLAND

There have long been rumors of buried treasure on the island, although it is doubtful any was ever buried here. However, Blackbeard probably did seek refuge on the island at some point because it was almost uninhabited and close to Topsail, one of his favorite spots. Furthermore, the shallow waters around the island would have made a good place to lay in wait for passing merchant ships. Settlers were forced to build protective structures, including a fort near Bear Inlet in 1749, which no longer exists.

Confederate soldiers were stationed on Bear Island during the War Between the States to defend the area from Union troops stationed on nearby Bogue Banks.

In 1914, Dr. William Sharpe and friends, led by African-American hunting guide, John Hurst, came to

Bear Island to do some duck hunting. Sharpe, a renowned New York brain surgeon, became so enchanted with the land that he had a large house moved onto the island. He named his home the Hammocks and hired his former guide, John Hurst and his wife, Gertrude, as caretakers. Many locals did not like that Sharpe had hired a black man as caretaker and sent anonymous, threatening letters to Sharpe. Sharpe retaliated by advertising a $5,000 reward in the local newspaper for information leading to the arrest of anyone who harmed his friends, the Hursts, or his beloved home. No harm ever came to either. North Carolina decided to build a road on the island in 1937. It is not clear why the state deemed a road necessary at this particular point in time. The road was set to run through the Hammocks, destroying Dr. Sharpe's huge house. Dr. Sharpe appealed to the state legislature, but his pleas fell on deaf ears. Dr. Sharpe, a very determined man, finagled a brief meeting with President Franklin Roosevelt, by means of the president's personal physician. Within days, road work stopped and was never resumed.

View of ocean from porch of bathhouse at Hammocks Beach State Park 1964

During World War II, the Coast Guard used the island to monitor U-boat activity.

In 1949, Dr. Sharpe gave the Hammocks to the North Carolina Negro Teachers Association because there were no beaches open to African-Americans and both Sharpe and Hurst thought Bear Island would make a great retreat. However, the association did not have the monies needed for upkeep and eventually turned it over to the state. On May 3, 1961, the public land officially became Hammocks Beach State Park.

Thirty-five acres of the park are on the mainland and the rest is on the island, which remains undeveloped, with the exception of a few small buildings and a pavilion on the beach. The pavilion has showers, restrooms, picnic tables, and refreshments (cold drinks and snacks only). A naturalist and lifeguard are on duty seasonally. The island's three-mile-long beach remains unspoiled, with lots of big sand dunes—some up to sixty feet tall! There is also a small marine forest and a marsh filled with sea oats, wax myrtle, Virginia creeper, red cedar trees, Yaupon, flowering dogwood, pine trees, and live oak. Additionally, egrets, laughing gulls, oyster catchers, herons, and terns are among the many birds that can be found here. Endangered loggerhead turtles nest in the summer and Carolina tree frogs breed in the spring and summer. There are also foxes, diamondback terrapin turtles, deer, canebrake rattlesnakes, lizards, and raccoons.

In addition to swimming, beachcombing, nature study, birding, and sunning, fishing can also be accomplished. Fishermen will likely catch puppy drum, mullet, flounder, and bluefish. Camping is allowed but a permit must be obtained. Campfires are forbidden and flashlights or lanterns should be used minimally during the summer months so as not to disturb nesting loggerheads. Water is available mid-March through November from the island's bathhouse. If you plan to do much island explo-

A pelican at Hammocks Beach State Park

ration, wear good walking shoes and insect repellent. You may notice two other islands as you cross Bear Inlet: Brown's Island and Onslow Beach. Both are owned and used by nearby Camp Lejeune Marine Corps. No trespassing is permitted.

SWANSBORO   **Swansboro** was an Algonquian village from around 500 A.D. until colonial settlement began in 1730. The area was perfect for hunting and fishing because it is at the mouth of White Oak River. In 1730, Jonathan and Grace Green and Jonathan's brother, Isaac Green, moved here from Massachusetts. Jonathan Green was thirty-five years old when he died, only five years after arriving in Swansboro. Grace Green remarried Theophilus Weeks, who had also moved from Massachusetts to nearby Hadnot Creek. Weeks bought out Isaac Green and became the owner of the plantation.

Swansboro

Weeks was an ambitious man. He worked the plantation, ran a tavern, and was appointed inspector of exports at the town's port. He became known as the town's founder because he sold parcels of land from his extensive plantation in 1771. He called the forty-eight lots "Weeks Wharf" and the deeds were registered as being part of a "...plan of a town laid out by Theophilus Weeks." Called Weeks Wharf, Weeks Point, and New-Town-upon-Bogue at different times, it officially became a town and was renamed Swannsborough in 1783. The name was chosen by the North Carolina Assembly to honor Samuel Swann, former speaker of the state's House of Representatives and

Swansboro Lifesaving Station

Onslow County representative. Over the years, the spelling was changed to Swansboro.

The town has been populated by some colorful characters, including Otway Burns. He became a privateer during the War of 1812. After the war, he was hailed as a hero when he returned to pursue ship building. He was also appointed lighthouse keeper at Portsmouth Island. Upon his death in 1850, he was buried in Beaufort's Old Burying Ground. You can see an impressive statue of Otway Burns in Bicentennial Park on the Swansboro waterfront.

Swansboro (circa 1940's)

Over the years, pine lumber, tar, and pitch were exported from Swansboro. It was a budding port until the Civil War, which changed the direction and prosperity for most of the Carolinas. It was occupied by Union soldiers in 1862 and 1864. After the war, the town reinvented itself as a fishing and farming community.

Today, Swansboro is a small, but pretty, waterfront town, dubbed "Friendly City by the Sea." Its downtown area has a historic district that is on the National Register of Historic Places. There are antique stores, gift and specialty shops, quaint restaurants, and lots of good fishing in the Swansboro area. You can reach Swansboro by taking either NC 58 if coming from Bogue Banks, or NC 24 if coming from Morehead City. Contact the Swansboro Chamber of Commerce for sites and attractions information. 910-326-1174, www.swansboroncchamber.com

Bear Island is five miles southeast of Swansboro on NC 24, between Beaufort and Wilmington. Turn off NC 24 onto SR 1511 and continue two miles to the parking lot and ferry terminal. The park office is here. Visitors need to register at the office. Private boats may tie up at the island ferry dock or along the shore. It is a popular place for kayakers and has a three-mile kayak trail with twenty-four markers posted by the state park service. A free, thirty-six-passenger ferry runs several times a day from June 1 to Labor Day, and then on weekends for the rest of September and May. Call for a current schedule. Although the island is only 2.5 miles from the mainland, it is a twenty-five minute ferry ride. It is a half mile walk from the ferry landing to the beach. Hammocks Beach State Park: 1572 Hammocks Beach Road, Swansboro, NC. 910-326-4881 or 910-326-3553. www.ils.unc.edu/parkproject/visit/habe/home.html

14. MISCELLANEOUS ISLANDS

There are so many islands along the Outer Banks and Crystal Coast that boaters cruising these waterways may wonder what they are used for and who owns them. For this reason, I've briefly discussed the islands of consequence.

The National Audubon Society (www.ncaudubon.org) has purchased or leased more than twenty North

Carolina islands to provide habitats to protected birds. **Beacon Island** is home to one of the largest brown pelican populations. **Battery Island** accommodates close to ten thousand nesting ibises, as well as three hundred egrets and herons. Additional tracts of land, such as **Lea Island,** have been designated Important Bird Areas (IBA).

The Nature Conservancy (www.nature.org) also owns many North Carolina islands, including **Money, Monkey, Swan, Narrows, Dews,** and **Mary Islands**. These were all owned formerly by wealthy Northern businessmen who operated hunting clubs on them. For example, American Tobacco Company executives bought Monkey Island in 1919 and formed the Monkey Island Club, an exclusive hunting club with only nine members. One member, Ashby Penn of Reidsville, North Carolina, eventually bought the others out in 1931. The Penn heirs sold the land to the Nature Conservancy in 1975. The Nature Conservancy leases the Monkey Island Lodge and hunting blinds to hunters who come from all over the country.

Goose Creek Island accommodates two fishing communities: Hobucken and Lowland. Access to the island is afforded by taking NC 33/NC 304 across the Intracoastal Waterway (ICW) by bridge. If you're in the area, you may want to visit **Goose Creek State Park**. Hiking, canoeing, fishing, camping, wildlife viewing, walking along the Palmetto Boardwalk Trail, and picnicking are permitted. More than two hundred bird species, seventy-five reptile species, and forty mammal species reside here. The park's wetlands are designated a National Natural Landmark. The education center, in the ten-thousand-square-foot visitors center, offers roughly one thousand special programs annually. North of Pamlico River and ten miles east of Washington. Take US 264 E and turn right onto SR 1334. Follow signs denoting the park entrance (2.5 miles up on the right). Park office is at 2190 Camp Leach Road, Washington, NC 27889. 252-923-2191. www.ils.unc.edu/parkproject/visit/gocr/home.html

Carrot Island, located across from Shackleford Banks, is accessible by boat only. There is good shelling here and it is a secluded picnic spot. This island, as well as **Horse Island**, **Bird Shoal**, and a few other islands are part of the 2,625-acre **Rachel Carson Research**

Reserve. Developers tried to build condominium complexes here in 1977, but their plan came to an end when the North Carolina Nature Conservancy bought 474 acres of Carrot Island.

HUGGINS
ISLAND

Huggins Island is due east of Bear Island, at the mouth of Bogue Inlet. This 225-acre island is part of the state's parks system and is deemed a Globally Rare and Significant Area because of its maritime swamp forest. The island has been used for hunting and fishing by Native Americans, by pirates lying in wait for merchant ships, and by a six-cannon battery of Confederates from 1861–1862. It can easily be seen from Swansboro but is accessible by boat only. There are no amenities or facilities.

JONES ISLAND

Jones Island lies two miles south of Hobucken, across the ICW. The five-thousand-acre island once housed one of the top fishing and hunting lodges on the eastern seaboard. Many migratory ducks and other waterfowl use the island, which is accessible only by boat.

LEA ISLAND

Lea Island, just off Topsail Beach, is accessible only by boat. It's interesting that nearly forty lots were platted on the island and some people plan to build, despite the fact that five or six lots are already under water! Some lots can support a septic tank, but no electricity or telephone service has been extended to the island. Due south of Lea Island is **No Name Island**, a 2.5-mile privately owned but uninhabited island.

NO NAME
ISLAND
PERMUDA
ISLAND

The uninhabited **Permuda Island** is actually one of three islands that make up a large part of the North Carolina National Estuarine Research Reserve, which is the third largest in the United States. The state's system consists of more than two million acres. Ninety percent of all seafood harvested commercially in the state derives from the estuary. These reserves are a vital part of North Carolina economy and ecology. Estuaries are created when fresh water from rivers mixes with salt water, as in a bay or a coastal lagoon. Each reserve is a "living laboratory." Therefore, research stations, as well as weather stations, are usually located on these islands. This fifty-acre barrier island is near Topsail Beach and is accessible only by boat. When some developers suggested developing the island in 1985, the Nature Conservancy stepped in and purchased the entire island for $1.7 million. The state bought half the land from the Conservancy two years later, in 1987, to include in the North Carolina Coastal Reserve.

It is used as an outdoor research lab as well as for educational purposes and for traditional uses. Visitors are allowed on the 1.5-mile-long island as long as they are respectful of its inhabitants and ecosystem, but there are no amenities and insect repellent is recommended. Many birds can be found here such as black skimmers, willets, warblers, and songbirds. There is also good fishing and hiking. 7205 Wrightsville Avenue, Wilmington. 910-256-3721. www.ncnerr.org

A fine summer day on the NC coast

Pivers Island is a tiny place, accessible by boat only. There is a marine science lab on the island used by Duke University marine science students and there is a National Marine Fisheries Station. The boat dock is shared by the school lab and fisheries station and is not for public use.

PIVERS ISLAND

Locals like to swim and picnic at **Radio Island**, but several years ago the North Carolina State Ports Authority bought a large tract of the island and has since restricted access by leasing a twelve-acre area to the county for public use. Carteret County constructed a parking lot but there are no other amenities. The island is between Morehead City and Beaufort, off US 70.

RADIO ISLAND

Wainwright Island lies at the junction of Pamlico and Core Sounds. Its name comes from James Wainwright, who founded a porpoise fishery near Hatteras Village in 1880. The uninhabited island has no amenities but is good for those seeking a secluded picnicking or camping spot.

WAINWRIGHT ISLAND

RECREATIONAL ACTIVITIES AND SPORTS—THE CRYSTAL COAST

In this section you will find listings of boat ramps, marinas, and fishing piers, along with some resources for practicing golf and tennis and for taking eco-tours of the Crystal Coast. This information is not meant to be comprehensive since it is constantly changing and the venues are sometimes too numerous to list here. For the most complete and up-to-date list of venues, companies, and outfitters, contact the **Crystal Coast Tourism Authority** at 3409 Arendell Street, Morehead City (in the Crystal Coast Visitor Center). 800-786-6962 or 252-726-8148. www.sunnync.com

BOATING

Boaters arriving along the Intracoastal Waterway may drop anchor in Taylor's Creek (Beaufort) in the *designated* anchorage on the south side of the channel. There is no charge for anchoring nor restrictions on length of stay. A public dinghy dock and restrooms are available at Beaufort Town Docks.

There is a launch spot for canoes and kayaks at the **Cape Lookout National Seashore.** Follow the signs to the picnic area and the launch site is posted. 252-728-2250. www.nps.gov/calo

Curtis A. Perry Park is a public ramp providing four launch areas into Taylor Creek. The park is located at the east end of Beaufort's Front Street. No phone or website available.

The **Grayden Paul Jaycee Town Park** has a wide pier that enables boats to be docked and launched from it. Parking is available on Front Street. No phone or website available.

There is a boat launch on **Harkers Island.** Go to the west end of the island at the Fisherman's Inn fish camp.

The camp offers a free launch but charges a parking fee for overnight parking. No phone or website available.

Municipal Park offers parking and several launch spots. 3409 Arendell Street, behind the Crystal Coast Visitor Center, Morehead City. No phone or website available.

Beside **Town Creek Marina** are two public ramps and a dock. Off W. Beaufort Road, Beaufort. No phone or website available.

BOAT MARINAS

70 West Marina. Morehead City. 252-726-5171. No website available.

Airport Marina. Beaufort. 252-728-2010. No website available.

Anchorage Marina. Atlantic Beach, Bogue Banks. 252-726-4423. No website available.

Atlantic Beach Causeway Marina offers thirteen wet slips, repair and fuel services, and a store. 300 Atlantic Beach Cswy., Atlantic Beach, Bogue Banks. 252-726-6977. No website available.

Barbour's Harbor Marina. Harkers Island. 252-728-6181. No website available.

Beaufort City Docks. Beaufort. 252-728-2503. No website available.

Beaufort Gulf Dock. Beaufort. 252-728-6000. No website available.

Calico Jack's Inn & Marina. Harkers Island. 252-728-3575. No website available.

Casper's Marina. Swansboro. 910-326-4462. No website available.

Coral Bay Marina. Morehead City. 252-247-4231or 247-6900. No website available.

Dockside Marina. Morehead City. 252-247-4890. No website available.

Dudley's Marina North of Swansboro on NC 24, Cedar Point. 252-393-2204. www.dudleysmarina.com

Fort Macon Marina. Atlantic Beach, Bogue Banks. 252-726-2055. No website available.

Harbor Master. Morehead City. 252-726-2541. No website available

Harkers Island Fishing Center. Harkers Island. 800-423-8739 or 252-728-3907. No website available.

Island Harbor Marina & Marine Center. Emerald Isle, Bogue Banks. 252-354-3106. No website available.

Morehead City Yacht Basin. Morehead City. 252-726-6862. www.moreheadcityyachtbasin.com

Morehead Gulf Docks. Morehead City. 252-726-5461. No website available.

Morehead Sports Marina. On the Morehead-Beaufort Causeway. 252-726-5676. No website available.

Morris Marina. Atlantic. Near Cedar Island. 252-225-4261. No website available.

Portside Marina. Morehead City. 252-726-7678. No website available.

Radio Island Marina. On the Morehead-Beaufort Causeway. 252-726-3773. No website available.

Sea Gate Marina Off NC 101, one mile north of Intracoastal Waterway's Core Creek Bridge. 252-728-4126. No website available.

Sea Water Marina. Atlantic Beach Causeway, Atlantic Beach, Bogue Banks. 252-726-1637. No website available.

Spooner's Creek Yacht Harbor. South of Morehead City, off Intracoastal Waterway. 252-726-2060. www.spoonerscreek.com

Swansboro Yacht Basin. North of Swansboro on NC 24, Cedar Point. 252-393-2416. No website available.

Town Creek Marina and Yacht Sales. North of the Beaufort drawbridge at Town Creek. 252-728-6111. www.towncreekmarina.com

Triple S Marina Village Atlantic Beach, Bogue Banks. 252-247-4833. No website available.

FISHING

Inshore fishing yields bluefish, spot, flounder, sea mullet, black drum, red drum, pompano, speckled trout, Spanish mackerel, king mackerel, sailfish, grouper, mahi mahi, cobia, amberjack, bluefish tuna, and tarpon (seasonally). A list of fishing piers follows:

Bogue Inlet Fishing Pier, Emerald Isle, Bogue Banks. 252-354-2919.

Iron Steamer Resort, Pine Knoll Shores, Bogue Banks. 252-240-7793.

Oceanana Fishing Pier, Atlantic Beach, Bogue Banks. 252-726-0863.

Sportsmans Pier, Atlantic Beach, Bogue Banks. 252-726-3176.

Triple "S" Fishing Pier, Atlantic Beach, Bogue Banks. 252-726-4170.

Best Times to Fish

- One hour before and one hour after high tides, as well as one hour before and one hour after low tides.
- During "the morning rise," after sunup for a spell, and "the evening rise," just before sundown and the hour or so after.
- When the water is still or rippled, rather than during a wind.
- When there is a hatch of flies, caddis flies or mayflies, commonly. (The fisherman will have to match the hatching flies with his fly, or go fishless.)
- When the breeze is from a westerly quarter rather than from the north or east.
- When the barometer is steady or on the rise. (But, of course, even in a three-day driving nor'easter, the fish aren't going to give up feeding. Their hunger clock keeps right on working, and the smart fisherman will find something they want).
- Starting on the day the moon is new and continuing through the day it is full. Always fish on the growing moon.

Taken from *The Old Farmer's Almanac* (also available on its website, www.almanac.com)

See the fishing schedule in the Outer Banks section (pages 63-64) to obtain an exact listing of offshore fish found in this area and the best times of year to catch them. Contact the Crystal Coast Tourism Authority for a current list of companies offering fishing charters, supplies, and lessons.

Tips for buying seafood. The best way to tell if a fish is fresh is by its eyes. They should be clear and bright, not cloudy and dull. Red gills are a sign of freshness while brownish gills means the fish is not fresh. The fish should smell mild and pleasant, not old and "fishy."

When cooking, be careful not to overcook. As a rule of thumb, allow ten minutes of cooking per inch of thickness. When fish flakes, it is ready. When cooking or boiling shrimp, allow no more than three minutes.

The most nutritious way to eat seafood is broiled, baked, smoked, boiled, steamed, or grilled. Avoid frying as much as possible because it disguises flavor and adds a significant amount of fat and calories. A good marinade is to brush the fish with olive oil, lime juice, and salt and pepper to taste. Fish, like other foods, continues to cook after you remove it from heat, so be careful not to overcook it.

GOLF

The following courses are open to the public:

Belvedere Plantation. 2368 Country Club Drive, Hampstead, off Hwy. 17. 910-270-2703. No website available.

Bogue Banks Country Club. 152 Oakleaf Dr., Pine Knoll Shores. 252-726-1034. www.boguebankscc.com.

Brandywine Bay Golf. Hwy. 70, Morehead City. 252-247-2541. No website available.

Castle Bay. 2516 Hoover Road, Hampstead (two miles off Hwy. 17). 910-270-1247. No website available.

North Shore Country Club was rated among the top twenty new courses of the decade by *Golf Reporter*.

One of its many unique qualities is an underground tunnel built beneath NC 210. Watch out for the ninth hole! NC 210. 101 North Shore Drive, Sneads Ferry. 800-828-5035 or 910-327-2410. www.northshorecountryclub.com

Olde Point Golf and Country Club. US 17 N., Hampstead. 910-270-2403. www.oldepoint.com

---

TENNIS

For those who enjoy tennis, the **Island Beach & Racquet Club** sponsors year-round tennis camps for all levels. Its academy is supervised by a tennis pro and is for those with serious ambitions. The club has six courts, a pro shop, and equipment rentals. Year-round and seasonal memberships are available for both area residents and visitors. 201 Salter Path Road, Atlantic Beach, Bogue Banks. 252-247-7900. www.ibrctennisresort.com. The **Bogue Banks Country Club** at Pine Knoll Shores has tennis courts as well and is open to the public. See golf listings above for contact information.

DIVING

There are some excellent diving spots and several companies that offer good dive packages. Online listings can be found at www.nc-wreckdiving.com or www.charternet.com, or contact the tourism bureau for a complete listing.

ECO-ADVENTURES

The **Cape Lookout Studies Program**, offered by the North Carolina Maritime Museum, takes place at the Cape Lookout National Seashore Field Station. The workshops, retreats, and programs are designed to educate children and adults about the area's islands and waterways. Some of the most popular programs include the annual Wooden Boat Show and Junior Sailing Program. North Carolina Maritime Museum. 315 Front Street, Beaufort. 252-728-7317. http://capelookoutstudies.org/

North Carolina Coastal Federation offers coastal adventures which include nature hikes, canoe outings, and workshops. These are great ways to explore and learn more about Bear Island, Croatan National Forest, Sharks Tooth Island, and Huggins Island. Sharks Tooth Island and Huggins Island are sandbar islands. Huggins has some Civil War earthworks but little else of interest to tourists. 3609 Hwy. 24 (Ocean), Newport, between Morehead City and Swansboro. 252-393-8185. www.nccoast.org

Morehead City Parks and Recreation Day Camp runs for eight weeks. The summer day camp offers preschool and school-age kids arts and crafts, swimming, skating, field trips, music, drama, sports, and games. The camp is open to both residents and nonresidents. 1600 Fisher Street, Morehead City. 252-726-5083.

Photography Tips. There are some great photo ops in these coastal hamlets and nature preserves but sometimes it can be hard to capture them. I recommend using a polarizer to enrich colors and reduce glare. A UV filter will protect your lens from scratches or harmful salt water/air. Go to your local camera store and ask a knowledgeable person about filters.

When trying to capture action scenes, use a high shutter speed to prevent blurring, such as 1/250 or 1/500. Many cameras have manual and automatic modes for controlling such settings.

Try different angles: straight on, from above, from below, horizontal, vertical, close up, etc.

Watch for distracting elements in the shot, such as a trash can, tree branch, pole, or vehicle. Try another angle or position to eliminate them. You may also want to exchange lenses from a wide angle to a telephoto or zoom lens to enhance detail. (continued on next page)

Photography Tips (continued). When shooting people and animals, try to capture movement and action. A picture should tell a story. Have the kids building a sand castle rather than just posing on the beach. Take a picture of your spouse feeding the ducks rather than just standing there. I also prefer action in my landscapes. Instead of just taking a pretty picture of the water or park or beach, try to include a sailboat, windsurfer, bicyclist, people playing Frisbee, a fisherman tossing his line, or sea gulls soaring overhead.

The best light for photography is early in the day and late in the day. Mid-day sun creates harsh shadows. This can be corrected by adding fill flash, which helps to balance out the bright sun and dark shadows.

Take care that your equipment doesn't suffer from sand and salt air. Put it in a zippered, waterproof camera bag when not in use. Don't load film directly in the sun. Also, don't keep camera gear or film in a hot car or on the beach to "bake" in the sun. I leave my good 35 mm and video cameras behind and buy a waterproof disposable camera for boating and beach scenes. I learned the hard way that sand and salt are *not* friends of the ol' camera. Rest in peace, Minolta 750.

For 35 mm cameras, 100 speed film is best for daytime shooting. Use 400 speed film for indoor or high action. For general purpose, 200 speed is recommended. When using digital cameras, make sure you have enough storage space to accommodate all the pictures you want to take. Some of the lower-end digitals can only store a few dozen images before you have to stop photographing or start deleting stored images.

NATURE PRESERVES, PARKS, AND SANCTUARIES–THE CRYSTAL COAST

Cape Lookout National Seashore is comprised of Cape Lookout/South Core Banks, Portsmouth Island/North Core Banks, and Shackleford Banks. It is a great place for swimming, sunbathing, shelling, picnicking, birdwatching, hunting (as per regulations), and primitive camping. No pets are allowed. Cape Lookout National Seashore offers primitive camping. This means no restrooms/showers or drinking water. There is a public bathroom nearby at the Cape Lookout Lighthouse. Also, there are some rustic cabins with toilets, hot showers, and kitchens (no cooking utensils provided). 131 Charles Street, Harkers Island. 252-728-2250. www.nps.gov/calo

Nature lovers, bird-watchers, and hikers will find much to appreciate in the **Cedar Island Wildlife Refuge.** The refuge accommodates many species of birds, waterfowl, and mammals, including woodpeckers, peregrine falcons, raptors, river otters, and bears. The fourteen-thousand-acre sanctuary is open to hikers, boaters, picnickers, bird-watchers, and hunters (according to regulations). There are two boat launches: one at the refuge office and the other (for canoes and kayaks) at the base of the Monroe Gaskill Memorial Bridge. Take US 70 East and NC 12 East from the Morehead City/Beaufort

Kayaking along the seashore

area for forty-five miles east to Cedar Island. Or, you can reach the island by ferry from Ocracoke Island. The Cedar Island–Ocracoke Ferry carries passengers and vehicles on the two-hour-and-fifteen minute ride. Reservations should be made. Cedar Island Ferry Terminal: 252-225-3551; Ocracoke Island Ferry Terminal: 252-928-3841. The refuge is under the management of the Lake Mattamuskeet National Wildlife Refuge. For information, contact the Refuge Manager at Route 1, Box N-2, Swan Quarter, NC 27885. 252-926-4021. http://southeast.fws.gov/cedarisland/ There are a couple of campgrounds and a motel with a restaurant on the island.

Croatan National Forest is home to the biggest group of carnivorous plants in any national forest. There are recreation areas, picnic areas, boat launches, and camping, as well as bathing and restroom facilities. Camping is permitted year-round in the 157,000-acre forest. Additionally, there are trails such as the Cedar Point Tideland Trail, a 1.4-mile loop trail that runs through the estuary, and the half-mile Island Creek Forest Walk Trail, which provide the opportunity for good bird watching and nature appreciation. For serious hiking, the Neusiok Trail extends twenty miles into the forest, starting at the Newport River Parking area and ending on the Neuse River at Pinecliff Recreation Area. Winter is best because of the lack of bugs, humidity, and snakes. There is lots of wildlife in the forest, such as black bears, owls, peregrine falcons, American alligator, and bald eagles. Croatan is located twenty-five miles north of Morehead City (between Morehead City and New Bern), off U.S. 70. The ranger station is at 141 E. Fisher Avenue, New Bern. 252-638-5628. www.cs.unca.edu/nfsnc/

Fort Macon State Park is visited by more than one million people every year, making it the most visited park in North Carolina. It is located at the eastern tip of Bogue Banks because the fort was erected to safeguard the Beaufort Inlet and harbor. During the 1700s and 1800s, this area was highly assailable by pirates and other enemies. In 1747, Spanish marauders captured Beaufort and in 1782 the British seized Beaufort. Two forts, Fort Dobbs and Fort Hampton, were built here prior to Fort Macon, but they weren't sufficient. Fort Macon was named after Nathaniel Macon, speaker of the House of Representatives and a

U.S. Senator from North Carolina. It was designed by Brigadier General Simon Bernard and built by the U.S. Army Corps of Engineers in 1834. The octagonal-shaped brick and stone edifice cost a whopping $463,790. Its exterior walls are nearly five feet thick and there are twenty-six, five-sided casements inside the fort.

Fort Macon

A 1924 Act of Congress gave the fort and land to North Carolina to be used as a public park. The four-hundred-acre park opened in 1936 and was the state's first public park. The fort was used in its official capacity for the last time during World War II. Many visitors come here because the park offers opportunities for birding, swimming, and fishing, and it has nice beaches, a bathhouse with restrooms, nature trail, museum and gift shop, concession stand, and picnic area complete with grills. The museum may be explored independently or by taking a tour. MM 0, NC 58, Atlantic Beach, Bogue Banks. 252-726-3775. www.ils.unc.edu/parkproject/visit/foma/home.html

Hammocks Beach State Park on Bear Island has much to offer visitors. Fishing is excellent year-round, especially in the fall. Puppy drum, bluefish, trout, and flounder are often caught on Bear Island. Federally protected loggerhead turtles come ashore from May to August to nest every three or four years. They nest up to six times a year, and each nest can produce up to 120 eggs! The tiny eggs have a two-month incubation period. Then the hatchlings have to get across the beach back to the water. Raccoons and foxes are fond of turtle eggs and will raid the nests whenever possible. The hatchlings are vulnerable to birds and ghost crabs. There are many other dangers waiting for them in the ocean. The island also accommodates many shore birds such as herons, egrets, and osprey. Bottlenose dolphins have been spotted offshore. Foxes and deer roam freely.

Primitive camping is permitted for just a few dollars a night, but campers must register with the park office at Swansboro Ferry Terminal on Hammocks Park Road. No hookups or conveniences, other than restrooms/showers, are available. There are two ways to reach the park. You can take a private boat over and dock, if you're good at navigating shallow water. Or you can take the state ferry from Swansboro—but you should be aware than it is more than a half mile from the ferry landing to the campsites. Sometimes it's closed to campers from June to August because of nesting loggerhead turtles. The park office is at 1572 Hammocks Beach Road, Swansboro. 910-326-4881. www.ils.unc.edu/parkproject/visit/habe/home.html

The **Rachel Carson Component** of the North Carolina National Estuarine Research Reserve, commonly called Carrot Island, or Bird Shoal, is actually comprised of a series of islands. Previously, the islands were privately owned and one of the owners decided to pursue development in 1977. His plan was to divide the 178 acres into lots and sell them. Luckily, some concerned citizens formed The Beaufort Land Conservancy Council and sought support for preservation from the Nature Conservancy. The two groups raised $250,000, which they used to buy the 178 acres.

Rachel Carson was a scientist who conducted a great deal of research on these islands in the 1940s. She wrote about her findings, thereby increasing public awareness of the importance of these environments. Today, the North Carolina Division of Coastal Management is responsible for preservation and maintenance. North Carolina manages the island reserve, whose estuarine habitat is a prime place for fish and shellfish, and which is home to 160 species of birds and feral horses.

This estuary is one of four the state safeguards. Zeke's Island, Currituck Banks, and Masonboro Island are the other reserves. Visitors may enjoy swimming, clamming, beach walks, kayaking, and nature exploration, as long as they leave the site as they found it. This means removing all trash but taking nothing else. Seasonal boat tours are offered from Pivers Island. Call for hours and reservations. Maps may be picked at the North Carolina Maritime Museum, ferry terminals, or online. 135 Duke Marine Lab Road, Beaufort (across from the waterfront and Taylor's Creek). 252-728-2170. www.ncnerr.org

Theodore Roosevelt Natural Area is the three-hundred-acre maritime forest surrounding the North Carolina Aquarium at Pine Knoll Shores. Donated to the state by the family of former President Theodore Roosevelt, it has freshwater ponds, trails, and birding opportunities. MM 7, Roosevelt Drive, Pine Knoll Shores, Bogue Banks. 252-726-3775. No website available.

STRANGE TALES AND GHOSTS

Blackbeard, Larger Than Life

Speaking of strange tales, there are more than a few involving the infamous Blackbeard. There's a wonderful story about Blackbeard in Charles Johnson's *A General History of the Pirates* (London, 1724).

> One day at sea, and a little flushed with drink: "Come," says he, "let us make a hell of our own, and try how long we can bear it." Accordingly, he, with two or three others, went down into the hold and, closing up all the hatches, filled several pots full of brimstone and other combustible matter and set it on fire and so continued till they were almost suffocated, and some of the men cried out for air. At length, he opened the hatches, not a little pleased that he held out the longest.

> The daring buccaneer is also purported to have made a deal with the Devil. Blackbeard once proclaimed no one, save the Devil and himself, knew where he had secured his booty (treasure). Whoever lived longer would get all the

riches. According to the legend of Teach's Lights, on clear nights the waters around Teach's Hole, Ocracoke Island, possess a unique shine and glimmer. It is said that the glimmer is caused by Blackbeard swimming these waters in search of his head, which was chopped off during a battle with the Royal Navy. Supposedly, anyone who follows the lights will eventually find Blackbeard's treasure, and the Devil himself will be seated on top of the chest!

Blackbeard

However, the "Skull Cup of Blackbeard" has to be the strangest and most fascinating folklore regarding the famous pirate. When Lt. Maynard brought the buccaneer's head back to Virginia, it was suspended from a pole at the harbor in Hampton, Virginia. Legend has it the skull eventually turned up in some secret "bones society" at Yale University. This is disputed by some who claim Blackbeard's friends stole the skull off the pole. It's also believed that the skull once belonged to one of the fraternities at William and Mary College. The skull ended up in North Carolina, supposedly, in the possession of an anonymous businessman. At some point, the skull was covered or plated with silver.

It's believed that the skull was once in the possession of former North Carolina judge, legislator, and author, Charles H. Whedbee. Some time in the 1930s, an anonymous group reportedly arranged a secret rendezvous at "Blackbeard's Castle," a nickname given to the pirate captain's former refuge house on Ocracoke Island, near Silver Lake. Supposedly, Whedbee drank from the skull, also referred to as "Blackbeard's Cup." Sadly, Whedbee is deceased, the house no longer exists, and no one has any idea who the other people in the group were, so the strange story cannot be verified.

The silver-plated skull came to belong to Edward Rowe Snow in 1949, who was also fascinated with piracy. After his death, his widow gave the skull to the Peabody Essex Museum in Salem, Massachusetts. Peabody Museum Assistant Curator Lyles Forbes told me it is not really silver-plated, just painted silver. Also, the lower jaw is missing—most likely a casualty resulting from age and rough handling. Forbes says it will never be possible to prove or disprove that the skull is Blackbeard's.

Why is this tall, dark, and rugged pirate one of the most famous sea robbers in the history of piracy? And why, after all this time, do we remain mesmerized by Blackbeard? Quite simply, it's because he pulled off some of the most spectacular feats imaginable, including defeating the Royal Navy, taking the town of Charleston, South Carolina hostage, and engaging in one of the bloodiest battles ever fought along the North Carolina coast. It took five gunshots and twenty cutlass wounds to kill Blackbeard!

TRADITIONS—THE CRYSTAL COAST

Many fun-filled events are held along the Crystal Coast every year, ranging from seafood festivals to holiday flotillas. Further information can be obtained about these events by contacting the appropriate tourism resources found in Additional Resources at the end of the book.

The **American Music Festival** concerts take place every month and feature chamber music ensembles and renowned performers. Downtown Morehead City.

Crystal Ballios an optional–black tie evening including dinner and dancing. It is hosted by the Carteret County Chamber of Commerce. Location varies.

Waterfowl Watching Weekend. Excursion to Lake Mattamuskeet and Pea Island guided by the North Carolina Maritime Museum. Beaufort.

Winter Trails: Cedar Point. Croatan National Forest is explored during a guided hike with the North Carolina Maritime Museum at Beaufort. Croatan National Forest.

Beaufort Walk is a guided tour by the North Carolina Maritime Museum of Beaufort's historic sites and scenic places. Beaufort.

Carolina Chocolate Festival. It is described as "a day of chocolate, chocolate and more chocolate..." The fundraiser benefits all Crystal Coast non-profit organizations. Crystal Coast Civic Center, Morehead City.

Living History Dramatization includes costumed volunteers performing various tasks, such as cooking, weaving, candlemaking, and other types of demonstrations. Beaufort Historic Site.

Winter Trails: Patsy Pond. Croatan National Forest is explored during a guided hike with the North Carolina Maritime Museum at Beaufort. Croatan National Forest.

Cape Lookout Lighthouse opens to visitors for one day only to celebrate Cape Lookout National Seashore's birthday on March 10. Those who would like to climb the Cape Lookout Lighthouse for the unforgettable view and a historic experience will be allowed to by reservation only.

Coastal Home Show. In this big event, many coastal home-related products are showcased by vendors at Crystal Coast Civic Center, Morehead City.

Easter Egg Hunt (March or April). Prizes, refreshments, and lots of eggs are available to children seven or younger. Beaufort Historic Site.

Emerald Isle St. Patrick's Day is a one-day festival of all things green on the Emerald Isle. There is music, dancing, green beverages, corned beef, and cabbage, along with contests and fun for kids. Emerald Isle.

North Carolina Seafood Festival. Beaufort offers music, dancing, and of course, great seafood. Beaufort.

St. Patrick's Day Pet Parade starts with the morning parade. There are events throughout the day, such as "Best Dressed" and "Best Look-A-Like Pet/Pal!" Downtown Morehead City

Swansboro Oyster Roast happens around St. Patrick's Day each year. Swansboro.

APRIL

The **Beaufort by the Sea Music Festival** (not to be confused with the North Carolina Seafood Festival) offers several stages with different musical performances. The International Choral Fest is also in attendance, treating guests to outstanding choral music. Beaufort.

Civil War Encampment includes historical reenactment, demonstrations, and more. Richlands.

Emerald Isle Homes Tour & Art Show. Features guided tours of four or five beautiful coastal homes. Local artists exhibit and sell their work in the Western Carteret Public Library. Door prizes and book sales are offered at the library. Tour begins at the Western Carteret Public Library on Taylor Notion Road, Cape Carteret.

Public Day is a colonial-style flea market and a unique event worth attending. Beaufort Historic Site.

MAY

Coming Home Weekend. Core Sound Waterfowl Museum puts on this event, complete with food, heritage entertainment, and many events. Harkers Island.

Memorial Day King Mackerel & Blue Water Tournament. Swansboro.

The **Morehead City Homes and Gardens Tour** offers participants a rare glimpse into the private homes and gardens of some of its residents. The guided tours discuss each property's historical significance, as well as general area history. Various locations in Morehead City.

North Carolina Blackbeard Fest is a "must-attend" event for pirate enthusiasts. The two-day event includes a pirate costume contest, pirate battle, pirate lore, treasure hunt, and tours of the repository of artifacts from Queen Anne's Revenge (Blackbeard's flagship which was recently found near Beaufort). Beaufort.

North Carolina International Choral Fest is a renowned musical event. Swansboro.

Quilt Show. This weekend event is sponsored by the Crystal Coast Quilt Guild, and includes items for sell, quilt-making demonstrations, and more. Crystal Coast Civic Center, Morehead City.

Salter Path Clam and Scallop Festival. Bogue Banks.

Spring Show is a juried show and sale of the Carteret County Arts and Crafts Coalition. Beaufort Historic Site.

Woodenboat Show. A weekend event that includes exhibits, demonstrations, and boat races at the Maritime Museum, Watercraft Center, and on the Beaufort waterfront

Arts By the Sea Festival. Art show and sale. Swansboro.

JUNE

Beaufort Antiques Show and Sale features roughly fifty antiques dealers and exhibitors during the same weekend as the Beaufort Old Homes and Gardens Tour. What a great weekend for antique lovers! Crystal Coast Civic Center, Morehead City.

Beaufort Old Homes and Gardens Tour is a fundraising event. Proceeds go towards the maintenance and preservation of Beaufort Historical Association's buildings, museum shop, galleries, and double-decker tour bus. Participants gain access to private homes and gardens, as well as witnessing living history demonstrations and more. Beaufort.

Big Rock Blue Marlin Tournament is a big fishing competition with approximately 100 participants. Morehead City.

Big Rock Lady Anglers Tournament. Morehead City.

Concert In The Park (June-August). This summer concert series provides free concerts each Friday night, and is sponsored by the Morehead City Parks and Recreation Department. Performances vary from Cajun zydeco to gospel music. At the waterfront Jaycee Park in Morehead City.

The **Decoy Carving, Colonial Music, Antique Tools and the BHA Militia** includes living history, decoy carving, and other demonstrations. Beaufort Historic Site.

JULY

Bogue Sound Kayak Festival. Bogue Banks.

Fourth of July Fireworks in Morehead City, Emerald Isle, Atlantic Beach and Swansboro.

Fourth of July Parade and Community Picnic is a fun tradition that includes a Beaufort waterfront parade, families and pets, concessions, music and a potluck community picnic. Carteret County Courthouse.

Fourth of July Underwater Bike Race. This underwater race takes place on the wreck of the *Indra*. It is sponsored by Discovery Diving Company, www.discoverydiving.com

Historic Beaufort Road Race includes a little of everything—timed walks, baby jogs, wheelchairs, 10K and 5K runs, etc. Downtown Beaufort.

Jazz Festival. Bogue Banks.

Summer Show is an annual juried show and sale of the Carteret County Arts and Crafts Coalition. Beaufort Historic Site.

AUGUST

The **Coastal Women's Fair** features food, entertainment, specialty vendors, and a fashion show. Crystal Coast Civic Center, Morehead City.

Outer Banks Wildlife Shelter Sand Castle Contest. Bogue Banks.

Atlantic Beach King Mackerel Tournament is the country's biggest all-cash fishing tournament. Bogue Banks.

Carteret County Big Sweep. Volunteers pick up litter and debris to keep our beaches clean. Bogue Banks.

North Carolina Annual Shell Show is the state's biggest. Come learn about the state's seashells. Bogue Banks.

Atlantic Beach Surf Fishing Tournament. Approximately one hundred anglers compete for various prizes. It is sponsored by the town of Atlantic Beach and the Carteret County Chamber of Commerce. Bogue Banks.

Carolina Kite Fest. Fun kite-flying competition and more. Bogue Banks.

Fall Gala & Art Show. Beaufort Historical Association's benefit is said to be the social event of the year in Beaufort. A different private home is selected each year as the site of the gala evening and one artist is featured each year, with works of art for sale. Location varies.

Harvest Time is filled with colonial actors demonstrating weaving, candlemaking, and much more. Special demonstrations and reenactments are held for school groups. Beaufort Historic Site.

North Carolina Seafood Festival All Kids' Pier Fishing Classic is a junior fishing competition and festival. Bogue Banks.

Swansboro Mullet Festival. Games, music, and food highlight this festival. Swansboro.

Candlelight Gallery Tour and Ball is a prestigious fundraiser. Bogue Banks.

Community Thanksgiving Feast is prepared by Beaufort restaurants to be enjoyed on site or for takeout. Beaufort Historic Site.

Kindergarten Thanksgiving (throughout November) welcomes touring students of kindergarten age to witness living history demonstrations of preparations for Thanksgiving in colonial times at the Leffers Cottage. Kids are shown how the Leffers family prepared for winter. Beaufort Historic Site.

Mill Creek Oyster Festival. Bogue Banks.

Santa's Seaside Workshop is open between Thanksgiving and Christmas on weekends. Beaufort (downtown waterfront boardwalk).

Swansboro By Candlelight is a holiday candlelight tour. Swansboro.

Swansboro Christmas Flotilla is a holiday boat parade and festivities. Swansboro.

Swansboro Speckled Trout Tournament. Swansboro.

The Jumble Sale gathers crafts, food, arts, antiques and more. The one-day sale relives the atmosphere of a Colonial Publick Day and is a good chance to find some great bargains! Beaufort Historic Site.

DECEMBER   **Beaufort-By-The-Sea Carolina Christmas Walk** includes stops at beautifully decorated inns and the Beaufort Historic Site. This will put you in the Christmas spirit! Beaufort.

Core Sound Decoy Festival is a show and sale of decoys carved by members of Core Sound Decoy Carvers Guild. Loon-calling contest and other fun events take place. Harkers Island.

Core Sound Waterfowl Weekend. Exhibits include boat building, conservation activities, vendor booths, and more. Core Sound Waterfowl Museum, Harkers Island.

Crystal Coast Christmas Flotilla is a parade of yachts and workboats decorated for Christmas. Morehead City and Beaufort waterfronts.

TEST YOUR KNOWLEDGE

Quiz

Just for fun, test your knowledge by taking this quiz.

1. True or False: Diamond City boasts one of the largest populations on the Crystal Coast.
2. Where is the Old Buying Ground?
3. Nowadays, Oriental is best known for what?
4. What is Harkers Island's principal industry?
5. The National Park Service towed away more than 2,500 broken-down old trucks, cars, boats, and farm equipment when it took possession of what place?
6. In 1753, a community was established on what island? (Hint: The place where river pilots used to help heavy ships by transporting their excessively heavy cargo across the tricky inlet.)
7. What is the oldest community on Bogue Banks?
8. What island has accommodated fishermen, whalers, planters, Neuse and Corees, and a nudist colony?
9. What city is on the National Register of Historic Places and is also dubbed "Friendly City by the Sea?"
10. Where is the only seaside ghost town in North Carolina?
11. Which park receives more than one million visitors annually?
12. What lighthouse has a black-and-white, diamond-shaped pattern?
13. True or False: Horse-pennings (or pony roundups) were events in which islanders round up their horses to sell.
14. What is "The Circle?"
15. What are the two most important industries along the Crystal Coast?
16. The Apothecary Shop is part of what historic attraction?
17. What are the two most sought-after volunteer positions with the National Park Service?

18. What port city has more than one hundred historic sites and buildings?

19. Name one of Beaufort's most famous citizens?

20. What is the 14,000-acre wildlife sanctuary that is home to many species of reptiles, birds, and mammals, such as raptors, bears, and otters, and is also a great place to canoe and kayak?

[Answers can be found at the end of the chapter.]

FUN WAYS TO LEARN

Teachers and parents may wish to tackle the activities below to teach their kids or students about North Carolina's coastal history and nature.

• Take an online field trip to see and hear "first hand" the final battle of **Blackbeard** and the excavation of what is widely believed to be his flagship, *Queen Anne's Revenge.* Visit the website of the North Carolina Department of Cultural Resources' *Queen Anne's Revenge* Shipwreck Project, www.ah.dcr.state.nc.us/qar/

• Have everyone make their own **pirate flag.** The most popular was the Jolly Roger, which was a black and white flag with a skull and crossbones. However, pirates usually personalized their flags. Some excellent examples can be found at *The Depot* and the *News & Record's* "Blackbeard Lives" website, www.blackbeardlives.com. What would your flag say about your personality?

• There are some interactive games and activities available for downloading from the **North Carolina Aquariums** website, www.ncaquariums.com/newsite/kids.htm. Activities include "Build a Shark," "Aquarium Coloring Book," and "Interactive Touch Tank."

• Have kids write their own **ghost story** or legend. To get them started, have them draw cards that suggest a person, location, or even provides the first sentence. These can be original stories or existing ghost tales that have a different beginning, middle, and/or end. This is a great creative writing exercise.

• **Shelling** is a fun family activity that combines amusement, exercise, and learning. For the classroom, have your students bring in shells collected on previous beach vacations and compare them to pictures found in books—especially ones about North Carolina's seashells—to identify them. Here are a few good books on the subject: *Carolina Seashells* by Nancy Rhyne, *Seashells of North Carolina* by Huge J. Porter and Lynn Houser, and *National Audubon Society Pocket Guide to Familiar Seashells* by National Audubon Society.

Crabby Facts. Did you know that horseshoe crabs have been swimming the ocean since before dinosaurs roamed the earth? Did you know that blue crabs mates only one time in their life, for 6–12 hours? Did you know that the hermit crab sheds its shell during growth and then takes a shell from a dead gastropod to replace it?

• **Crabbing** is an easy and fun activity for all ages. There is minimal equipment involved. You'll need a string or cord and some bait. Blue crabs can be caught by wrapping the string or cord around the bait (fish heads, chicken necks, or chicken wings work best). Gently lower the string or cord back into the water for a few minutes. When you feel a slight pull or after a few minutes, check it. If you see a crab or crabs hanging on, eating the bait, slowly pull the string out of the water and slide your crab net under it as quickly as possible. You will probably lose the first couple of crabs by jerking the cord out of the water too fast. But just try again. Wherever you vacation, ask the locals where the best crabbing spots are. Shallow water (less than twelve feet deep) and warm weather (at least 60 degrees) are best. Also, there shouldn't be any waves or surf—if the water isn't relatively calm, you can't tell if there's a crab pulling on your line. And don't waste your money buying expensive bait. Fish or chicken parts work just as well or better. A chicken wing or neck will bring all the crabs you want if you're in a good crabbing spot. Keep in mind that you should throw the crab back into the water if it is less than 5 inches from tip to tip. Have fun!

Atlantic Beach, Bogue Banks 1952

Southern Tea. Beach activities can make any-one thirsty, especially in the intense summer heat. Nothing quenches thirst better than an iced cold glass of sweet tea.

In case you are not from the south, here are directions for making Southern Tea (sweet is redundant!). First, bring a pot of water to a full boil and add one or two family size tea bags, such as regular or decaffeinated Lipton, or Luzianne. Be sure to let the tea steep for at least 3-5 minutes. Pour into pitcher and add a cup or so of sugar. Chill for a few minutes and then pour over ice and add fresh lemon wedges. If entertaining, you may want to add a sprig of mint.

QUIZ ANSWERS

1. False. It no longer exists! Residents relocated to Morehead City and Harkers Island after two huge hurricanes destroyed their community.

2. Beaufort

3. Sailing

4. Boat building

5. Shackleford Banks

6. Portsmouth Island

7. Atlantic Beach

8. Bear Island

9. Swansboro

10. Portsmouth Island

11. Fort Macon State Park

12. Cape Lookout Lighthouse

13. False. The pennings or roundups took place to brand the colts and "break them in" so they could be ridden.

14. "The Circle" is the center of Atlantic Beach, at the southernmost end of the Atlantic Beach Causeway.

15. Tourism and fishing

16. Beaufort Historic Site

17. Cape Lookout National Seashore Lighthouse caretaker; Portsmouth Island caretaker

18. New Bern

19. Privateer Captain Otway Burns

20. Cedar Island Wildlife Refuge

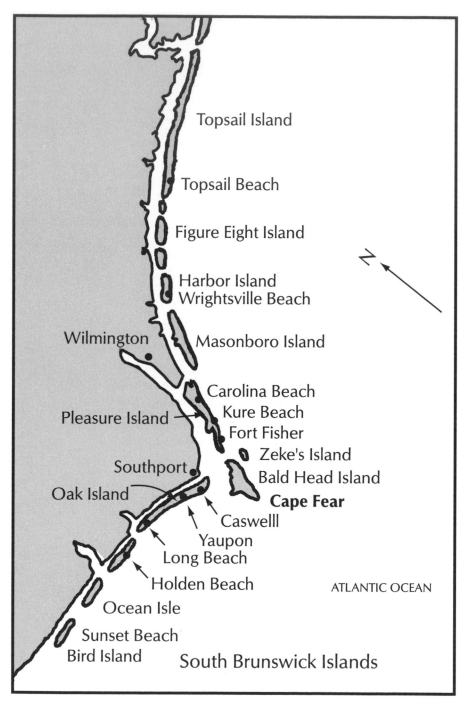

Topsail Island

Topsail Beach

Figure Eight Island

Harbor Island
Wrightsville Beach

Wilmington

Masonboro Island

Carolina Beach
Kure Beach
Pleasure Island
Fort Fisher
Zeke's Island
Southport
Bald Head Island
Oak Island
Cape Fear
Caswelll
Yaupon
Long Beach
Holden Beach
ATLANTIC OCEAN
Ocean Isle
Sunset Beach
Bird Island
South Brunswick Islands

N

The Lower Coast

3

Lower Coast

CAPE FEAR COAST

Introduction

The Cape Fear/Lower Coast is comprised of New Hanover and Brunswick Counties. New Hanover County includes Figure Eight Island, Wrightsville Beach, Wilmington, and Pleasure Island (Carolina and Kure Beaches). Bald Head, Oak Island, Southport, and the South Brunswick Islands fall under the jurisdiction of Brunswick County. With 19 municipalities, 856 square miles of coastal communities and inland towns, and close to 78,000 inhabitants, Brunswick County is the fastest growing county in the state.

However, New Hanover County is still the "big brother," boasting a population of more than twice Brunswick's. Wilmington alone has a population of more than 90,000. What's especially appealing about this stretch of coast is its diversity. Take, for instance, Southport: although it is growing in leaps and bounds, it has maintained its quaint, small waterfront town charm. Bald Head Island's lure is its limited development. While there are lots of homes and condominiums on the island, there is minimal commercial development. You also won't find overhead utility lines on the island or even automobiles. Only bicycles and golf carts are permitted on Bald Head, so there is no need for paved streets, traffic lights, or signs. This also means no noise pollution or road rage! And while cars are permitted

167

on Figure Eight Island, its residents also support a minimal development policy. If you could gain admittance onto this private island, all you would see are the clubhouse facilities, lots of homes, and the beach.

Contrasting these locations are Carolina and Kure Beaches. There are family beaches filled with lots of mom-and-pop motels, eating establishments, and family amusements. The most notable attractions (other than the beaches, of course) are Carolina Beach Boardwalk and Carolina Beach State Park. At the end of Kure Beach you'll find one of the state's most important historic sites, Fort Fisher. You'll also find one of three state aquariums, all of which have undergone major renovations and expansions to create impressive must-see facilities.

The Lower Coast also includes historic Oak Island and the scenic Brunswick Island, each boasting three beach communities including a fort, planetarium, winery, lighthouse, and museum. Topsail Island, located in both Onslow and Pender Counties, is approximately halfway between Cape Fear and Cape Lookout. Because it is closer to Wilmington than Cape Lookout, it is discussed in this section. Topsail has an engaging history, including being a missile testing site and pirate hideout.

FAST FACTS

CAPE FEAR COAST

Brunswick, New Hanover, Pender, and Onslow Counties comprise the Lower North Carolina Coast. The Cape Fear River is the outlet to the Intracoastal Waterway and Atlantic Ocean. The biggest city is Wilmington, which not only has the largest population, but also the most tourist attractions, ranging from a serpentarium to hundreds of restaurants and shopping outlets.

TOURIST SEASON

Officially runs from **Easter to Thanksgiving**. However, many attractions, accommodations, restaurants, and souvenir shops are closed or have limited hours except during the summer. The exception is Wilmington, which caters to tourists year-round. There are four rental rate seasons: prime season (expensive, runs from June 10 to August 20), holiday season (expensive, runs Easter week, Memorial week, and Labor Day week), mid season (moderate, runs from April 1 to Easter week, from May 1 to Memorial week, and from after Labor Day week to October 31), and winter season (least expensive, runs from January 1 to March 31 and from November 1 to December 31).

Average Temperatures for Cape Fear Coast

	High	Low
January	56	35
February	58	37
March	65	43
April	74	52
May	81	60
June	86	67
July	89	71
August	87	71
September	84	66
October	75	54
November	67	44
December	59	37

*These statistics are from
The National Weather Service and
Cape Fear Convention and Visitors Bureau.*

MOST POPULAR ATTRACTION

The **Fort Fisher Recreation Area and Historic Site** contains a nice four-mile beach, monument, visitor's center, recreation area, and underwater archaeology center. Fort Fisher played a vital role in the Civil War because it was the biggest Confederate fort and the Confederacy's last stronghold. At the Fort Fisher State Historic Site there is a Visitors Center which houses displays and shows an interesting film depicting the fort's history. Nearby is the Fort Fisher Monument, which was erected in 1932. 1610

Fort Fisher Blvd. South, Kure Beach. 910-458-5538. The adjacent, state-of-the-art North Carolina Aquarium at Fort Fisher also draws many visitors. Twenty miles south of Wilmington, south of Kure Beach on US 421 at 1610 Fort Fisher Blvd. 910-458-9042/8206. www.arch.dcr.state.nc.us/UW-LIGIT.htm

BEST VIEW Driving **across the Cape Fear Memorial Bridge into Wilmington,** one can see the impressive Cape Fear River, *Battleship North Carolina*, and the city's historic waterfront.

MOST UNIQUE ANNUAL EVENT **Christmas in Wilmington**. Nobody makes a bigger fuss over the holiday than this port city. December is filled with a myriad of festivities: Old Wilmington by Candlelight Tour, Kwanza Festival, Moravian Candle Tea, Reindeer-drawn Trolley and Caroling, Holiday Pops Concert, Lighting of the World's Largest Living Christmas Tree, Holiday Lighting of the *Battleship NC*, and culminates with a New Year's Eve River Cruise. Various locations. 800-222-4757 or 910-341-4030. www.cape-fear.nc.us

MOST IMPORTANT INDUSTRY **Tourism**.

MOST IMPORTANT HISTORICAL EVENT **British reign over North Carolina came to an end in Southport in 1775.** After fleeing New Bern in May 1775, Royal Governor Josiah Martin sought refuge at Fort Johnston, which was ideally located on a bluff overlooking the mouth of the Cape Fear River. The governor escaped by ship on July 18, 1775. The next day 500 Minutemen raided the British fortress and it remained "off limits" for the British for the rest of the Revolutionary War.

To this day, Southport-Oak Island host the biggest three-day party in the state celebrating America's independence.

Early Map of North Carolina

ISLANDS & TOWNS

15. TOPSAIL ISLAND

History

Topsail is a twenty-six-mile barrier island, located approximately halfway between Cape Fear and Cape Lookout. It was used by Native Americans for hunting and fishing and later colonized by European explorers in the 1500s. The island became a favorite hiding spot for pirates, who attacked merchant ships as they passed. Ships carrying valuable cargo posted crews to watch out for buccaneers. If the tops of sails were seen beyond the dunes, that most likely meant "Beware, pirates are waiting to ambush." That's how the island got its name.

Because of its remote location and inaccessibility, the island was not inhabited by many folks until the late 1800s and early 1900s. These early settlers came to work in the island's main industry—salt production. Up until the Civil War, salt was produced employing a technique most likely learned from area Native Americans. An easier method was perfected around the 1860s. I don't know how the Native Americans did it, but in the 1860s, saltwater was pumped from the sound, concentrated in brine pools, and later the water was boiled off in large pans so the salt could be extracted. It's remarkable that there were more than 100 salt production facilities in the greater Cape Fear area, including Topsail Island. Salt was vital in those days, not so much as an additive, but to preserve meat. These businesses were worth about $8 million in 1863!

Topsail remained sparsely populated and accessible only by boat until World War II. In 1940, the federal government developed part of the island as a training center, Camp Davis. This was later expanded to include a missile launch pad and nine concrete towers used to record missile launches and Operation Bumblebee flights. At the end of World War II, the Navy worked with Johns Hopkins University's Physics Lab to develop a supersonic guided missile with the ability to hit airplanes up to twenty miles away. No one was allowed on the island without proper credentials and the Navy kept two patrol boats in operation to keep fishermen at a safe distance.

Topsail Beach 1950

By October 1946, 600 Navy sailors, marines, and civilian scientists were working on World War II's Operation Bumblebee. During the next two years, two hundred missiles were launched into the ocean. They traveled up to 1,400 mph and achieved their goal of twenty miles. Area population grew so much that the Navy feared the island was no longer the best place to conduct their tests. When they realized that Cape Canaveral, Florida, would be better suited for such activities, the pad and towers were deserted, but most still exist. Some have been converted to private homes and the former Assembly Building is now the Topsail Island Missiles and More Museum. Barnacle-encrusted missiles still wash ashore occasionally.

The government returned the island to its residents in 1948, and since that time, the island has become a popular resort. Topsail Island is made up of three towns: Surf City, which was founded in 1949; Topsail Beach, which was incorporated in 1963; and North Topsail Beach, which was officially established in 1990. The Greater Topsail area includes Holly Ridge and Sneads Ferry, a small fishing community.

SURF CITY Of the three island communities, **Surf City,** which is located on the center of the island and extends to the mainland, has the most shops, restaurants, vacation properties, and motels. It was incorporated in 1949, has the largest population (1,400), and the only traffic light. Surf

City is in both Onslow and Pender Counties. The only way to get to **Topsail Beach** is through Surf City. Topsail Beach is the smallest, with a population of just 425, although it has been incorporated since 1963. Pender County residents must like it the way it is, because they don't allow high rise development on it. **North Topsail Beach,** population 843, is a quiet residential community that has only a few oceanfront condominiums and rental cottages. There are virtually no restaurants or shopping facilities, but there is a fishing pier, several public beach accesses and a soundside park complete with covered picnic areas, a basketball court, and a playground. This Onslow County community was incorporated in 1990.

TOPSAIL BEACH

NORTH TOPSAIL BEACH

Surf fishing on Topsail Beach

Topsail Island is five miles east of Hwy. 17, between Wilmington and Swansboro. From Raleigh take I-40 East to NC 210. Topsail is linked to the mainland by two bridges, NC 50 at Surf City and a span bridge on NC 210 at North Topsail Beach. Topsail Island is 25 miles north of Wilmington, 28 miles south of Jacksonville, and 150 miles south of Raleigh. For detailed information, contact the **Greater Topsail Area Chamber of Commerce and Tourism** at 13775 Treasure Coast Landing, Suite 101, Highway 50, Surf City. 800-626-2780 or 910-329-4446. www.topsailcoc.com

Sites and Attractions–Topsail Island

Camp Lejeune Marine Corps Base Tour is a self-guided tour of "the largest marine expeditionary force in the world" and is also the most comprehensive training base of its kind. Camp Lejeune was established in 1941 as a Marine Corps Training Center, and was named after Lt. General John A. Lejeune. The base encompasses New River Air Station and 151,000 acres. The brochure and map, available at the gate and at the Topsail Area Chamber and Tourism office, disclose two dozen points of interest. Back Gate Base Entrance is off NC 172, Sneads Ferry. You may want to call first to determine accessibility. Most bases have closed to tourists since 9/11/01, although Camp Lejeune says that it will remain open to visitors. 910-455-1113. No website available.

Topsail Island Museum: Missiles and More has displays highlighting the island's history, as well as an extensive shell collection. Exhibits include Native American artifacts, piracy history, and of course, information on World War II operations that took place on the island or at nearby Camp Davis. The museum offers storytelling and refreshments for children once a week during the summer. Assembly Building, 720 Channel Blvd., Topsail Beach 800-626-2780 or 910-329-4446. http://topsailmissilesmuseum.org

---

16. WILMINGTON

History

Wilmington had many names including New Liverpool, New Carthage, New Town, and Newton, before it finally came to be called Wilmington, in honor of the Earl of Wilmington, Spencer Compton. The newly appointed Governor Gabriel Johnston came up with the idea to honor Compton, who had appointed him to the position. The town was established in 1729, but wasn't officially incorporated until 1739.

During the mid-1700s to late 1800s, Wilmington was one of the state's largest ports. The port city's strong econ-

View of vessels loading at the Wilmington wharves. March 22, 1890.

omy was also based on its shipbuilding and lumber production. It was even one of the biggest cotton exchanges
in the world and a producer of naval stores (tar, pitch, and
turpentine). Nothing significant occurred here during the
Revolutionary War, except that the citizens revolted
against Britain's Stamp Act and helped end the use of
British stamps. There was also an important battle at nearby Moore's Creek (twenty miles north of Wilmington) in
1776. Although the Patriots won this battle, the British
overtook the city in 1781. It is believed that General

*Corner of Fourth and Orange streets, looking toward
the railroad, 1873. Photo by Rufus Morgan.*

Cornwallis stayed in the Burgwin-Wright House, which still exists today. He surrendered later that year in Yorktown, and Wilmington continued to grow and prosper.

The Wilmington Railroad was built in 1840, and, within ten years, Wilmington became the largest city in North Carolina. Thalian Hall was built in 1858. The first-rate theatre brought performers and patrons from all over, helping Wilmington achieve significant cultural, as well as economic, stature.

Then came the Civil War. The Cape Fear River, Wilmington, and Fort Fisher, were all vital throughout the Civil War. In fact, Fort Fisher was the most important stronghold, so when it was finally conquered by the Union on January 15, 1865, the war ended less than six months later. In 1866, the town of Wilmington officially became a city.

Like most of the South, Wilmington suffered economically after the war. Cotton production and exporta-

Wilmington's historic riverfront remains as important today as it was during the 1800s. Freighters, cruise ships, and pleasure crafts are often spotted cruising Cape Fear River and tourists linger along its riverwalk, enjoying the view.

tion revitalized the area. Later, the Great Depression took its toll on Wilmington, but economic stability returned when the demand for ships increased during World Wars I and II. The port city was one of nation's biggest shipbuilders during this time. In 1947, Wilmington College, which is now the University of North Carolina at Wilmington, was established. The North Carolina Ports Authority was established in Wilmington in 1952. It was a booming place until the railroad moved its headquarters, just a few years later, to Jacksonville, Florida.

City officials turned to tourism to replace previous sources of revenue. The *Battleship North Carolina*, a World War II battleship, was brought to Wilmington as a tourist attraction. In 1974, much of Wilmington's waterfront area was put on the National Register of Historic Districts. In fact, the city has one of the state's largest historic districts—230 blocks are listed on the register. Visitors will note that most of the streets are named after streets in Liverpool, England such as Castle, Princess, Market, Queen, and Church Streets.

As North Carolina's main deep-water port, more than eight hundred ships from around the world come to Wilmington every year. The Cape Fear River was recently dredged and deepened to accommodate mega-sized cruise ships and whopper freighter ships.

One especially interesting feature of Wilmington is its underground tunnels, partially created by feeder streams that empty into the Cape Fear River. Historically, these streams provided water for both homes and businesses as well as sewage removal. They also brought mosquitoes and periodic flooding. Eventually, property owners bricked over the streams to prevent such problems and possible interference with traffic and commerce, which had increased significantly by the late eighteenth century. These tunnels sometimes reached five feet or higher and ran from three to seventeen feet underground. Every stream tunnel had a name such as Jacobs' Run or Tanyard Branch. The tunnels made up a rather intricate system that has been used for many different purposes. Revolutionary War soldiers, pirates, slaves, and prisoners escaping from Cornwallis' dungeon, all have allegedly used the tunnels for their various missions. There hasn't been a need for these stream tunnels in many years and most have substantially deteriorated.

Wilmington Regatta at Wrightsville Beach 1946

While the tunnels aren't used anymore, the busy streets and sidewalks that cover the city's 198-square miles are used by hundreds of thousands of tourists every year. *Money Magazine* recently named the Cape Fear Coast one of its Top 12 Best Places to Vacation.

To get to Wilmington, from the northwest, take I-40 or US 421 and follow the signs. From the west, take US 74/US 76 and follow the signs. From the south, take Hwy. 17 and follow the signs. Wilmington has a large airport, Wilmington International Airport. 1740 Airport Blvd, Wilmington. 800-282-3424 or 910-341-4125/4333. www.fly-ilm.com. Wilmington is 65 miles from Myrtle Beach, SC; 413 miles from Atlanta, GA; 360 miles from Washington, DC; 797 miles from Nashville, TN; and 123 miles from Raleigh, NC.

Sites and Attractions–Wilmington

African-American Heritage Trail can be explored by obtaining a free booklet and map at Cape Fear Coast Convention and Visitors Bureau (CVB). Admission fees are charged to enter some buildings included on the trail, such as the Bellamy Mansion Museum and Slave Quarters. CVB is at 24 North Third Street, in the historic courthouse, Wilmington. 800-222-4757 or 910-341-4030. www.cape-fear.nc.us

The Cape Fear River brought good and bad to Wilmington. Goods were easily transported along the river, but along with that convenience came the ships filled with sailors. Sailors were a rowdy, uncouth bunch for the most part. Townspeople didn't like them hanging around too long. So laws were passed barring them from staying in port for more than six hours. And no merchant was to extend credit to them—they had to pay cash only! Sailors didn't like traveling the Cape Fear River, either. The river got its name because sailors feared its labyrinth of channels and treacherous sandbars.

Battleship North Carolina is on Eagles Island, which was named in honor of Richard Eagles, an area planter. During the eighteenth century, the island produced large quantities of rice, which was exported via the Wilmington harbor. The battleship, which was brought to the area by Captain B. M. Burris, actually sits on the New Hanover County–Brunswick County line. It was stationed in the Pacific Theater during World War II and was part of every significant offensive during the war. The vessel was decommissioned in 1960; area residents raised funds to bring the ship to Wilmington. The ship may be seen by taking a self-guided tour of its nine decks. There is also a Sound and Light Show nightly, seasonally. Bring insect repellent if you plan to attend the show. There is a shipboard museum complete with historical photographs and displays (including a "Roll of Honor" list of all North Carolina men who died during World War II), gift shop, snack bar, picnic area, and large parking lot. The island is located at the junction of Highways 17, 74, 76, and 421, which is across from Wilmington's historic district. Take the Cape Fear Memorial Bridge out of Wilmington. Eagles Island is linked to the mainland by a causeway. The ship is just across the bridge on the right. Or hire a water taxi, which departs from the foot of Market Street. 910-350-1817 or 251-5797. www.battleshipnc.com.

Bellamy Mansion and Museum (circa 1859) was once used as a Union headquarters. The antebellum mansion and two-story former servants house behind it are open for guided tours. The museum offers a History-Mystery Tour in October. Corner of Fifth and Market Streets, Wilmington. 910-251-3700. www.bellamymansion.org

Burgwin-Wright House Museum and Garden (circa 1770) is an outstanding example of Georgian architecture. Offers a Colonial Christmas celebration in December. 224 Market Street, Wilmington. 910-762-0570. www.geocities.com/PicketFence/Garden/4354

Burgwin-Wright House Museum and Garden

Cape Fear Museum is the state's oldest history museum, founded in 1898 by the Daughters of the Confederacy. Exhibits in the two-level facility range from colonial to contemporary—including, for instance, Civil War and Michael Jordan collections (Jordan is from Wilmington and played college basketball there). There is also a nice gift shop in the museum. 814 Market Street, Wilmington. 910-341-4350. www.co.nhcgov.com/cfm

Cape Fear Serpentarium only recently opened and has already been featured on Discovery Channel. See rare, exotic, and dangerous snakes, crocodiles, dragons, and more. Programs and shows are also offered at various times. 20 Orange Street, downtown Wilmington. 910-762-1669. www.bushmastersonline.com

Latimer House Museum (circa 1852) is a fully furnished Victorian house and home to the Cape Fear Historical Society. Offers a Old Wilmington by Candlelight Tour in December. 126 South Third Street, Wilmington. 910-762-0492. www.latimerhouse.org

Louise Wells Cameron Art Museum. Art lovers will surely appreciate this collection of North Carolina ceramics, decoys, sculptures, and paintings housed in a 42,000-square-foot facility with fifteen galleries. There's also an on-site restaurant and Civil War Battlefield and Sculpture Park on the 10-acre property. 33201 South 17th Street, Wilmington. 910-395-5999. www.cameronartmuseum.com

Racine Center for the Arts has an "eclectic collection of local, regional, and national artists." The center also provides a dance and drama school and instructional art programs, as well as an indoor/outdoor cafe. 203 Racine Drive, Wilmington. 910-452-2073. www.racinecenter.com

The Tallship Nighthawk is an 82' gaff-rigged schooner that now operates as a pirate ship, offering demonstrations, cruises, and tours by costumed "pirates" who sail the Cape Fear River. Its permanent home is Harbor Point Marina, 1500-A Point Harbor Road (next to Isabella Holmes Bridge on the southwest side of the Cape Fear River). 910-251-0015. www.nighthawkpirates.com

Wilmington Railroad Museum is a small museum packed with informative displays and exhibits, including a steam locomotive and caboose. It is located at the corner of Water and Red Cross Streets. 910-763-2634. www.wilmington.org/railroad

Wilmington's Children Museum has interactive exhibits and play stations, including a pirate ship and puppet theatre. It is located at Second and Orange Streets, Wilmington. 910-254-3534. www.wilmingtonchildrensmuseum.org

Theater in Wilmington

Wilmington has many community theaters and one major film studio. Since 1983, more than four hundred projects have been filmed in the Wilmington area. Many of them have been produced at Screen Gem Studios, which is the largest movie production facility east of Los Angeles. Since the first movie was filmed here in 1983, more than three hundred movies and six TV shows, including *Matlock, Dawson's Creek,* and *One Tree Hill* have been filmed in the Wilmington area. Stars such as Bruce Willis, Richard Gere, Kim Basinger, Sharon Stone, Patrick Swayze, John Travolta, and Anthony Hopkins have been seen around town. On the weekends, guided walking tours of the studios are conducted. Tours include a video presentation and walk through some studio sound stages and sets for projects currently in production. There is an on-site commissary where you just may spot a rising star!

City Stage Theatre, once owned by famous actor Dennis Hopper, offers theatrical productions in the Masonic Temple (circa 1899). 21 North Front Street, Wilmington. 910-342-0272. No website available.

Opera House Theatre Company presents many shows year-round. 2011 Carolina Beach Road (between Wilmington and Carolina Beach). 910-762-4234. www.oper ahousetheatrecompany.net

Scottish Rite Temple offers theatrical productions in its 360-seat theatre. 1415 South 17th Street, Wilmington. 910-762-6452. No website available.

Screen Gem Studios. Access to all sets is not guaranteed. Tour starts at the studio gate and advance reservations are advised. 1223 North 23rd Street, Wilmington. 910-343-3500. www.screengemstudios.com

Thalian Hall (circa 1858) offers top quality theatrical productions. Tours of this historic and reportedly haunted theater are available for a fee. 310 Chestnut Street, Wilmington. 800-528-2820 or 910-343-3664. www.thalian hall.com

University of North Carolina-Wilmington theater department produces various shows in Kenan Auditorium and SRO Theatre. 601 S. College Road, Wilmington. 800-732-3643 or 910-962-3500. No website available.

While there are walking tours, there are also many other unique ways for visitors to tour Wilmington:

• **By boat.** *Henrietta III* Riverboat Cruises offer narrated tour cruises, lunch and dinner cruises, and private party charters aboard a steamer-style boat. Docked at the foot of Dock Street, Wilmington. 800-676-0162 or 910-343-1611. www.cfrboats.com

• **By horse or trolley.** Horse-drawn carriage and trolley tours, including costumed drivers, are offered several times a day. Special events include a Halloween ghost ride, Christmas caroling, Easter "bunny" ride, and Valentine ride. Private rides/events can be arranged. Tours depart at the corner of Market and Water Streets. 910-251-8889. www.horsedrawntours.com. Also, Wilmington Trolley Company provides a narrated tour that covers eight miles of historic sites. Departs daily, except Mondays, from the corner of Dock and Water Streets. April – October. 800-676-0162 or 910-763-4483. www.wilmingtontrolley.com

• **On your own.** You can take a two-hour independent tour or a ferry tour (forty minutes aboard Southport–Fort Fisher ferry) of the Wilmington and Cape Fear area. The self-paced tour includes seven major attractions: *Battleship North Carolina*, Orton Plantation Gardens, Brunswick Town and Fort Anderson, Southport Maritime Museum, CP&L's Brunswick Nuclear Plant, North Carolina Aquarium at Fort Fisher, and Fort Fisher Civil War Museum. Free maps highlighting this route are available at the Cape Fear Convention and Visitors Bureau. 24 North Third Street. Wilmington. 800-222-4757 or 910-341-4030. www.cape-fear.nc.us. Or just take a walk along Wilmington's Riverwalk, which rewards strollers with excellent views of the historic waterfront district and scenic Cape Fear River.

• **The scary way!** Take the Haunted Pub Crawl or the Ghost Walk of Old Wilmington. The **Haunted Pub Crawl** starts at 7:30 P.M. year-round at an underground pub (directions are given upon confirmation of reservation) and is for adults only. **The Ghost Walk** is appropriate for all ages except small children. It departs from riverfront at the corner of Market and Water Streets. Ghost Walk of Old Wilmington, Inc. 910-602-6055. www.hirchak.com

Wilmington Trolley Company,
Horse-drawn carriage tour

Nearby

Brunswick Town Historic Site contains the ruins of Brunswick Town and Fort Anderson. Brunswick Town was founded in 1726 and was the first permanent European settlement between Charleston, SC, and New Bern, NC. It was one of the biggest communities in the state until New Bern and Wilmington were established. Fort Anderson was built by the Confederacy in 1861. Near the end of the war, the Federals won control of the fort after three days of fierce fighting. Not much remains of the old town or fort, but there is a visitor's center with a gift shop and many exhibits, plus a fifteen-minute slide show and picnic area. Eighteen miles south of Wilmington on NC 133. 8884 St. Phillips Road SE, Winnabow. 910-371-6613. http://www.ah.dcr.state.nc.us/sections/hs/

Duplin Winery offers tours and tastings of its special wines, scuppernong and muscadine. Dinner shows are sometimes offered, plus they host several events, such as the Down Home Country Christmas and annual Grape Stomp. Forty miles north of Wilmington on US 117 at Rose Hill (watch for signs). 800-774-9634 or 910-289-3888. www.duplinwinery.com

Moore's Creek National Battlefield is the site of the first Patriot victory of the Revolutionary War and is considered to be one of the most important battlefields in

North Carolina. It has a visitors center, complete with exhibits and a video presentation. Twenty miles north of Wilmington on US 421 in Currie. 910-283-5591. www.nps.gov/mocr

Orton Plantation and Gardens was once a thriving rice plantation. The house (circa 1725) is closed to the public but the lavish gardens may be toured. On NC 133 between Wilmington and Southport (eighteen miles south of Wilmington). 910-371-6851. www.ortongardens.com

Poplar Grove Plantation was once a 628-acre peanut plantation that now extends 16 acres. It features a circa 1850 Greek-revival–style manor house, slave cabin, outdoor kitchen, restaurant, gift shop, barn, and more. Free classes and plantation life demonstrations are conducted year-round. Don't miss their annual Halloween festivities, including hayrides. Ten miles north of Wilmington on US 17. 910-686-9518, Ext. 26. www.poplargrove.com

Tregembo Animal Park (formerly Tote-Em-In Zoo) is eastern North Carolina's largest zoo, featuring more than one hundred kinds of animals. It is located between Wilmington and Carolina Beach. 5811 Carolina Beach Road. 910-791-0472. No website available.

---

17. ZEKE'S ISLAND

History

Zeke's Island is surrounded by Fort Fisher State Recreation Site to the north, Smith Island to the south, the Atlantic Ocean to the east, and the Cape Fear River to the west. It is actually one of three islands (North Island and No Name Island are the others) that make up a large part of the North Carolina National Estuarine Research Reserve, which is the third largest in the United States.

Artillery was positioned on the island during the Civil War in defense of Fort Fisher. There was also a turpentine factory and gill net fishing center on the island. These structures were destroyed by a big hurricane in 1889. The island has remained uninhabited ever since.

The 1,200-acre, uninhabited island reserve off the coast of Fort Fisher is open to the public. Fishing, sunbathing, birding, boating, camping, and regulated hunting are all permitted. However, the terrain is rugged and there are no established trails. Bottle-nosed dolphins, loggerhead turtles, and many species of birds, such as red-tailed hawks and ospreys, can be found here. There are no amenities on the island. Insect repellent is recommended. Trash and other foreign items should be disposed of properly.

The best way to get there is by boat, but it can be done by foot with some diligent effort. Go to the boat ramp at Federal Point (beyond the ferry terminal). At low tide, carefully walk "The Rocks," a breakwater that extends three miles past Zeke's Island. If you do this, be sure to head back before high tide or it becomes dangerous to cross "The Rocks." For the less adventurous: From Wilmington, take US 421 South for twenty-two miles and you'll reach a parking lot and public boat launch at the North Carolina Wildlife Resources Commission (due north of the Aquarium at Fort Fisher) that can be used by visitors to Zeke's Island. Another option is to take the Fort Fisher-Southport Ferry, which yields a good glimpse of the island during the thirty-minute ferry ride. US 421, south of Kure Beach. 910-457-6942 or 800-BYFERRY.

The North Carolina Aquarium at Fort Fisher offers educational excursions to the island. School field trips, adult workshops, and outreach programs are offered by the North Carolina National Estuarine Research Reserve (NCNERR). For more information on visiting Zeke's Island, contact the NCNERR, 1 Marvin Moss Lane, Wilmington, 910-962-2470, www.ncerr.org; the North Carolina Division of Coastal Management, 888-4COAST, http://dcm2.enr.state.nc.us/; or the North Carolina Aquarium at Fort Fisher, 910-458-8257, www.ncaquariums.com

18. FIGURE EIGHT ISLAND

History

This picturesque little island extends five miles from Rich Inlet to Mason Inlet. Most of its homes have been built on the waterfront, either on the sound or on the beach. The island supposedly got its name when several pilots ended up sailing past the island in a perfect figure eight.

Over the years, the picturesque island has hosted many visitors and inhabitants, including wild ponies, many species of birds, nesting turtles, illegal whiskey distillers, marijuana smugglers, Coast Guard Auxiliary, fishermen, picnickers, and the Army Air Corps, who used it for target practice.

Figure Eight Island

The land was first owned by James Moore, who received a land grant for it in 1762. It was sold to Cornelius Hartnett in 1775. Hartnett was one of the signers of our Declaration of Independence. James Foy, who also owned Wilmington's Poplar Grove Plantation, bought a large tract of the island in 1795. During the 1950s, two brothers, Bruce and Dan Cameron, began buying all the land and eventually owned the entire island. Because so little development had occurred and because Hurricane Hazel annihilated the area in 1955, the men got the land cheap—$100,000 netted them the idyllic five-mile island. Figure Eight Island is now worth roughly $200 million.

During Prohibition, there were quite a few illegal stills in the area. An area fisherman operated one on the north end of Figure Eight. It was accessible only by boat at high tide. He reportedly produced more than five gallons of whiskey a week. During World War II, the Coast Guard Auxiliary stationed themselves in the inlets around Figure Eight, watching for enemy submarines. Beach patrols also kept vigil for German boats. An Army military barracks and Coast Guard shack were constructed during the war. A fisherman later made his home in the abandoned Coast Guard shack. The squatter was the island's only resident when the Cameron brothers began developing it in the late 1950s.

What was their objective? "We have the last area of unspoiled privately owned beach property in North Carolina and we're going to keep it that way," Bruce Cameron stated. Little development has occurred on Figure Eight other than single family dwellings and a yacht club complete with a restaurant, marina, and tennis courts. There are no tours, attractions, or organized activities (except at the club). An architectural review board must approve a project before it can proceed. This means that the building plans, all building materials, and landscaping plans must receive approval or construction is not permitted.

Figure Eight is a private island. Pictured here are the guard gate and the bridge that links island to mainland.

Home sites initially sold for $5,000. Today, there are only a few lots left for sale—at close to one million dollars each. The island is very private and exclusive, making it a favorite of celebrities and politicians such as Oscar-winning actress Kim Basinger (and twenty-six of her family members), Dustin Hoffman, Gene Hackman, Alan Alda, and former Vice President Al Gore. Even though the island has graciously harbored many celebrities, homeowners still call the shots. Barbara Streisand's request to film some scenes for "Prince of Tides" on the island's beach was denied. It would have been too disruptive for islanders, the Homeowners Association informed her manager.

How different things were in 1973 when a couple of men rented houses on the island and claimed to be sports fishermen. Suspicious behavior led to the discovery of a drug smuggling operation. Approximately fourteen thousand pounds of Colombian marijuana brought over on a two-masted ketch was seized by officials off Figure Eight. Fifteen people were indicted, leading to six convictions, in August 1974.

Figure Eight Island Beach Path

No scandals or publicized criminal wrongdoings have happened on this sleepy island since that time. Nowadays, vacationers and homeowners seem to have found utopia on Figure Eight Island. However, its one big drawback is that it suffers horrific erosion on the northern end. In fact, in 2003, Duke University brought coastal studies students to the island to witness its extreme erosion. About one-third of the island was renourished a couple of years ago, but the sand washed out to sea after only a couple of months. Some experts believe the only feasible long-term solution is to remove the homes on the northern tip of Figure Eight Island.

There are no timeshares, hotels, or motels on this private island; in fact, there are no restaurants, except at its yacht club. There are several rental properties such as The Stubbs House. To give you an idea of rental costs, The Stubbs House is a six-bedroom, six-bath house that rents for $2,800 a week in the low season and $4,500 a week in the high season (according to its website at time of publication). 800-279-6085 or 910-686-4400. www.figure8island.com

Figure Eight Island is eight miles north of Wilmington, just north of Wrightsville Beach. From the Wilmington area, take Hwy. 17 North to Porter's Neck Road. Make a right and continue to Edgewater Road. Make another right onto Edgewater, which dead-ends into Figure Eight Island. It is only a couple of miles off Hwy. 17. As soon as you cross the swinging drawbridge from the mainland, there is a guard gate. Access is granted only to residents and their guests.

---

19. HARBOR ISLAND

History

WRIGHTSVILLE
BEACH

Harbor Island consists of four-mile Wrightsville Beach and one-mile Shell Island Beach, which is at the island's northern end. **Wrightsville Beach** became one of the state's earliest beach resorts when a group of businessmen began developing it in 1853. They built the Carolina Yacht Club, which is one of the oldest yacht clubs in the state, on "the Banks." Development increased when the Wilmington Sea Coast Railway was built in 1888. The rail system provided easy access from the mainland to Hammocks Island, which once existed in Wrightsville Sound. A manmade footbridge from the railway to Wrightsville Beach completed the journey. Four years later, in 1905, an electric rail system (also called electric trolleys) was constructed that extended along Wrightsville Beach.

Wrightsville Beach was called Ocean View until 1900. A nearby community was called Wrightsville, so it made more sense. The town was incorporated that same year. Moore's Inlet once separated Wrightsville Beach from Shell Island, which got its name because it was a great shelling spot before the inlet was removed. In 1965, the Army Corp of Engineers filled in the inlet and made the two beaches into one five-mile long island.

Wrightsville Beach Holiday Flotilla

In 1910, **Shell Island** was used by two Wilmington businessmen to test an airplane they had built. In 1923, some Wilmington businessmen opened an upscale summer resort for African Americans on Shell Island. They outfitted it with every conceivable amenity, including restaurants, piers, a boardwalk, pavilion, bathhouses, sewers, water, electricity, and beach houses. A highway linking the island to the mainland was built in 1926. Many came from across the U.S. and even other countries, until some suspicious fires destroyed most of the dwellings. The remaining structures, as well as one hundred homes and buildings on Wrightsville Beach, were destroyed by a massive fire on January 28, 1934.

Once known as the crowning jewel of Wrightsville Beach, the Lumina Hotel, established in 1905, was torn down in 1973. The two-story resort had many amenities, including bowling alleys, slot machines, bleachers, a movie "theater" on the beach, a ladies' parlor, dance hall, and

SHELL ISLAND

restaurant complete with a grand fireplace. Famous musicians, including Louis Armstrong, Tommy Dorsey, and Guy Lombardo played the Lumina during its heyday. The magnificent Seashore Hotel and the grand Hotel Tarrymore (later renamed The Oceanic) were destroyed in the big fire of 1934. The Blockade Runner Resort Hotel is located where the Seashore Hotel once stood.

Harbor Island is now covered with beach houses and commercial businesses. After years of development and the work of Mother Nature, erosion has taken a big toll. The Army Corp of Engineers pursued beach nourishment by building a 2.5-mile artificial dune line and pumping 3 million cubic yards of sand onto the beach in 1965. Five years later, they added another 1.5 million cubic yards of sand.

Beach Biking

The only thing built on the northernmost tip of Shell Island is the Shell Island Beach Resort. The problem is that the hotel was built on an artificial inlet, meaning one that was created by filling it with large amounts of sand. It was also built on the beach with only a seawall between it and the pounding surf. Seawalls tend to have long-term detrimental effects on beaches, which is why it is hard to get governmental approval to build them. The Shell Island Beach Resort has been in and out of court for years pursuing options such as dredging and creating additional seawalls to protect something that never should have been built.

Hurricanes haven't helped matters either. Hurricanes Hazel and Fran caused serious damage and destroyed many homes. Yet, homes or home sites are hard to come by on Harbor Island and are quite expensive. That's because it is a small island in close proximity to Wilmington that has managed to keep commercial development to a minimum. Many of the houses are vacation homes that have been owned by the same family for generations. Public parking remains a big problem and is even more so now that parking meters have been installed. If you find a parking space, be sure you bring enough change to feed the meter.

Harbor Island is one mile east of Wilmington on US 74 or US 76. This public island is connected to the mainland by a drawbridge, which yields right of way to mariner traffic. Town of Wrightsville Beach, 321 Causeway Drive, Wrightsville Beach. 910-256-7900. www.townofwrightsville beach.com

Sites and Attractions–Harbor Island

Wrightsville Beach Museum of History is a small, interpretive museum that is located in the fourth oldest cottage on the island. This is one of the few structures that survived Hurricane Hazel in 1954. Visitors will be rewarded with a slide show, recorded oral histories, and historical exhibits. The walls are lined with historical images, such as black-and-white enlargements of the old Lumina Hotel hosting one of its spectacular summer parties. Immediately after you cross the drawbridge, veer left at the "Welcome to Wrightsville Beach" sign. The museum is on the right just past the fire station. 303 West Salisbury Street, Wrightsville Beach. 910-256-2569. www.wbmuseum.com

Wrightsville Beach Park offers visitors tennis and basketball courts, a playground, and a sports field. It also offers The Loop, a 2.5-mile walking, jogging, or bicycling path that extends from downtown to the park. 1 Bob Sawyer Drive, in the middle of Harbor Island. 910-256-7900. www.townofwrightsvillebeach.com/parksandrecreation

Money Island. The best way to see this small, uninhabited island from the mainland is to take South Lumina Avenue to the end of the southern end of Harbor Island (Wrightsville Beach). Somewhere near the Wrightsville Beach Coast Guard Station is the best place to see the it.

There's not much to see or do on Money Island. It is best known for the legend of Captain Kidd and his buried treasure. Legend has it Captain Kidd hid part of his treasure here. This may very well be true. In doing research for *Pirates of the Carolinas,* I discovered Captain Kidd reportedly dropped off one of his crew and some of his treasure on a remote, uninhabited South Carolina island on his way to England to answer charges for piracy.

According to a story that ran in the *Wilmington Herald* in 1858, a fisherman saw some men on Money Island but thought better of investigating. Instead, he went to the island the next morning—and discovered a large hole that many believe held one of Captain Kidd's treasure chests! The island got its name because of this story. Over the years, treasure seekers flocked to the island looking for hidden loot, but no one has claimed to have found any. The closest success was in 1939, when two Wilmington men found a huge, ancient iron chest sealed with a big lock. When the lock was broken and the lid opened, nothing was inside. Did the trunk once house pirate treasure?

20. MASONBORO ISLAND

History

Navigator Giovanni da Verrazano, hired by King Francis I of France, first saw Masonboro Island in 1524 and described it in glorious terms, noting its "sweet and odoriferous flowers" and "trees greater and better than any in Europe." This island, which is 8.5 miles long and as wide as a football field at its widest point, is located just ten miles southeast from downtown Wilmington off the southern tip of Wrightsville Beach, and was privately owned until the 1980s. In fact, it was still part of the mainland until 1952, when Carolina Beach Inlet was cut, thus making this land an island. In 1983, the nonprofit Society for Masonboro Island was formed after Wilmington area resident Edith Friedberg read an ad announcing oceanfront lots were available on Masonboro Island. Like many other area residents, she felt the island is a special place that should be spared the fate of development. The nonprofit group suggested North Carolina should buy the 5,046 acres, which it did between 1985 and the early 1990s.

Masonboro Island is the only island in the NC Coastal Reserve, which includes NC National Estuarine Reserve Research System, that permits primitive camping (meaning no amenities!).

This uninhabited island, as well as Zeke's Island, Currituck Banks, and Rachel Carson now comprise the National Estuarine Reserve Research System and remains protected land. It is also the largest undeveloped barrier island on the lower coast of North Carolina. It's home to a wide variety of plants and animals, including otters, foxes, and many species of birds. Endangered loggerhead and sea turtles nest on the island's unspoiled beach.

To its north is Masonboro Inlet and Wrightsville Beach, to the south is Carolina Beach, to the west is the Intracoastal Waterway, and to the east lies the Atlantic

Ocean. It is five miles southeast of Wilmington and can only be accessed by private boat. Public boat launches are available at Wrightsville Beach and Carolina Beach. There is no dock or conveniences. Insects can be a nuisance, depending on the time of year, so bring repellent to be on the safe side. This is a great spot for boaters seeking a quiet refuge to sun, swim, and picnic. Please be respectful and remove everything you brought with you to the island when you leave, such as food and trash. School field trips, adult workshops, and outreach programs are offered by the North Carolina National Estuarine Research Reserve. 1 Marvin Moss Lane, Wilmington. 910-962-2470. www.ncnerr.org

Wrightsville Beach Scenic Cruises offer narrated harbor cruises as well as sunset cruises and charters. They also provide ferry service to Masonboro Island. Departs from Banks Channel in South Wrightsville Beach, across from the Blockade Runner Resort. Call 910-350-BOAT for a schedule. www.cruiseinc.net

---

21. PLEASURE ISLAND

History

Although 7.5-mile Pleasure Island is often referred to as a peninsula and was once called the Federal Point Peninsula, it is an island because the land mass is surrounded by water: to the east is the Atlantic Ocean, Cape Fear River is to the west, Corncake Inlet is to the south, and Snows Cut is on the north side.

CAROLINA
BEACH

There were only a few summer retreats on the island before the Civil War, all owned by wealthy planters. **Carolina Beach** is the big sister to Kure Beach and one of the oldest beach communities in the state. In 1857, Wilmington businessman Joseph L. Winner decided to make Carolina Beach a resort. He bought 108 acres for development but was never able to further his dream. However, other developers did pursue such ambitions and by the late 1800s, several hotels and dozens of homes had been built.

Aerial view of Carolina Beach 1945

In 1866, a steamship began carrying vacationers down the Cape Fear River to Snow's Cut. A small railroad took the passengers on the last leg of their trip onto Carolina Beach. During the late 1800s and early 1900s, the island grew in popularity with vacationers, so much so that in 1912, Southern Realty & Development Company bought one thousand acres of it, including two miles of prime oceanfront property. Their goal was to establish a first-class resort. In keeping with this plan, electricity was brought to the island three years later and a paved highway linked the beach to the mainland.

In 1925, Carolina Beach was incorporated and continued to grow and prosper until Hurricane Hazel hit in 1954. Like many other area coastal communities, Carolina Beach was devastated. More than 360 structures were annihilated and another 360 or so were severely damaged.

Erosion plagues Carolina Beach to the extent that there is no beach on the north end. An artificial inlet, Carolina Beach Inlet, was created in 1952 despite protests from the Army Corp of Engineers, because locals wanted a shortcut to the ocean. Ever since the inlet was made, millions of dollars have been spent combating the erosion the Army Corp of Engineers predicted. A seawall was constructed and dredging has been done to try to prevent further erosion.

KURE BEACH

To the south, Carolina Beach merges into the town of **Kure Beach,** which was named after its first owner, Hans Kure of Denmark. During a fishing excursion in 1891, he decided it would make a good suburban summer resort, and so he bought oceanfront property including a bowling alley and saloon.

In 1933, Dow Chemical Company and Ethyl Corporation built the first facility for removing bromine from seawater. During World War II, the plant was unsuccessfully attacked by a U-boat. In 1946, the plant was replaced by a bigger, newer facility in Texas. Ten years later the North Carolina plant was dismantled, and the following year Kure Beach was incorporated.

Surf fishing on Kure Beach 1945

Today, Kure Beach is overwhelmingly residential, dotted with beach cottages and small, locally owned motels and restaurants. Other than a few condominiums, there are few tall buildings. In fact, code prevents structures from exceeding thirty-five feet in height. Its crowning jewels are a picturesque fishing pier and boardwalk. It is one of the few beaches along the coast that has managed to keep development in check. Thanks to its size and location, Kure Beach should realize no further development. It would be impossible to extend the coastal community because Fort Fisher Historic Site is to its immediate south, Carolina Beach to the north, the government owns the land to the west as a buffer for its Sunny Point military installation, and to the east is the Atlantic Ocean.

Once upon a time, some of the best beach real estate deals could be found in Kure Beach. Today, this sleepy beach town is growing in popularity by leaps and bounds. Two of the newest developments, Kure Beach Village and Beachwalk, feature moderately expensive homes and town-houses, complete with tennis courts, pools, and clubhouses.

There are two ways to get to Pleasure Island, which is approximately thirty minutes from Wilmington's Historic District. From Wilmington, drive south for twelve miles on US 421. Or, take the free Southport–Fort Fisher car and passenger ferry. Carolina Beach is on the north side of the island, while Kure Beach and Fort Fisher are on the south end. The ferry terminal is on Ft. Fisher Blvd. South, Kure Beach.

Four-wheeling. At the northern tip of Pleasure Island's Carolina Beach, four-wheel-drive vehicles are permitted on the beach. Because the erosion is so severe, this activity is not considered to be detrimental, but be sure your vehicle is up to the challenge

Sites and Attractions–Pleasure Island

Carolina Beach Boardwalk has been a longtime icon, dating back to World War II. Soldiers and Marines stationed at nearby bases spent their time off here. The boardwalk and pier underwent major renovations in 1987. It is now concrete rather than wooden, and the amusement park is gone. Tourists will find taverns, eateries, gift and novelty shops, an arcade, and rides such as the Ferris wheel and a carrousel in colorful stucco buildings. Enjoy a foot-long hot dog at "The Dollar Dog" hot dog stand and then a handmade glazed doughnut at Britt's (founded in 1939). Carolina Beach. 910-458-8434. www.carokure.wil mington.net

*Carolina Beach, on the north side of Pleasure Island,
is one of the best NC beaches because it is less developed
and therefore not as crowded as other state beaches.*

Fort Fisher Historic Site and Recreation Area
contains a nice four-mile beach, the Fort Fisher Monument
(1932), a recreation area, and an underwater archaeology
center. Additionally, there is a visitors center which houses displays and shows an interesting film depicting the
fort's history. Fort Fisher played a vital role in the Civil
War because it was the biggest Confederate fort and last
stronghold. It was needed to protect the Wilmington port.
In 1865, thousands of Union troops, along with a heavy
naval assault, forced a Confederate surrender. Once the
Confederacy lost Fort Fisher, the war was all but over. The
fort was named after Charles Fisher, a Colonel from North
Carolina who died at First Manassas. 1610 Fort Fisher
Blvd. Just south of Kure Beach. 910-458-5538.
www.ils.unc.edu/parkproject/visit/fofi/home.html(park/rec.
info) or www.arch.dcr.state.nc.us/(historical info)

**North Carolina Underwater Archaeological
Center** at Kure Beach. Learn all about islands, including
how they are formed and what hurricanes do to them.
There are hands-on displays and aquariums. 1610 Fort Fisher
Blvd., Kure Beach. 910-458-9042. No website available.

North Carolina Military History Museum offers
indoor and outdoor exhibits that detail all branches of
service and their respective roles in state history. Near Fort
Fisher at the National Guard Training Center, Kure Beach.
910-251-7325. No website available.

22. BALD HEAD ISLAND

History

Bald Head Island, comprised of fourteen miles of maritime forests, marshes, and beach, is located at the mouth of the Cape Fear River. First used by Native Americans and later by French and Spanish explorers in the sixteenth century, Bald Head also hosted pirates during the early part of the 1700s. A lighthouse was built in 1795 to help sea traffic maneuver Cape Fear River's dangerous shoals. It was built too close to the river, which made it necessary to construct another beacon in 1816, which was completed the following year. This tower, affectionately known as Old Baldy, still shines brilliantly. Many British troops were stationed on the island during the Revolutionary War; the island was used by Confederate blockade runners during the Civil War.

Bald Head was once called Smith Island, after its original owner, Thomas Smith, who bought it in 1690. Later, Thomas Boyd bought it, envisioning the island as a great resort destination. However, the Depression dashed Boyd's dream and he was forced to turn it over to the state in 1933. The Coast Guard used it until it was deeded back over to Brunswick County because of unpaid taxes.

In 1970, Carolina Cape Fear Corporation paid $5.5 million for the island and began developing it. Environmentalists were outraged at their plans for a large marina. The next seven years were spent in court arguing over environmental impacts. Carolina Cape Fear Corporation ended up selling the land to Bald Head Island Limited, which was given permission to build the marina as long as it set aside ten thousand acres for the North Carolina Nature Conservancy.

Today, the three-thousand-acre island is mostly developed, blending residential communities with vacation properties. The owners have given Middle and Bluff Islands to the North Carolina Nature Conservancy. The Bald Head Island Conservancy is a nonprofit organization that was founded to guarantee that development doesn't compromise the island's nature. Bald Head Island accounts for nearly half of all sea turtle eggs laid in North

Carolina. Additionally, The Audubon Society comes to the island annually to track the many different species of birds that can be found on Bald Head.

All home plans must be submitted to a review board to ensure they meet certain criteria, such as not exceeding tree lines and maintaining island integrity. No cars are permitted on the island with the exception of contractors. Residents and visitors walk, bicycle, and use golf carts. That is one of the best things about this island—there are no traffic jams, or air or noise pollution from car engines. That also means there is no road rage!

Take Hwy. 211 South to Howe Street and turn right onto West Ninth Street. Proceed for 1.7 miles until you reach Indigo Plantation. Indigo Plantation Drive ends at the marina and ferry terminal. It is a twenty-minute ride aboard a private passenger ferry. For ferry reservations, call Bald Head Island Ferry office at 910-457-5003. Since no cars are allowed on the island, you may wish to rent a golf cart or bicycles (if they are not included in your vacation package). Bald Head Island is sixty miles north of Myrtle Beach, thirty miles south of Wilmington (45 minutes from New Hanover International Airport), and three miles east of Southport.

Bald Head Island

Sites and Attractions–Bald Head Island

Bald Head Island Conservancy is a nonprofit group that operates a facility filled with interesting island and ecological exhibits (including turtles) and a delightful gift shop filled with educational games, toys, and gifts. 7000 Federal Road, Bald Head Island. 910-457-0089. www.bhic.org

Bald Head Island Historic Tour is a guided tour of the island that includes Old Baldy, Smith Island Museum of History, and Captain Charlie's Station. The guide tells stories about the history of the island and stops at all island highlights. Reservations are required because transport to the island is aboard the Bald Head Island private ferry service. Departs from Indigo Plantation. West Ninth Street, Southport. 910-457-5003. No website available.

Captain Charlie's Station was once Cape Fear Lighthouse Station keepers' houses. Cap'n Charlie Swain was a keeper at Cape Fear Lighthouse, which was destroyed after being decommissioned for more than thirty years. Later, the three wooden houses were used for meetings and educational programs of The Bald Head Conservancy. The former keepers' cottages, which are listed on the National Register of Historic Places, are now used as rental accommodations. Bald Head Island beach. 800-432-RENT. No website available.

Bald Head Island Lighthouse is an octagonal tower made of brick and coated with cement. The squat tower, lovingly nicknamed "Old Baldy," is only 109 feet tall. Built in 1817, it is the oldest lighthouse in the state. The beacon was decommissioned in 1935 and was sold several times before it was given to the Old Baldy Foundation, a nonprofit organization dedicated to restoring the lighthouse. The keeper's house was destroyed by fire in 1931, as was the former Coast Guard Station in 1968. However, the adorable old lighthouse remains open to visitors. At the marina on Bald Head Island. 910-799-4640. www.old baldy.org

Smith Island Museum houses island-related exhibits and artifacts. Adjacent to Bald Head Lighthouse. 910-457-7481. www.oldbaldy.org or www.baldheadisland.com

23. SOUTHPORT

History

This waterfront town, formerly called Smithville, is steeped in history. North Carolina's first fort, Fort Johnston, was established here in 1754. Over the years, a small community of river pilots, fishermen, and tradespeople formed around the fort. In 1792, Smithville was created. In 1808, Smithville became the county seat of Brunswick County. For the rest of the century, the town grew and made plans to pair rail service with river commerce in order to create a major southern port. And so this coastal town was aptly renamed Southport in 1887. For nearly two hundred years, it remained a relatively small fishing community. However, its population has steadily increased since the 1970s. Outlying communities, such as incorporated St. James Plantation, have significantly contributed to the town's growth. A larger area population creates more business growth opportunity, which in turn makes Southport more desirable to retirees and those looking to relocate to the coast.

Historic Southport waterfront

Southport was one of the first places in the state to celebrate July Fourth and is widely regarded as the "Fourth of July Capital" of North Carolina. History records reveal that citizens gathered at Fort Johnston and observed a thirteen-gun military salute to the original thirteen states in 1795. In 1813, a Russian warship anchored in

The Intracoastal or inland Waterway around Southport
was a favorite among mullet fishermen
and mullet remain a good catch in the spring and fall.

the harbor fired a thirteen-gun salute and fireworks were used as part of the celebration. In 1972, the Fourth of July Festival was chartered and incorporated as the official state July festival. Over the years it has grown in popularity and become a three-day event. Southport and neighboring Oak Island put on quite a spectacle. Among the festivities are a yacht race, parade, pancake breakfast, and huge fireworks spectacle. A word of warning: 25,000 to 35,000 people descend on the Southport–Oak Island area for the patriotic party. Traffic and finding a good spot on the parade route can be problems.

It makes sense for Southport to put on such a big celebration. After all, it was here that British reign over North Carolina came to an end in 1775. After fleeing New Bern in May 1775, Royal Governor Josiah Martin sought refuge at Fort Johnston, which was ideally located on a bluff overlooking the mouth of the Cape Fear River. The governor escaped by ship on July 18, 1775. The next day, five hundred Minutemen raided the British fortress and it remained off limits for the British for the rest of the Revolutionary War.

This quaint town is listed on the National Register of Historic Places and ranked by both Kiplinger and Rand McNally as one of the most desirable places in America for retirees. Southport is also a great locale for day trippers. History buffs will appreciate the town's beautiful old homes and historic cemeteries. For example, the Captain Thompson House offers visitors a glimpse into the life of a Civil War blockade runner. Literary enthusiasts should stop to see author Robert Ruark's boyhood home, the Adkins-Ruark House. Additionally, there are many excellent area restaurants, as well as several antique and specialty stores along Howe and Moore Streets. Long-time icon The Christmas House, should definitely be included with any visit to Southport. The gift shop is inside a huge Victorian-style home and inside is a two-story shop filled with ornaments, decorations, gifts, books, nautical items, dolls, fudge and candy, and more. 104 W. Moore Street, Southport. 910-457-5166.

There are a couple of ways to get to Southport. Motorists may take NC 87 or NC 211 into Southport, or take the Southport–Fort Fisher car and passenger ferry from Pleasure Island and Fort Fisher over to Southport. 800-293-3779. 800-BY-FERRY). www.ncferry.org

Sites and Attractions–Southport

Adkins-Ruark House is the boyhood home of author Robert Ruark, who wrote *The Old Man and the Boy*. Ruark was also a well-known journalist. The dwelling is now a private residence but can be seen from the street. 119 North Lord Street, Southport. 800-457-6964 or 910.457-6964. No website available.

Fort Johnston is the state's first fort and remains the world's smallest military installation. It has been used to aid navigation of the treacherous shoals and mouth of Cape Fear River and by Confederate troops during the War Between the States. The fort itself no longer exists but the compound does contain other original structures which now accommodate personnel assigned to nearby Sunny Point Military Ocean Terminal. At Davis and Bay Streets, Southport. You cannot go inside the compound but an excellent view is afforded from the road. 910-457-7927. No website available.

Keziah Memorial Park is a small park complete with a picturesque gazebo. Its most exceptional feature is an eight-hundred-year-old unusually bent live oak, called the

Indian Trail Tree. It is said that Native Americans deliberately bent the tree so it would be a landmark, preventing them from getting lost. At West Moore and South Lord Streets, Southport. 800-457-6964 or 910.457-6964. No website available.

North Carolina Maritime Museum at Southport, while relatively small in size, has many exciting exhibits highlighting the history of the lower Cape Fear area, including some treasures retrieved from local shipwrecks and famous pirate Stede Bonnet's plea for clemency, which he wrote shortly before he was hanged. 116 North Howe Street, Southport. 910-457-0003. http://www.ah.dcr.state.nc.us/sections/maritime/branches/southport_default.htm

Old Smithville Burial Ground dates back to 1804 and is worth a visit to examine the tombstones of occupants, many of whom were lost at sea. East Moore and South Rhett Streets, Southport. 800-457-6964 or 910.457-6964. No website available.

Riverwalk is a meandering walkway that extends 0.7 mile past the City Pier, boat harbor, and boardwalk. It is ideal for walking and bicycling. 800-457-6964 or 910-457-6964. No website available.

Southport Museum displays more than one hundred years of art. There is a museum store on site and custom framing is available. 309 N. Howe Street, Southport. 910-457-6166. No website available.

Southport Trail is a mile-long self-guided walking trail that is a must-see for visitors. Along the route are twenty-five historic sites, such as the Stede Bonnet memorial, Southport Baptist Church (1871), and the Old Brunswick Jail. A brochure detailing each site is available from the visitors center, which is the starting point of this self-paced tour. 113 W. Moore Street, Southport. 910-457-7927. www.southport-oakisland.com/attractions

St. Philip's Episcopal Church, built in 1843, is the town's oldest church still in use. The picturesque clapboard church houses every flag that has flown over it and the original Brunswick Town St. Philip Church. Architectural enthusiasts will delight in the various influences. East

Moore and Dry Streets, Southport. 910-457-5643. No website available. The original St. Philip's Church is the only Colonial church in this part of the state. North of Southport at the Old Brunswick Town State Historic Site, off Hwy. 133. 910-371-6613. No website available.

The Grove is an absolutely lovely park in the heart of Southport. The walls and entrances are comprised of ballast stones dating back over one hundred years. Highlights of the park include huge, old live oak trees and the Franklin Square Art Gallery, which was once a schoolhouse. Franklin Square Park at 130 E. West Street (corner of E. West and Howe Streets), Southport. 800-457-6964 or 910.457-6964. No website available.

Waterfront Park provides visitors with an exceptional view of Bald Head ("Old Baldy") Island Lighthouse and Oak Island Lighthouse. Bay Street at the foot of Howe Street, Southport. 800-457-6964 or 910.457-6964. No website available.

Battery Island and **Striking Island** host the largest population of shorebirds (including a considerable pelican population) in North Carolina. The private islands, leased by Audubon Society, are located off Southport on Cape Fear River. Be on the lookout and you may see some of these birds while you're in the Southport area.

24. OAK ISLAND

History

Adjacent to Bald Head Island is Oak Island, which got its name because of the island's magnificent oak trees. The view there is terrific because the island is bounded by the

Atlantic Ocean and the Intracoastal Waterway. However, it offers far more than pretty scenery. There are fourteen miles of beaches, including Yaupon, Caswell, and Long Beaches. Plus, Oak Island boasts a rich history. **Fort Caswell** was constructed on **Caswell Beach** in 1827. Since the military fortification played such a vital role during the Civil War, it was expanded and reinforced during the war.

CASWELL
BEACH

The island served mainly as a good summer haven until World War II. At the beginning of this war, there were only a few homes on the island. By the end of it, three hundred homes had been built. Sadly, Hurricane Hazel destroyed all but five of these houses in 1954. Many were rebuilt, and the island population continued to grow.

In 1999, the towns of **Yaupon Beach** and **Long Beach** consolidated to become the town of Oak Island. The town of Oak Island also annexed additional land on the mainland, including the new housing, marina, and commercial community of South Harbor.

YAUPON
BEACH
LONG
BEACH

To get there, take NC 133, 87, or 211 South, which end at the bridge to Oak Island. The island is thirty minutes from downtown Wilmington and six miles from Southport. The closest airport is Brunswick County Airport, which is on the eastern end of Long Beach Road on the mainland, near Oak Island. 910-457-6483.

Sites and Attractions–Oak Island

Fort Caswell, built in 1826, once occupied 2,800 acres on the island's east side. It was a critical line of defense during the Civil War and remained so until Union soldiers conquered nearby Fort Fisher in 1865. The fort was also used during the Spanish American War and World Wars I and II. Today, Fort Caswell is owned by the North Carolina Baptist Assembly and used as a spiritual retreat. Caswell Beach Road, Caswell Beach. 910-278-9501. www.fortcaswell.com

Oak Island Lighthouse is part of the Coast Guard Station and therefore not open to the public. However, you can get a good view of it from the road or Caswell Beach. This lighthouse, built in 1958, is one of the last beacons built in America and the last manually operated one in the world. It is switched on each evening from the base of the tower at thirty minutes before sunset, and switched off each morning at thirty minutes past sunrise. Using eight 480-volt mercury arc bulbs, Oak Island is one of the most powerful lighthouses in the world. Its light shines so brightly that black panels have been placed over the lantern room windows to prevent "spotlighting" the surrounding homes. Additionally, protective gear must be used to perform lantern room maintenance when the lights are on. Caswell Beach Road, Caswell Beach. No phone number available. www.carolinalights.com

Oak Island Lighthouse is one of the last beacons built in America, 1958, and the last manually operated one in the world.

Oak Island Scenic Walkways is an extensive sidewalk system affording bicyclists and pedestrians scenic vistas, including two bridges extending along the waterway. SE 19th Street, behind the Recreation Center on Oak Island. Oak Island Recreation Department. 910-278-5518. www.oakislandnc.com/recpages

---

25. SOUTH BRUNSWICK ISLANDS

History

Holden Beach is the biggest of these three islands, extending ten miles. This coastal tract was purchased by the Holden Family in 1756 when Benjamin Holden bought one hundred acres from Lockwood Folly to Bacon Inlet. It was used primarily for commercial fishing during the early 1900s. A ferry was put into use in 1934, which spurred development. However, the impressive high-rise bridge you cross to enter the island wasn't built until 1988.

HOLDEN BEACH

Shrimp boats, Holden Beach Ferry

OCEAN ISLE

Ocean Isle, which is seven miles long, is situated between Holden and Sunset Beaches. It originated in the 1950s when a young soldier returned from World War II and bought the land. This soldier, Odell Williamson, envisioned a nice, family beach. In keeping with this plan, he laid out a commercial district and made the rest residential. Williamson had a great deal of initiative and foresight. He even had canals dug to create more waterways. A modern bridge transports travelers onto the island, which offers a beach, airstrip, fishing pier, boat docks, golf and tennis courts, and more.

Sunset Beach

SUNSET
BEACH

It's interesting that **Sunset,** being the smallest at only three miles in length, has the largest population. In fact, the 1990 census showed a population of only 311 which has swelled to nearly 1,900 during a ten-year period. Development of this little coastal haven is due to Manlon Gore and his son, Ed Gore. The island's vistas are breathtaking from any angle. Adding to its charm is the one-lane swinging bridge that links the beach to the mainland. There has been talk of getting rid of this bridge to erect something more modern, but it has been vetoed by area residents for many reasons. One is that it may result in too much development and tourism, and secondly, this swinging bridge is the last one of its kind remaining on the East Coast. Let's hope it stays this way.

Each beach is reached by a separate bridge adjoining it to the mainland. As noted, the only way onto Sunset Beach is by crossing a one-lane bridge, so there may be traffic delays during the summer. The island is mostly residential and there is a nice fishing pier in the center of Sunset Beach. Fishing remains as important an industry as tourism.

The South Brunswick Islands are about 30 miles south of Wilmington (off Hwy. 17) or 30 miles north of Myrtle Beach (off Hwy. 17). Bridges connect each of these island communities to the mainland. The Ocean Isle Airport is located on the mainland (910-579-2166) and the Brunswick County Airport is on the eastern end of Long Beach Road near Oak Island (910-457-6483).

Oyster shuckings, complete with music and cold beverages, always draw large crowds to the South Brunswick Islands.

Sites and Attractions–South Brunswick Islands

Ingram Planetarium, a state-of-the-art facility, opened in late 2002. The two-million-dollar planetarium has a forty-foot dome with seating capacity for nearly one hundred, a science and education center, numerous displays, and a "space age" gift shop. The Village Sunset Beach, Sunset Blvd. North. 910-575-0033. www.ingram-planetarium.org

Museum of The Coastal Carolinas has six exhibit halls showcasing the area's natural history and offers many programs such as "Story Time," "Native American Lore," "Live Snake and Reptile Show," and "Nesting Sea Turtle." 21 E. Second Street, Ocean Isle. 910-579-1016. www.museummofcc.org

Silver Coast Winery covers forty acres on the wooded side of Ocean Isle. Take a tour, browse their gift shop and art gallery, enjoy a picnic, or attend one of their annual festivals. 6680 Barbeque Road, Ocean Isle. 910-287-2800. www.silvercoastwinery.com

Nearby

BIRD ISLAND

Bird Island. This undeveloped island was privately owned by the Janie Price family from Greensboro, North Carolina, until the state bought it for $4.2 million in 2002. Ralph Price, heir to the Jefferson Pilot fortune, bought Bird Island in the late 1950s to build a summer home. He also had a bridge constructed to link it to Sunset Beach, but a mysterious fire destroyed the bridge. Fire trucks were delayed by flat tires caused by tacks. The arsonists were never found and Ralph Price died in 1989. In the 1990s, the family spent three years in court fighting to rebuild the bridge, but the state rejected the proposal because the bridge would be in an inlet hazard area, so that development never occurred. Bird remains one of the few noteworthy islands that hasn't been developed. It contains 1.2 miles of ocean shoreline and 1.5 miles of shoreline along the Intracoastal Waterway. The state has made the 1200-acre island (including dry land and wetlands) into a coastal reserve, ensuring it will remain pristine.

This little barrier island is popular with picnickers, campers, and sunbathers—especially nude ones. Since the island is accessible from Sunset Beach during low tide and the sunbathers sometimes wander over to Sunset Beach, town officials have posted a sign that reads "Entering Sunset Beach, No Nudity Allowed" to discourage such activity. Nonetheless, you may want to venture over to Bird Island to partake of a unique island tradition: reading or posting an entry in "the journal," a book that is stored in a mailbox and which first appeared mysteriously on a tiny bit of sand near Tubbs Inlet. Erosion claimed this sandy spot that was once located between Sunset Beach and Ocean Isle.

Legend has it that "the Kindred Spirit" moved the mailbox to Bird Island, where it has withstood tropical storms and hurricanes, including Fran and Hugo. I suppose it is the same kindred spirit who has supplied most of the blank journals year after year. If you have any doubt as to how special a place this little island is, you won't after reading a few entries of "the journal":

March 17, 2002

"Such riches I have held in this lifetime, but none so rich as this moment in time. God has touched this moment, this place, and this love. I stand in absolute awe."

August 19, 1994

"Dear Kindred Spirit: Still the hearts of those who want to change your beauty. Inspire us to be good stewards of your shores. Engrave on us a passion to seek your love and peace. Grant us appreciation of what's here forevermore."

Other entries aren't nearly so inspirational. Some are just notations of good times that were had while vacationing in the area and of successful reunions and vacations with old friends or family. There is even a story about a couple who got married at the Kindred Spirit mailbox in 1987. In late 2002, the Kindred Spirit put up a notice that he or she is trying to collect all the journals and use them in a special project featuring more than twenty-one years of entries. In return, the Keepers of the Journals would receive a special print autographed by the Kindred Spirit itself! The print depicts an early Kindred Spirit standing at the mailbox overlooking the ocean.

CALABASH

Nearby **Calabash,** near Sunset Beach, has been dubbed the "Seafood Capital of the World." You can enjoy calabash-style seafood in one of the twenty or so area restaurants that fill this little community (population 600). Casual attire is accepted at all restaurants, which have extensive menus (including children's and seniors') and are reasonably priced. Or, bring a cooler and buy some fresh shrimp right off the fishing boats. Fishermen return to the marina around 4 P.M., from about May to November. www.ohwy.com/nc/c/calabash.htm

MYRTLE BEACH

Myrtle Beach, South Carolina, (fifty miles from Wilmington) is one of the biggest beaches in the state. For more information on the thousands of restaurants, outlet stores, golf courses, and attractions in the greater Myrtle Beach "Grand Strand" area, contact the Myrtle Beach Area Convention and Visitors Bureau at 800-356-3016 or 843-626-7444. www.myrtlebeachinfo.com

Building sandcastles

Myrtle Beach Trivia

• The first oceanfront lots sold for $25 in 1905. If a property owner spent at least $500 on home construction, he received a second lot for free!

• "The Grand Strand" is a phrase that was coined by a newspaper columnist in 1949. The Grand Strand encompasses the area between Little River, NC, and Georgetown, SC, including Myrtle Beach and North Myrtle Beach.

• Average annual temperature is 65 degrees Fahrenheit.

• "The Shag" is the official dance here. It is widely believed to have begun on Ocean Drive in the 1940s as a variation on the Jitterbug. Beach music remains popular. Seafood specialties, featuring Calabash-style and Lowcountry cooking, are favorites of locals and vacationers alike.

• There are more than 120 golf courses and 50 miniature golf courses in the Grand Strand. More than four million rounds of golf are played here every year!

• Myrtle Beach offers sixty miles of beaches. There are also hundreds of museums, amusement parks, theatres, and shopping centers and outlets, which is why 13 million visitors flock to Myrtle Beach every year.

RECREATIONAL ACTIVITIES AND SPORTS—
THE LOWER COAST

The Cape Fear Coast offers a myriad of possibilities for active vacationers. Below you will find listings of boat ramps, marinas, and fishing piers, along with some resources for practicing golf, tennis, scuba diving, and surfing as well as for taking eco-tours of the area. This information is not meant to be comprehensive since it is constantly changing, and—especially in the case of golf and tennis resorts in the Cape Fear Coast—the venues are sometimes too numerous to list here. For the most complete and up-to-date list of venues, companies, and outfitters, contact the **Cape Fear Coast Convention and Visitors Bureau** at 24 North Third Street, Wilmington. 800-222-4757 or 910-341-4030. www.cape-fear.nc.us

BOAT RAMPS AND MARINAS

Boating is a big deal on this part of the Intracoastal Waterway (ICW). Everything from small pleasure crafts to immense yachts can be found along the Cape Fear River and ICW. A listing of ramps and marinas follows.

The public ramp at 55th Street East or West 57th Place, Oak Island, allows access to the ICW, Davis Canal, and Lockwood Folly River. There is also canoe/kayak ramp at 39th Place West, Oak Island.

The ICW can also be accessed from the North Carolina Wildlife Commission ramp off the junction of NC 133 South and Fish Factory Road, SR 1101 in the Southport–Oak Island area. Tidalwaves Park also offers a canoe/kayak ramp at 31st Street on Davis Canal, Southport.

There is a free public boat ramp that is north of the first bridge onto Harbor Island (Wrightsville Beach).

There are also three public launches on the South Brunswick Islands: the North Carolina Wildlife Commission ramp at NC 130, Holden Beach, under the NC 130 bridge; Pelican Pointe Marina at 2000 Sommersett Road S.W., Ocean Isle Beach; and Bonaparte Landing, off NC 179 in Shoreline Drive, Sunset Beach (please note that is nearly impossible to take a boat out or put in at low tide from Bonaparte Landing).

Local Marina

There are also many marinas in this area:

Airlie Marina. Wilmington. 910-256-1199. No website available.

Atlantic Marina. Wrightsville Beach. 910-256-9911. No website available.

Baker Marine. Wilmington. 910-395-5008. No website available.

Bald Head Island Marina. Bald Head Island. 910-234-1666. www.baldheadisland.com

Bennett Brothers Yachts. Wilmington. 910-772-9277. www.bbyachts.com

Blue Water Point Marina. Oak Island. 910-278-1230. No website available.

Canady's Yacht Basin. Wilmington. 910-686-9116. No website available.

Cape Fear Yacht Works. Wilmington. 910-395-0189. www.capefearyachtworks.com

Carolina Beach Municipal Marina. Carolina Beach. 910-458-2985. No website available.

Carolina Beach State Park Marina. Carolina Beach. 910-458-7770. No website available.

Coastal Carolina Yacht Yard. Wilmington. 910-686-0004. www.coastalcarolinayachftyard.com

Creekside Yacht Club. Wilmington. 910-350-0023. No website available.

Dockside Marina and Restaurant. Wilmington, just before crossbridge to Wrightsville Beach. 910-256-3579. No website available.

Dockside Marina. Wilmington. 910-256-3579. No website available.

Holden Beach Marina. Holden Beach. 910-842-5447. No website available.

Hughes Marina. Shallotte (near Ocean Isle). 910-754-6233. No website available.

Indigo Plantation Marina. Southport. 910-457-7380 www.baldheadisland.com

Inlet Watch Yacht Club. Wilmington. 910-392-7106. No website available.

Johnson Marine Services. Wilmington. 910-686-7565. www.johnsonmarineinc.com

Marsh Harbour Marina. Calabash. 910-579-3500. No website available.

Masonboro Boat Yard & Marina. Wilmington. 910-791-1893. No website available.

Oak Winds Marina. Wilmington. 910-509-1942. No website available.

Pelican Pointe Marina. Ocean Isle. 910-579-6440. No website available.

Scott's Hill Marina. Wilmington. 910-686-0896. No website available.

Seapath Yacht Club. Wrightsville Beach. 910-256-6681. No website available.

South Harbour Village Marina. Oak Island. 910-454-7486. No website available.

Southport Marina. Southport. 910-457-5261. No website available.

St. James Marina. St. James Plantation, St. James (outside Southport). 800-245-3871. www.stjamesplantation.com

The Beach House Marina. Topsail Island. 877-496-2131 or 910-328-BOAT. www.beachhouse-marina.com

The Bridge Tender Marina and Restaurant. Wilmington, just before crossbridge to **Wrightsville Beach.** 910-256-6550. No website available.

Wilmington Dock Master. Wilmington. 910-520-6875. No website available.

Wrightsville Marina Yacht Club. Wrightsville Beach. 910-256-6666. No website available.

FISHING

Contact the **North Carolina Marine Fisheries Department** for more fishing information at 910-395-3900. Some fishing piers follow.

Carolina Beach Pier. Pleasure Island. 910-458-5518. No website available.

Holden Beach Pier. Supply and Holden Beach. 910-842-6483. No website available.

Johnnie Mercer Pier. Underneath the pier lies the remains of the shipwrecked *Fanny and Jenny*, which sank in 1864 following a skirmish with the *Florida* at

Harbor Island (Wrightsville Beach). 910-256-4469. No website available.

Jolly Roger Pier. Topsail Beach. 910-328-4616. No website available.

Kure Beach Pier. Pleasure Island. 910-458-5524. No website available.

Long Beach Pier. Oak Island. 910-278-5962. No website available.

Ocean City Pier. Ocean Isle. 910-579-6873. No website available.

Ocean Crest Fishing Pier. Oak Island. 910-278-6674. No website available.

Ocean Pier. Topsail Beach. 910-328-3161. www.oceanpierinn.com

Oceanic Pier. Harbor Island. No phone or website available.

Seaview Pier. North Topsail Beach. 910-328-3171. No website available.

Sunset Beach Pier. Sunset Beach. 910-579-6630. No website available.

Surf City Ocean Pier. Surf City. 910-328-3521. No website available.

Topsail Sound Pier. Topsail Island. 910-328-3641. No website available.

GOLFING

While the best fishing takes place along the Outer Banks, the best golfing can be found along the Cape Fear Coast. There are fifty championship golf courses in the Cape Fear area that are open to the public and another hundred in the Grand Strand (greater Myrtle Beach area). To obtain a booklet detailing these courses, contact the Cape Fear Coast Convention and Visitors Bureau or the Myrtle Beach Area Convention and Visitors Bureau at 800-356-3016 or 843-626-7444, www.mbchamber.com The Bald

Head Island Club offers a championship course and golf getaways that include one-day golf and ferry packages. 910-457-7310 or 457-7381. www.baldheadisland.com Another good resource for golfers is www.golfcarolina.com

TENNIS

There are also numerous resorts, clubs, and schools that allow the public to use their tennis courts. For a comprehensive list, contact the Cape Fear Coast Convention and Visitors Bureau.

SCUBA DIVING

As for watersports, you can scuba dive with the Scuba South Diving Company, which takes participants on interesting shipwreck dives such as to the sunken steamship *City of Houston* and the blockade runner *Sherman*. Southport Marina. 910-457-5201. For more information on area diving, contact the Cape Fear Descenders Dive Club at 910-845-2330 or check out the North Carolina Dive Shops and Charter Boats website for a complete list: http://www.nc-wreckdiving.com/shops.html

SURFING

Surfing conditions are good all along the Cape Fear Coast. There are two Wrightsville Beach surf camps with programs open to all ages and levels (residents and vacationers are welcome): Crystal South Surf Camp, 910-395-4431, www.crystalsouthsurf.com; and Wrightsville Beach Surf Camp, 866-844-SURF, www.WBSurfCamp.com

Other resources include the website of the Cape Fear Chapter of the Surfrider Foundation, www.surfrider.org/capefear, and the website of Blowing in the Wind, a Wilmington kitesurfing shop, www.blowinginthewind.com

ECO-ADVENTURES

There are a handful of companies that offer sightseeing cruises, kayaking ecotours, bird-watching excursions, and kayak and bicycle rentals. One such company, **Carolina**

Coastal Adventures, offers a wide variety of fun family-oriented adventures along the Cape Fear Coast, including fishing with experienced guides, kayaking (tours and rentals), kids camps, nature tours, sightseeing tours, day camps, sunrise and sunset tours, bird-watching, bicycling tours, and walking tours. Surfing equipment and boat rentals are also available. Bridge Barrier Road, Carolina Beach. 910-458-9111. www.coastaladventures.com

The **Bald Head Island Conservancy** sponsors several fun programs, such as Alligator Walks and Beachcombing. Loggerhead turtles nest on the southern end of the beach. It is illegal to jeopardize their well-being in any way so it is best to steer clear of the nests. However, the Conservancy has turtle hatching "parties," which allow participants to join the Conservancy for a brief talk and then on to the beach to wait and (hopefully) witness turtles being born. Their building contains exhibits and a gift shop. 7000 Federal Road, Bald Head Island. 910-457-0089. www.bhic.org

Roughly 140 to 165 species of birds can be found in the area. Take a bird-watching tour with the **National Audubon Society** of Wilmington or contact them for a birding checklist. 910-251-0666. www.ncaudubon.org

NATURE PRESERVES, PARKS, AND SANCTUARIES–THE LOWER COAST

Airlie Gardens is a sixty-seven-acre, post-Victorian European style garden showcasing twelve acres of freshwater lakes and gardens filled with wax myrtles, jasmine, honeysuckle, live oaks (including the 450-year-old Airlie Oak), and birds such as egrets, geese, and herons. Two miles west of Wrightsville Beach at 300 Airlie Rd., Wilmington. 910-793-7531 or 910-452-6393. www.airliegardens.org

Bald Head Woods is 173 acres comprised of Bald Head Island, Middle Island, and Bluff Island. This maritime forest contains huge, old stately oak trees, as well as yaupon, holly, and wild olive shrubs. There are freshwater ponds that are home to several species of amphibians and waterfowl. Bird watchers will find all kinds of birds, including blue jays, Carolina wrens, and cardinals. Bald Head Woods is part of the North Carolina Coastal Reserve. Bald Head Island. No telephone available. www.ncnerr.org

Carolina Beach State Park is a 1,773-acre park along the Cape Fear River that was initially established in 1969 as Masonboro State Park. The name change occurred in 1974. The park is comprised of several different ecosystems and unusual plants, such as Venus flytrap and terrestrial bladderwort. The Venus flytrap grows only in the Carolinas and it is against the law to violate this plant. There is a five-mile trail system, complete with five different walking trails. Don't miss Sugar Loaf, a sixty-foot-tall sand dune named by explorer William Hilton. There is a campground with RV hookups, a picnic area, an amphitheater where summer programs are held, a pier, and a marina. It is a fishing mecca for both surf and pier fishing. Nineteen miles south of Wilmington on US 421. 910-458-8206. www.ncsparks.com

EV-Henwood Nature Preserve is part of University of North Carolina-Wilmington. The 174-acre nature area offers fifteen nature trails, ponds, a forest, and many species of plants and animals. Ten miles south of Wilmington off Hwy. 17 (Town Creek Road Exit). 6150 Rock Creek Road. 910-962-3487. No website available.

Fort Fisher State Recreation Area offers visitors a four-mile beach, snack bar, picnic area, and restrooms with showers. At the Fort Fisher State Historic Site, US 421, south of Kure Beach. 910-458-9042/8206. www.arch.dcr.state.nc.us/

Greenfield Park and Gardens is a 200-acre city park that is great place for bicycling, walking, playing at its large playground, picnicking, or just appreciating the many blooming flowers. Additionally, canoes and paddleboats may be rented to take out on the large lake. Music is offered in its amphitheater during summer months. Take US 421 South to Carolina Beach Road(off Wilmington's Third Street, follow signs). 800-380-3485 or 910-341-7868/7855. www.ci.wilmington.nc.us/prd/greenfield_park.htm

Karen Beasley Sea Turtle Rescue and Rehabilitation Center cares for turtles in need (loggerheads, Kemp's ridley, hawksbill, green, and leatherbacks). It is the only sea turtle hospital in the state and its purpose is also to educate the public about endangered turtles. Turtle talks are held once a week during the summer at a Topsail Island area location. The facility is located on Topsail Island because it is among the most northern nesting sites in the world. There are 100-150 nests on the island when the turtles are nesting. 822 Channel Blvd., Topsail Beach. 910-328-3377. www.seaturtlehospital.org

Sea turtles are protected under the Endangered Species Act of 1973. It is illegal to harass, harm, pursue, hunt, shoot, wound, kill, trap, capture, or collect sea turtle eggs, hatchlings, or adults. Violators can be prosecuted under civil and criminal laws and be assessed heavy penalties. The protection of sea turtles is taken very seriously because six of seven species are in danger of becoming extinct. Do not shine lights or take flash photos of turtles. Do not disturb nest markers. Do not crowd, disturb, or pick up a turtle or hatchling

New Hanover County Arboretum consists of seven acres and thirty-three gardens, including four thousand classifications of plants. Nature trails and boardwalks meander through the themed gardens. Tours are taken independently, but volunteers will lead tours when requested. There is also a Japanese Tea House and Children's Cottage. 6206 Oleander Dr., Wilmington. 910-452-6393. www.nhcgov.com/ces/cesmain.asp

Oak Island Nature Center offers a talking tree trail, interpretive trail, walkway along the marsh, picnic area, live animal exhibits, and restrooms. Located at the end of 52nd Street, Oak Island. 910-278-5518. No website available.

Strange Tales and Ghosts

The following story, "Buried Alive," is from my book *Ghosts of the Carolina Coasts.*

It was a cruel turn of events. The boy had been out horseback riding, jumping fallen logs and tree branches. What an excellent rider he was! What a wonderful way to pass an afternoon, he thought.

Overly cocky, Sam tried to cross a wide hurdle. The horse stumbled and threw him, and he hit his head on a large stone and lost consciousness. When he was found, his parents rushed the young man to the doctor, but it was too late. The physician pronounced him dead.

The young man, barely eighteen years of age when the terrible accident occurred, was buried at Wilmington's St. James Cemetery. His tombstone reads: Samuel R. Jocelyn, 1792–1810.

St. James Cemetery, downtown Wilmington

His best friend since childhood, Alexander Hostler, was overtaken by grief and guilt. If only he had gone riding with him, maybe he could have done something. The death of his friend pulled at his heart and conscience.

Alex couldn't sleep for several days after the funeral, as he kept seeing Sam's face every time he closed his eyes. One night, unable to stand it any longer, he decided to visit the grave and say his goodbyes to his longtime friend. He thought maybe that would help him put it behind him and get on with his life. As Alex thought about all the things they would never do together again and how much he missed Sam, a voice interrupted.

"How could you?" it hissed. "I thought you were my friend. You buried me alive! You buried me alive! Open my coffin and free me."

Thinking he had lost his mind, Alex ran out of the cemetery and tried to forget the incident, but Sam's voice plagued the young man day and night. He could get no

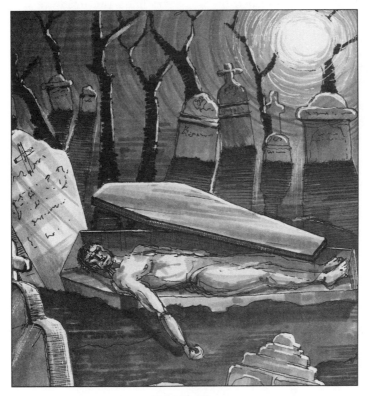

Buried Alive

peace from it. What if they had all made a mistake? Didn't he owe it to his friend to make sure? Knowing no one would believe him, he told only one person, a very close mutual friend, Louis Toomer.

Hysterically, he asked Toomer to go with him to dig up their friend. Although shocked by his friend's plea, he agreed to accompany him since he could see how distraught Alex was. The two waited until well after midnight the following night before going to the gravesite. Upon arrival, Alex fervidly began digging up Sam's plot.

Even though they worked steadily, it took hours to dig up the coffin that had been embedded deep in the earth. When they finally were able to open the coffin, the sight made Louis Toomer cry out in disbelief, while the Alex fell to his knees. Sam's body was face down! When they turned him over, Sam looked much as he had when Alex had last seen him, only his fingernails were different. They were all broken and bloody, obviously from the boy's efforts to open the lid. Scars lined the inside of the coffin around the hinges where Sam had pawed and scraped with all his strength. It must have been a brief struggle, for the boy would surely have quickly suffocated.

The surviving friend was never the same again. He felt he was responsible, although the doctor had said Sam was dead. The senile physician had obviously mistaken unconsciousness for death!

Alexander lost his mental faculties, now diagnosed as a nervous breakdown. From that point on, he spent most of his time at the cemetery pulling up weeds, putting out fresh flowers, and keeping the gravesite in excellent condition.

Many years later, a group of teenagers sneaked into the cemetery. They got more than they bargained for when they stopped at Sam's burial site.

Soon after they gathered around the headstone, a muffled voice cried out, "Get off of me! Can't you see I've been buried alive?" Before the frightened and confused kids could figure out what to do, a figure was seen coming towards them.

As they scattered among the graves and headed for the gate, they heard the staggering figure exclaim, "I didn't know. I didn't mean to. Please forgive me, Sam, and leave me in peace . . ."

TRADITIONS–THE LOWER COAST

For the most up-to-date event information, contact tourism resources found at the end of this book.

Antique Show. Big antiques displays and sales event. Wilmington.

JANUARY

Civil War Battle Reenactment of Fort Fisher. History buffs will enjoy this reenactment of the battle at Fort Fisher, as well as demonstrations and other related events. Fort Fisher.

Sundown Shindig on the River (one day every month). Entertainment, food, and more. Wilmington.

Moore's Creek National Battlefield Anniversary Celebration. Special events honoring this historical battle, including music and food. Moore's Creek National Battlefield.

FEBRUARY

North Carolina Jazz Festival. Renowned performers come together to delight audiences. Wilmington.

A Day At The Docks is the annual blessing of the boats followed by a boat parade. South Brunswick Islands.

MARCH

Coastal Living Show. Huge show featuring coastal living products and vendors. Wilmington.

Southport Spring Festival (Easter weekend, March or April). Arts and crafts, food, music, and vendors are part of this event. Southport.

Spring Art Show. Artists display and sell their works. Southport.

Art in the Park. Artwork is displayed and sold. Southport.

APRIL

Marsh Harbour Inn Cooking School and Wine Weekend. Bald Head Island.

North Carolina Azalea Festival and Parade. This is one of the biggest and best events of the year. In addition to the brilliant azaleas, there is a parade, street fair, concert, and home and garden tour. Wilmington.

North Carolina Azalea Festival and Parade

APRIL

Oak Island Garden Tour. Oak Island.

Oak Island Lighthouse 10K Run/Walk. Fundraiser event with run/walk, music, and vendors. Oak Island.

Robert Ruark Chili Cook-off. Music, vendors, and a big chili-making contest make this a fun event. Southport.

Spring Fling. Spring festival filled with music, food, games, and vendors. Topsail Island.

Surf and Turf Triathlon. Athletic land and water competition. Topsail Island.

MAY

Annual Bald Head Island Fishing Rodeo. Competition and games. Bald Head Island.

Cape Fear Folk Festival. Folk tellers gather from near and far. Features lots of vendors, and more. Wilmington.

Coastal Classic Celebrity Golf Tournament. Big golf tournament featuring celebrity golfers. Wilmington.

Concerts on the Coast take place every week, from May to September. They are sponsored by the Brunswick County Parks and Recreation Department and held at Franklin Square Park (corner of Howe and West Streets). Southport.

Greek Festival. Features Greek music and bands, dancing, and food. Wilmington.

Flounder Tournament (June). Southport. **JUNE**

Shakespeare on the Green Festival. A celebration honoring the Bard. Wilmington.

Camp Lejeune Fireworks. July Fourth festivities. Topsail Island. **JULY**

East Coast Classic King Mackerel Tournament. Pleasure Island.

Fireworks Celebration. July Fourth festivities. Wilmington.

Fourth of July Celebration. Bald Head Island.

Fourth of July Festival (July 2-4). The biggest and oldest July Fourth festivities in the state. Southport.

July National Art Show. Huge art show. Southport.

Surf City Fireworks. July Fourth festivities. Topsail Island/Surf City.

Ladies King Mackerel Tournament. Fishing tournament. Southport. **AUGUST**

Sneads Ferry King Mackerel Tournament. Two-day fishing tournament . Sneads Ferry/Topsail Island.

Sneads Ferry Shrimp Festival. This fun two-day event includes a parade, arts and crafts, food, carnival rides, military displays, entertainment, and fireworks. Sneads Ferry/Topsail Island.

Children's Crab Derby. Children race crabs, play games, and more. Southport. **SEPTEMBER**

SEPTEMBER

Labor Day Arts and Crafts Fair. Oak Island.

South Brunswick Islands King Classic King Mackerel Tournament. Fishing tournament. South Brunswick Islands.

Spot Festival. Three-day fishing tournament and festivities. Topsail Island.

OCTOBER

Autumn with Topsail Festival. Topsail Island.

Captain Charlie's Kids Fishing Tournament. Southport.

Carolina Beach Surf Fishing Tournament. Pleasure Island.

Celebration of Oak Island. Games, competitions, food, and music highlight this annual celebration. Oak Island.

Fall Brawl Kingfish Tournament. Fishing tournament. South Brunswick Islands.

Fall Festival. Arts and crafts, food, music, and more. Wilmington.

Marsh Harbour Inn Cooking School and Wine Weekend. Bald Head Island.

North Carolina Festival by the Sea. Food, music, and games are part of this event. South Brunswick Islands.

North Carolina Oyster Festival includes crowning of the North Carolina Oyster Shucking Champion. South Brunswick Islands.

Poplar Grove

Pleasure Island Seafood, Blues, and Jazz Festival. Pleasure Island.

Poplar Grove Halloween Festival. Hayrides, ghost stories, games, food, and more. Poplar Grove, outside Wilmington.

Riverfest. Big event featuring music, food, vendors, and other entertainment and special events. Around Wilmington's Riverwalk.

U.S. Open King Mackerel Tournament. Southport.

Wilmington Dog Jog. Fundraiser for humane societies and animal shelters (you can walk, jog, or run). Wilmington.

Airlie Gardens Holiday Light Show runs from late November to December 31st. Light display with holiday scenes and special events. Wilmington.

NOVEMBER

Annual Ocean Isle Beach Christmas Parade. South Brunswick Islands.

Antique, Art, and Garden Show. Wilmington.

Festival of Trees. Seasonal celebration. Wilmington.

Holly Days. Seasonal celebration featuring traditional festivities. Southport.

Holly Ridge Holly Festival. Holiday festival. Holly Ridge/Topsail Island.

Island of Lights (November–January). Tour of homes, holiday flotilla, and parade. Pleasure Island

Island of Lights Festival. Holiday festival. Wrightsville Beach.

Maritime Classic Road Race. Sponsored by the Bald Head Island Shoals Club Recreation Department (800-234-1666). Bald Head Island.

North Carolina Holiday Flotilla. Decorated boat parade. Wrightsville Beach.

Topsail Island Holiday Boat Flotilla. Boats decorated for the season will take part in a flotilla (boat parade). Topsail Island.

Christmas by the Sea Festival. Festivities include music, food, and Christmas activities. Oak Island.

Holiday Lighting of the *Battleship North Carolina*. Eagle Island/Wilmington.

New Year's Eve River Cruise. Wilmington.

Holiday Pops Concert. Wilmington.

Kwanza Festival. Holiday celebration. Wilmington.

Lighting of the World's Largest Living Christmas Tree. Since 1928, the city has sponsored this spectacular event at Hilton Park. Wilmington.

Moravian Candle Tea. Moravian church tradition. Wilmington.

Old Wilmington by Candlelight Tour. Great way to combine the holidays with historic tour. Wilmington.

Reindeer-drawn Trolley and Caroling. Wilmington.

Sneads Ferry Winter Holiday Festival. This two-day event celebrates the Christmas holidays with traditional festivities. Sneads Ferry/Topsail Island.

Wilmington Holiday Parade. Features bands, community groups, and businesses. Wilmington.

Lighting of the World's Largest
Living Christmas Tree

TEST YOUR KNOWLEDGE

Quiz

Just for fun, test your knowledge by taking this quiz.

1. True or false: There are three dozen championship golf courses in the Cape Fear area.

2. What is the biggest family beach in the Cape Fear area?

3. True or false: The *Battleship North Carolina* is moored at Ocean Isle.

4. True or false: Salt production was a multi-million dollar business in the Cape Fear area in the1800s.

5. Where was one of the biggest salt production facilities?

6. Which coastal community has been dubbed the "Seafood Capital of the World?"

7. What island does not permit any vehicles except golf carts?

8. Which state park is the only place in North Carolina where you can find the rare Venus flytrap?

9. Which Topsail Island community boasts the largest population—Surf City, Topsail Beach, or North Topsail Beach?

10. Where was Operation Bumblebee conducted during World War II?

11. What is the name of the smallest military installation in the state?

12. Where is the smallest military installation in the state?

13. Where is Ingram Planetarium?

14. Where is the biggest July Fourth celebration held?

15. Where is the Karen Beasley Turtle Rehabilitation Center located?

16. Where was the last North Carolina lighthouse built? (Hint: It is also one of the last lighthouses built in the United States.)

17. True or False: Bald Head Island Lighthouse is the second oldest beacon in the state.

18. Where is one of the world's largest marine training bases and what is its name?

19. Which island has home sites that start at approximately one million dollars?

20. Where is the *Battleship North Carolina* anchored?

21. True or False: Fort Caswell has been used during the Spanish American War, Civil War, World War I, and World War II.

22. Which beach is entered via a one-lane swinging bridge?

23. What place has underground tunnels that were once used by pirates, Revolutionary War soldiers, slaves, and prisoners escaping from Cornwallis' dungeon?

24. Every year, the lighting of the World's Largest Living Christmas Tree takes place where?

25. Which barrier island has made so many nude sunbathers flock to it that it has erected a sign that reads "Entering _____Beach, No Nudity Allowed?"

[Answers can be found at the end of the chapter.]

Sea turtles' diet varies by species. Sea turtles may be carnivorous (meat eating), herbivorous (plant eating), or omnivorous (eating both meat and plants). The jaw structure of many species indicates their diet.

1. Green and black sea turtles have finely serrated jaws adapted for a vegetarian diet of sea grasses and algae. In adulthood, they are the only herbivorous sea turtles, but in an aquarium environment all sea turtle species can be maintained on a carnivorous diet.

2. Loggerheads' and ridleys' jaws are adapted for crushing and grinding. Their diet consists primarily of crabs, mollusks, shrimps, jellyfish, and vegetation.

3. A hawksbill has a narrow head with jaws meeting at an acute angle adapted for getting food from crevices in coral reefs. They eat sponges, tunicates, shrimps, and squids.

4. Leatherbacks have delicate scissorlike jaws that would be damaged by anything other than their normal diet of jellyfish, tunicates, and other soft-bodied animals. The mouth cavity and throat are lined with papillae (spinelike projections) pointed backward to help them swallow soft foods.

5. Researchers continue to study the feeding habits of flatbacks. There is evidence that they are opportunistic feeders that eat seaweeds, cuttlefish, and sea cucumbers.

FUN WAYS TO LEARN

Teachers and parents may wish to tackle the activities below to teach their kids or students about North Carolina's coastal history and nature.

• Have an in-depth discussion on **the importance of the Cape Fear River,** both in past times (how it was once used for shipping transportation, by Civil War blockade runners, pirates, etc.) and today (as part of Intracoastal Waterway, etc.).

• Write a short essay on what your **perfect beach vacation** would be like. Who would be with you—family? friends? pets? Where would you eat? What would you eat? What activities would you enjoy? How long would your vacation last? Would you stay in a motel, a hotel, or a house? If you could invite a famous person discussed in this book, who would it be—one of the Wright Brothers? Blackbeard? Anne Bonny? Privateer Otway Burns? One of the former lighthouse keepers? One of the former lifesaving station crew? What would you ask that person?

• Study **turtles** and learn the differences between them. A visit to the Karen Beasley Sea Turtle Rescue and Rehabilitation Center is an educational experience for all ages. The facility cares for turtles in need and is the only sea turtle hospital in the state. Its other purpose is to educate the public about endangered turtles. Turtle talks are held once a week during the summer at various Topsail Island area locations. The facility is located on Topsail Island because it is among the most northern nesting sites in the world. There are 100–150 nests on the island when the turtles are nesting. 822 Channel Blvd., Topsail Beach. 910-328-3377.

• Take an **ecotour or a sightseeing tour or a cruise**. Make a list or draw a picture of everything of importance that you see, such as a historical building, a dolphin, island, monument or memorial, state park, aquarium, lighthouse, etc. A point will be awarded for each item and whoever scores the most points wins! A prize can be awarded. A twist on this is to make up a list of items that have to be checked off during vacation.

The following is a list of suggestions:

alligator _____

any kind of park (write down the name) _____

cannon_____

cemetery_____

conch shell_____

crab_____

dolphin_____

ferry_____

fort_____

full moon_____

historical building (write down the name) _____

horse-drawn carriage tour or trolley tour_____

Hummer SUV_____

lighthouse_____

museum (write down the name) _____

pontoon boat or johnny boat_____

sand castle_____

seagull_____

someone dressed in nautical clothing_____

someone eating an ice cream cone_____

someone fishing_____

someone on a bicycle_____

someone skateboarding_____

someone walking a dog_____

someone with a sunburn_____

sunset_____

surfer_____

vehicle with Ohio license plates_____

white bird (not a seagull) _____

• This list can be made more difficult by adding qualifiers, for example: a conch shell (in perfect condition, meaning no piece broken off), a surfer (in the act of riding a wave), someone fishing (off a pier and wearing a cap), a seagull (eating bread crumbs), a sand castle (being built by two adults and/or children). This way, different age groups can appreciate playing the same game.

• Build a **sand castle** together or have a family sand castle building contest. Don't build too close to the water or high tide will wipe out your efforts! Some good ideas: make a fort, a ship, a treasure chest, an animal-shape (such as an alligator or dolphin), a castle, a pier, or a lighthouse. Or spell out a fun message.

Quiz Answers

1. False. There are fifty championship golf courses in the Cape Fear area and another hundred in the Grand Strand (Greater Myrtle Beach area).

2. Myrtle Beach (it's also one of the biggest beaches in the state).

3. False. It's moored at Wilmington on Eagle's Island.

4. True

5. Topsail Island

6. Calabash

7. Bald Head Island

8. Carolina Beach State Park

9. Surf City (Topsail Beach has the smallest population)

10. Topsail Island

11. Fort Johnston

12. Southport

13. Sunset Beach

14. Southport

15. Topsail Island

16. Oak Island, 1958

17. False. It is the oldest lighthouse in North Carolina.

18. Camp Lejeune Marine Corps Base, Topsail Island

19. Figure Eight Island

20. Eagle Island, across the bridge from Wilmington

21. True

22. Sunset Beach

23. Wilmington. The underground tunnels were partially created by feeder streams that empty into Cape Fear River. These streams provided water for both homes and businesses, as well as sewage removal. They also made good escape routes!

24. Wilmington

25. "Entering **Sunset Beach,** No Nudity Allowed"

ADDITIONAL RESOURCES

SECTION 1: OUTER BANKS

Currituck Chamber of Commerce (Currituck County)
6328-E Caratoke Hwy.
Grandy, NC
877-CURRITU (287-7488) or 252-453-9497
www.currituckchamber.org

Greater Hyde County Chamber of Commerce
(Ocracoke Island and mainland Hyde County)
P. O. Box 178
Swan Quarter, NC
888-493-3826
www.hydecounty.org

Ocracoke Island Visitor Center
NC 12 (near the Cedar Island and Swan Quarter Ferry
Docks)
Ocracoke Island, NC
252-928-4531

Outer Banks Chamber of Commerce
PO Box 1757
101 Town Hall Drive
Kill Devil Hills, NC
252-441-8144
www.outerbankschamber.com
(Includes Currituck County, Dare County including
Hatteras Island, and Ocracoke Island in Hyde County.)

Outer Banks History Center
Route 400, Ice Plant Island
P.O. Box 250
Manteo, NC
252-473-2655
www.ah.dcr.state.nc.us/sections/archives/arch/obhc/default.
htm

Outer Banks Visitors Bureau
One Visitors Center Circle/Hwy. 64/264
Manteo, NC
800-446-6262
www.outerbanks.org

SECTION II: CRYSTAL COAST

Cape Lookout National Seashore Visitors Center
131 Charles Street
Harkers Island, NC
252-728-2250
www.nps.gov/calo

Carteret County Chamber of Commerce
801 Arendell St.
Morehead City, NC
252-726-6350
www.nccoastchamber.com

Crystal Coast Tourism Authority (in the Crystal Coast
Visitor Center)
3409 Arendell Street
Morehead City, NC
800-786-6962 or 252-726-8148
www.sunnync.com

SECTION III: LOWER COAST

Bald Head Island Information Center
5079 Southport, Supply Road
Southport, NC
RENTALS: 800-432-RENT
SALES: 800-888-3707
www.baldheadisland.com

Cape Fear Coast Convention and Visitors Bureau
24 North Third Street
Wilmington, NC
800-222-4757 or 910-341-4030
www.cape-fear.nc.us

Jacksonville/Onslow Chamber of Commerce
P.O. Box 765
1099 Gum Branch Rd.
Jacksonville, NC 28540
910-347-3141
www.jacksonvilleonline.org

Onslow County Tourism (Topsail Island, Swansboro, Bear Island)
800-932-2144
www.onslowcountytourism.com

Pleasure Island Chamber of Commerce
(Carolina Beach, Kure Beach, and Fort Fisher)
1140-B North Lake Park Blvd.
Carolina Beach, NC
910-458-8434
www.carokure.wilmington.net

South Brunswick Islands Chamber of Commerce
4948 Main Street
Shallotte, NC
Visitor Information Only: 800-795-7263
800-426-6644 or 910-754-6644
www.ncbrunswick.com

Southport–Oak Island Area Chamber Commerce
4841 Long Beach Road SE
Southport, NC
800-457-6964 or 910-457-6964
www.southport-oakisland.com

Southport Visitor's Center
113 West Moore Street
Southport, NC
910-457-7927

GENERAL

North Carolina Association of Convention and Visitor Bureaus
4324 Mail Service Center
Raleigh, NC
800-VISIT NC
http://visit.nc.org

North Carolina Department of Commerce
310 N. Wilmington Street
Raleigh, NC
919-733-4151
www.nccommerce.com/tourism

North Carolina Division of Archives and History
109 E. Jones Street
Raleigh, NC
919-733-7862
www.ah.dcr.state.nc.us/sections/archives

North Carolina Division of Travel and Tourism
430 N. Salisbury Street
Raleigh, NC
800-VISITNC or 919-733-8372
www.visitnc.com

North Carolina Division of Marine Fisheries
P.O. Box 769
Morehead City, NC
800-682-2632 or 252-726-7021
www.ncfisheries.net

North Carolina Ferry System
113 Arendell Street, Morehead City
800-293-3779 (800-BY-FERRY)
www.ncferry.org

North Carolina State Parks and Recreation Areas
Division of Parks and Recreation
Dept. of Environment and Natural Resources
P.O. Box 27687
Raleigh, NC
919-733-PARK
http://www.ohwy.com/nc/n/ncparks.htm

The NC ECHO website, www.ncecho.org, is a service of
the State Library of North Carolina which links 600 North
Carolina museums, libraries, historic sites, and archives.
This is a great tourism resource.

RESOURCES/USEFUL PUBLICATIONS

Barnes, Jay. North Carolina's Hurricane History. Chapel Hill, North Carolina: University of North Carolina Press, 2001.

Nadeau, Nola. An Island Called Figure Eight. Wallace, North Carolina: Wallace Enterprise, 1991.

Riggs, Stan & Orrin Pilkey. From Currituck to Calabash. Durham, North Carolina: Duke University Press, 1982.

Riggs, Stan & Orrin Pilkey. The North Carolina Shore and Its Barrier Islands. Durham, North Carolina: Duke University Press, 1998.

Salter, Ben B. & Willis, Dot S. Portsmouth Island: Short Stories and History. Self-published, 1972.

Stick, Frank. The Outer Banks of North Carolina. Chapel Hill, North Carolina: University of North Carolina Press, 1958.

Whedbee, Charles. Blackbeard's Cup and Stories of the Outer Banks. Winston-Salem, North Carolina: John F. Blair, 1989.

Zepke, Terrance. Ghosts of the Carolina Coasts. Sarasota, Florida: Pineapple Press, 1999.

——. Pirates of the Carolinas. Sarasota, Florida: Pineapple Press, 2000.

——. The Best Ghost Tales of North Carolina. Sarasota, Florida: Pineapple Press, 2001.

INDEX

PHOTO CREDITS

All photographs by the author except for the following (which were used with permission):

Front cover: Dare County Tourist Bureau (left); NC Travel and Tourism (top right); Dare County Tourism Bureau (bottom right).

Spine: Photo courtesy of NC Division of Tourism, Film and Sports Development (top and middle); Photo courtesy of the Cape Fear Coast Convention & Visitors Bureau (bottom).

Back cover: From left to right: Photo courtesy of the Cape Fear Coast Convention & Visitors Bureau; Photo courtesy of NC division of Tourism, Film and Sports Development; Photo courtesy of the Cape Fear Coast Convention & Visitors Bureau.

Outer Banks: p. 4 N.C. State Archives; p. 5 Outer Banks Tourist Bureau (OBTB); p. 6 OBTB; p. 12 National Archives; p. 13 N.C. State Archives; p.17 OBTB; p. 18 N.C. State Archives; p. 20 OBTB; p. 21 N.C. State Archives; p.28 N.C. State Archives; p. 29 N.C. Travel & Tourism; p. 31 OBTB; p. 33 OBTB; p. 34 OBTB; p. 36 N.C. Travel & Tourism; p. 40 OBTB; p. 43 OBTB; p. 44 N.C. State Archives; p. 48 OBTB; p. 50 N.C. State Archives; p. 51 OBTB; p. 52 Hyde County Tourism; p. 56 Hyde County Tourism; p. 58 Hyde County Tourism; p. 59 N.C. Travel & Tourism; p. 67 OBTB; p. 69 N.C. State Archives; p. 71 OBTB; p. 72 N.C. Travel & Tourism; p. 77 Outer Banks History Center; p. 79 N.C. Travel & Tourism; p. 82 OBTB (upper photo) and Hyde County Tourism (lower photo); p. 83 Hyde County Tourism; p. 85 OBTB; p. 97 N.C. Travel & Tourism.

Crystal Coast: p. 103 N.C. Travel & Tourism; p. 106 N.C. Travel & Tourism; p. 107 N. C. State Archives; p. 109 N.C. Travel & Tourism; p. 110 N.C. State Archives; p. 111 N.C. Travel & Tourism; p. 112 N.C. State Archives; p. 113 NC. State Archives; p. 114 N.C. State Archives; p. 115 N.C. Travel & Tourism; p. 116 N.C. Travel & Tourism; p. 119 N.C. State Archives; p. 120 N.C. State Archives; p. 121 N.C. State Archives; p. 123 N.C. State Archives; p. 124 N.C. Travel & Tourism; p. 127 N.C. State Archives; p. 128 N.C. Travel & Tourism; p. 129 N.C. State Archives; P. 132 N.C. State Archives; p. 133 N.C. Travel & Tourism; p. 134 N.C. Travel & Tourism; p. 135 N.C. State Archives (both photos); p. 139 N.C. Travel & Tourism; p. 148 N.C. Travel & Tourism; p. 150 N.C. Travel & Tourism; p. 153 N.C. State Archives; p. 165 N.C. State Archives.

Lower Coast: p. 170 Brunswick County Tourism; p. 172 N.C. State Archives; p. 173 N.C. Travel & Tourism; p. 174 N.C. State Archives; p. 176 Cape Fear Convention & Visitors Bureau (CFCVB); p. 178 N.C. State Archives; p. 180 CFCVB; p. 184 CFCVB; p. 191 CFCVB; p. 192 N.C. Travel & Tourism; p. 195 CFCVB; p. 197 N.C. State Archives; p. 198 N.C. State Archives; p. 200 CFCVB; p. 202 Bald Head Island Ltd.; p. 204 Southport-Oak Island Chamber of Commerce and John Martin of Eastern Aviation; p. 205 N.C. State Archives; p. 211 N.C. State Archives; p. 212 N.C. Travel & Tourism; p. 213 N.C. Travel & Tourism; p. 214 Brunwick County Tourism; p. 216 N.C. Travel & Tourism; p. 218 CFCVB; p. 227 Julie Rabun; p. 230 CFCVB; p. 234 CFCVB; p. 222 N.C. Travel & Tourism.

MORE BOOKS FROM PINEAPPLE PRESS

If you enjoyed reading this book, here are some other books from Pineapple Press on related topics. For a complete catalog, write to Pineapple Press, P.O. Box 3889, Sarasota, FL 34230 or call 1-800-PINEAPL (746-3275). Or visit our website at www.pineapplepress.com

Also by Terrance Zepke

Best Ghost Tales of North Carolina and *Best Ghost Tales of South Carolina*. The actors of Carolina's past linger among the living in these thrilling collection of ghost tales. Experience the chilling encounters told by the winners of the North Carolina "Ghost Watch" contest. Use Zepke's tips to conduct your own ghost hunt. ISBN 1-56164-233-9 (pb); 1-56164-306-8 (pb)

Exploring South Carolina's Islands. A complete guide for vacationers, day-trippers, armchair travelers, and people looking to relocate to this charming area. What to see and do, where to stay and eat on South Carolina's fabled islands, with over 70 photos. ISBN 1-56164-259-2 (pb)

Ghosts of the Carolina Coasts. Taken from real-life occurrences and Carolina Lowcountry lore, these thirty-two spine-tingling ghost stories take place in prominent historic structures of the region. ISBN 1-56164-175-8 (pb)

Lighthouses of the Carolinas. Eighteen lighthouses aid mariners traveling the coasts of North and South Carolina. Here is the story of each, from origin to current status, along with visiting information and photographs. Newly revised to include up-to-date information on the long-awaited and much-debated Cape Hatteras Lighthouse move, plus websites for area visitors' centers and tourist bureaus. ISBN 1-56164-148-0 (pb)

Pirates of the Carolinas. Thirteen of the most fascinating buccaneers in the history of piracy, including Henry Avery, Blackbeard, Anne Bonny, Captain Kidd, Calico Jack, and Stede Bonnet. ISBN 1-56164205-3 (pb)

Bansemer's Book of Carolina and Georgia Lighthouses by Roger Bansemer. Written and illustrated in the same engaging style as Bansemer's Florida book, this volume accurately portrays how each lighthouse along the coasts of the Carolinas and Georgia looks today. ISBN 1-56164-194-4 (hb)

Georgia's Lighthouses and Historic Coastal Sites by Kevin M. McCarthy. With full-color paintings by maritime artist William L. Trotter, this book retraces the history of 30 sites in the Peach State. ISBN 1-56164-143-X (pb)

Guide to the Gardens of South Carolina by Lilly Pinkas. Organized by region, this guide provides detailed information about the featured species and facilities offered by South Carolina's public gardens. Includes 8 pages of color photos and 40 line drawings. ISBN 1-56164-251-7 (pb)

Haunted Lighthouses and How to Find Them by George Steitz. The producer of the popular TV series *Haunted Lighthouses* takes you on a tour of America's most enchanting and mysterious lighthouses. ISBN 1-56164-268-1 (pb)

Historic Homes of Florida by Laura Stewart and Susanne Hupp. Seventy-four notable dwellings throughout the state—all open to the public—tell the human side of history. Each is illustrated by H. Patrick Reed or Nan E. Wilson. ISBN 1-56164-085-9 (pb)

Shipwrecks of Florida: A Comprehensive Listing Second Edition by Steven D. Singer. General information on research, search and salvage, wreck identification, artifact conservation, and rights to wrecks accompanies a listing of 2100 wrecks off the Florida coast from the sixteenth century to the present. Loaded with photos. ISBN 1-56164-163-4 (pb)